group

ALSO BY PAUL SOLOTAROFF

The House of Purple Hearts

riverhead books · a member of penguin putnam inc. · new york · 1999

paul solotaroff

group

six people in search of a life

The names and certain characteristics
of individuals depicted in this book
have been changed to protect
their privacy.

RIVERHEAD BOOKS
a member of
Penguin Putnam Inc.
375 Hudson St.
New York, NY 10014

Library of Congress Cataloging-in-Publication Data

Solotaroff, Paul.
    Group : six people in search of a life / Paul Solotaroff.
      p.   cm.
    ISBN 1-57322-065-5
      1. Psychotherapy patients—Interviews.   2. Group psychotherapy—
Anecdotes.   3. Psychotherapist and patient—Miscellanea.   I. Title
RC480.5.S636   1999   99-14261   CIP
616.89'152—dc21

Printed in the United States of America
10   9   8   7   6   5   4   3   2   1

This book is printed on acid-free paper. ∞

Book design by Claire Naylon Vaccaro

For my two lights,
Elaine and Luke

group

prologue

This is what it felt like the first time, twenty years ago. Three in the morning on a bitter March Sunday, the wind bullying the elm trees on the other side of the dorm window, I lay awake worrying about an unwritten Blake thesis, and about my obdurate, pill-proof insomnia. Quietly, without my much marking it at first, the soles of my hands and feet began to tingle, and the muscles in my throat constricted. Sitting up in bed, I felt the sheet damp beneath me, and was so unnerved by the sudden racket of my heart that, for a moment, I thought it issued from *outside* me. I got up to check it out, but my legs were like tent poles, blocky and unbending at the knee. What the hell, I muttered, and made the alarming discovery that I could barely summon oxygen down my windpipe.

Now, like most asthmatics, I have reflexive concerns—What is the mold count today? Where's my backup inhaler? They all reduce, though, to one cardinal terror: *I can't breathe, and I'm going to die.* I have had that thought in racing ambulances, blue in the face and heaving, and I have had it, however briefly, at the bottom of a pileup, fighting for air while others fought for the football. I have never, however, been more disabled by it than I was that night in my dorm room. The fact of the matter is, my lungs were clear; it was my head that was clamping shut, as full-blown nightmare scenarios fired through at an interval of seconds, or split seconds. The longer I stood there, pop-eyed and gasping, the more preposterous the supposi-

1

tion. But with my circuits abuzz in fear and adrenaline, there was no telling mad from madder. Nor was there a means of formulating action, as every reasonable solution suggested its inverse—*I'll call for a cab and go to the infirmary; no, no, they'll put me in a straitjacket and drag me upstairs to the locked psych ward. . . .*

At some point, I either passed out from hyperventilating, or knocked myself cold in a fall. When I awoke, with a cut lip and a loosened front tooth, I found myself on the floor of my shower stall. I turned on the hot water and sat under the stream, vaporizing thought in a torrent of white noise, until sometime after sunup. Dragging off to bed, I went down for twelve hours into a drenching, bottomless sleep.

That evening, however, I wasn't awake for five minutes when the nightmare resumed in full cry. It was occasioned not by fear but by a fear *of* the fear, a shamelessly suggestible dread. From that moment on, I had only to think the word *panic* and, in short order, I was in its grasp. In those adrenaline boil-overs, I wanted to shed my own skin and run wildly in five directions. Nothing availed me when the panic set in, other than waiting it out. Alcohol, sedatives—they were of less than no use; often, they merely spiked the fear.

Over the next eleven years, I became less and less real to myself, floating in a kind of subcutaneous orbit. I lost forty pounds, wandered from grad school to grad school, and left no trace in the lives of other people, associating mainly with my TV. But if this began to feel like fate to me, I never stopped flailing against it. In the course of those years, I went to four different therapists, all competent, well-meaning people who tried to decipher my distress. But recounting to them my near-fatal asthma attacks in boyhood, or my preteen sadness over my parents' divorce, in no way relieved my terror as an adult, and I found myself increasingly sour and hopeless, thinking almost daily about suicide.

And then, in 1990, I got lucky. My therapist at the time, strapped for a way to help me, referred me to a former colleague of hers, a psychopharmacologist named Charles Lathon. I went to him grudgingly, having gotten nowhere with Xanax, to say nothing of Halcion and Valium (or, for that matter, yoga, shiatsu, and biofeedback). Settling into a two-thousand-dollar leather club chair (and calculating my bill by the Japanese art on his walls), I started on a by-then rote recitation of the exotic particulars of my condition. Lathon stopped me after five or six minutes.

"I don't mean to insult you," he said, "but what you have isn't complicated; it's a standard panic disorder. There are several medications that can help you."

"Th-there are?" I stammered, feeling three parts rage to two parts hope. It was the first time I'd ever heard the clinical term uttered, and the coolness with which he said it made me want to strangle my former therapists. To be fair, as I later learned, the drugs alluded to were new; moreover, at the time, only a handful of clinicians were literate in the biochemistry of panic. Happily for me, though, Lathon was one of them, and the drug he prescribed merely changed my life. A week on Anafranil, and I was sleeping through the night, awaking without the usual twinges of premonitory nausea. Within the year, I'd put on thirty pounds of new muscle, and was flying around the country in my new capacity as a journalist, having formerly been unable to board so much as an elevator. It was, I told Lathon, like being let out of jail, given the gift of the wide-open world before me and the courage to find my place in it.

But as soon became evident after my release from solitary, I was in need of something more than just smart-bomb medicine. I had to find out who I suddenly was, absent the overlay of fear and grievance. And so, when Lathon invited me to join a group he was forming, I said yes before he could furnish the details. In the month before it began meeting, however, I got mixed reports about group therapy. Said one friend, a veteran of several such groups, "They usually turn into contests about who's got the worst life, or whose narcissism makes them the teacher's pet." Another likened hers to "a really bad singles joint, where the same two guys cruise you over and over, and take 'no' as a sign of persecution."

Lathon's group, however, proved nothing of the kind. Instead, it was two years of powerhouse theater—of tears wrung out and terror faced up to, of lives disassembled and rebuilt. It would be hard to imagine five more unalike characters—and yet, such was the empathy shared among us that, after sessions, I would lie awake and tremble. It wasn't just the narrative of suffering that stirred me, nor the intimacy of five strangers in a lifeboat. What most transfixed me, and kept me coming every Tuesday, was the sight of us in transformation.

I have heard and read a lot over the years about the inutility of talk therapy. Indeed, for twelve years, I thought of myself as Exhibit A in the case against its efficacy. But what I saw firsthand in Lathon's office emphatically changed my mind. I watched as Sophie, a kind but defeated woman, stood up for the first time to her fire-breathing mother, then laid down the law to her stockbroker boss, who'd had his hands all over her for years. I watched as Mark, a moribund corporate attorney whose career and marriage had fizzled, came to life after kicking the booze and Ativan and launched a brilliant boutique business. And I, who'd begun as a reclusive editor, compulsively rewriting other people's prose on weekends, emerged from it with the confidence to write my own, shining a light on the black holes of our culture—the mindless carnage of L.A.'s gang wars, the sex trade of homeless children in New York. Better still, I met a sane and lovely woman and, instead of fleeing at top speed, stuck around to "make some history with her," per Lathon's firm request. I was eventually emboldened enough to marry the woman, and now find myself in a life that is passably adult, save for my inexplicable purchase of the *New York Post* each morning. Apparently, where matters of bad taste are concerned, no amount of good therapy will avail.

. . .

But if any of the above smacks of the gospel of recovery, then I do Lathon and the five of us great insult. Because what happened in his office over the course of those two years was about as epiphanic as ditch-digging. When you're bent over a trench with a shovel in your hands, you get familiar very quickly with the muscles in your shoulders, and with the tender ridge of skin between your thumb and forefinger. That, in essence, is what Lathon did for us: acquainted us, through hard work, with our neglected bodies, and the text of our wounds and wishes. He taught us many things, but none more important than how to listen to ourselves, to turn down the all-day racket in our heads and listen for the whisper of true self.

"It's painful to listen to yourself, at least in the beginning, but the alternative is endless suffering," Lathon told us. "Among the five of you, you've tried all thirty-one flavors of anesthesia—sex, food, drugs, TV, alcohol, shopping, overwork, et cetera—and what you've seen is that they make more misery than they mask. Because now, in addition to whatever pain you've been numbing, you've got a booze-related ulcer, or a clogged artery from overeating, or chronic back pain or a heart murmur or the whole catechism of misery. And that doesn't even include the thing that hurts most—all those wasted years on ether, when you could have been out living instead."

Though seldom brutal, Lathon minced no words, wielding what he called "the sword of ruthless compassion" to cut through our resistance. Griping about office politics, say, when your real pain lay elsewhere brought a swift and tidy rebuke from him, often in the form of the word *boring!* writ large and held up for all to see. "Go deeper," he kept exhorting us, "tell us where and how it hurts. The dignity of being human consists of the courage to acknowledge shame, and the refusal to be trapped or diminished by it."

With an eye for the dramatic, Lathon set the room up like a downtown stage: two black leather armchairs faced off from one another under the narrow arc of a spotlight, while the other four chairs, including his, formed a wing on either side. At the beginning of each session, he chose two of us at random to go sit in the black leather chairs, instructing one to interrogate the other closely for twenty minutes. "Be a bulldog, Mark, get to the bottom of what's going on between Sophie and her husband. What's he doing to her at home, or out with her family, that made her cry last session? And what's she so afraid of that she's kept silent all these years, worrying herself sick with colitis? Get the whole story from her, leave nothing out, and don't let her strike up the band again about how bad things are for her at work."

In the beginning, Lathon cut in early and often, taking over the questioning or passing notes about what to ask. But by the end of the first year, we had mastered his method, and were effectively running sessions ourselves. We all knew one another's stories cold—where a marriage had gone bad, where the deep wounds lay. Now, we were asking elemental questions: Who *are* you, underneath the symptoms, and what two or three things do you need to accomplish before you leave the planet? Having lain in wait for some blessed future, or run scared circles around the havoc of our past, we began to ask ourselves, "What do I need to live now? What will suffice for me to finally be, after a lifetime of failed becoming?"

"Happiness, or what we mean by it in this culture, is usually thought of as passive," said Lathon. "It's a feeling, a technicolor state of mind, two lovers in a field of daisies. But the truth is that it's exactly the opposite. Happiness consists entirely of *doing*, of making something rich with meaning and passion—a relationship, or a painting, or a body of work. I'm sure you've all known someone in the thrust of that passion; in fact, at some point or other, you've all *been* that person, whether it was while finger-painting in kindergarten or singing lead in the school musical. Your body was lost, transported somewhere in a voluptuous act of expression. It's a state that I call 'serious fun,' in which the body and brain are so in synch that you're not even aware of being. In the time we have left together, we're going to go over that ground thoroughly, because no matter how distant or irrelevant it seems, in it lie the seeds of true self."

The five of us passed a look around the circle; clearly, we had turned some sort of corner. For most or all of the foregoing year, Lathon had been hammering away at the notion of false self, the self that, from earliest age, takes its orders from the world. Said Lathon, "Good enough parents, of whom there are shockingly few in this world, have the grace and confidence to listen to their children, to allow them, within limits, to author themselves. Bad parents, on the other hand, do all the talking, dictating to the child who he or she is from the minute they're out of the womb: 'Why can't you start going to the bathroom like a normal kid?' Or, 'Your brother was reading by the time he was five; what's taking *you* so long?'

"And then," he went on, "there are the parents who say *nothing* to their kids, who pay them the insult of ignoring them altogether. Given either of those kinds of signals, kids form ideas of themselves that have nothing to do with who they are. Our job here is to *listen* to that text, to pay close attention to the dogma of false self—I'm ugly, or I'm weak, or I'm stupid, or No one loves me. Because in the back of your head, just out of earshot, those three or five words have been running your life, jerking you between shame and outrage."

In our anatomy of that text, however, we spent little time reviewing history. Instead, Lathon had us deconstruct the present, theorizing that we were better served by seeing the false self in action than by establishing its date of origin. And so, in listening to the particulars of Mark's doomed marriage, we began to hear the voice of a boy who had been raised without affection, the son of a pediatrician who ran his household like a waiting room. And, listening to me inveigh against the "bastards" in my office, the group soon made out the voice of my mother, telling me, over and over again, to fear the world.

"That—fear the world—is the very mantra of false self," said

Lathon. "It's the scared kid in flight from pain in his past, and living in fear of pain in the future. True self, on the other hand, is the parent that steps in, that says, 'It's okay now, I'm here,' and takes measures to treat the wound. It's the husband who defuses tensions by having an adult conversation with his wife. It's the woman who confronts her harasser at work and says, 'This is going to stop now, or else.' And it's the person who, from time to time, says, 'I'm sorry, I fucked up; what can I do to make it better?' It bravely accepts pain as the price of being human, and proceeds from a mature sense of its own decency."

Looking back now, it occurs to me that, more than anything Lathon said, it was precisely this rational optimism he embodied that most inspired us to change. Implicit in his confidence and respect for us was the sense that any life could be bettered, could yet be made to count for something, no matter how bleak its backstory. If we learned, by degrees, how to be adults in that room, it was as much from watching him as listening to him, measuring ourselves against the resilient cool with which he mediated our distress.

And soon enough, we began to mediate it ourselves, planning for and taking the kinds of "self-respecting action" he had been advocating since day one—starting afresh in a new line of work that challenged us, or fixing the downed lines of communication with the people who mattered most to us. Where once our miseries had seemed intractable, suddenly big changes were being reported in session. Maria cut the cord with her controlling ex-husband, and took up with a nice-guy science teacher, the first man to be introduced to her twin poodles in five years. Mark, buoyed by the success of his new business, got a more or less amicable divorce from his wife and met a charming woman on Block Island; within a year, they were married and expecting their first child. And Sophie, once so susceptible to the stunts of her grown children that she'd been hospitalized for exhaustion, decided instead to put her energy into her marriage, which had been lingering on life support for years.

"This is what I meant by the phrase 'authoring yourselves,' living lives of your *own* design," said Lathon, toasting us with cider at our last session together. "Most people get handed a script in childhood, and follow it all their lives. You guys said the hell with that, and had the guts to own your stories. Ultimately, our stories are all we've got, the one thing that separates us from the whales and white mice. *They* don't write novels about dead ancestors, or dedicate songs to unborn children. *We* do, or at any rate, some of us do, and it's those people who regain some title over their stories that lead lives of meaning and heft."

In the four years since our group broke up, I'd thought a lot about what Lathon taught us: about his elegant metaphor of self as art, the author of its own earned narrative; and about his notions of making, and serious fun, as they applied both to relations and career. But mostly, I thought about those stories, with their endless plot twists and defied expectations. A good deal of living went on within those walls, and a good deal of non-living, too—the adhesive urge to remain fixed in suffering, in the waist-deep mud of the familiar. All of it, in any case, hung on in me, kept shading me like the residue of a recurrent dream.

And so, in the fall of 1994, I approached Lathon for permission to tell those stories. He tactfully declined, saying that it would break faith with the group, and entail a wholesale reconstruction of the facts. A couple of months later, though, he called me back with an offer that went mine one better. Several new groups were in the process of forming, one of which was of particular interest. Each of its members was thoughtful and well-spoken, a vivid teller of his or her story. Each, moreover, was receptive to the idea of letting a writer in, provided that steps were taken to preserve everyone's privacy.

Each further agreed to sit for side interviews, and to furnish such facts and ephemera of personal history as hadn't come up in session.

In turn, I have kept my end of the bargain, changing members' names and descriptions. I have also gone to the length of changing Lathon's name, as it might identify members to their friends and loved ones. That said, I have changed nothing in their essential situation, let the nature of their condition come through as told. At a glance, they seemed to have little in common with their counterparts in my group. They were much less spooked and isolate, in general, and far more prosperous and articulate. Such, in fact, was their effluent charm that I remember thinking, early on, what good dinner company they would make. But it soon became clear that there was no lack of pain to go around, and that each of them had come in with a critical choice to make. That, said Lathon, was the operative idea. It was important that there be an air of mission in the room, a unifying sense of intensity. Styles might clash and agendas diverge, but intensity was indivisible.

"Diversity is great for mutual funds," he said, "but not, I find, for group therapy. People need to be able to *see* themselves as they look around the room, to have somebody they can measure against as the group gets on with its work. When the resistance kicks in, there's nothing like a little peer envy to nudge them off the dime."

That broad similarity aside, however, this group came in with the full complement of modern misery. Alcoholism, bankruptcy, clinical depression, drug abuse, erotomania, filial hatred—each letter of the suffering alphabet was represented here. It may follow, then, that readers will see something in these pages that causes them pain in their own lives. Those who do will likely be curious to hear what Lathon says on the subject. That is fine, as far as it goes. Lathon is an artful and expansive thinker, and has useful things to say about a range of human behavior.

But this is not a book about his methods, nor to be mistaken for a self-help text. Rather, it is a work of narrative journalism that documents, at close hand, a year in group therapy. As such, its intentions are strictly literary: to tell the following stories with power and specificity, and leave other implications to those so inclined. To that end, a cigar is just a cigar, and these six people are only who they are—not archetypes or paradigms but imperfect originals, in whose company various readers may just chance to meet themselves.

one

january

There may be fancier enclaves in New York City than University Place between Eighth and Twelfth Streets, but few, if any, with its recessed calm and heterodox self-possession. Bounded on either end by the blare of Greenwich Village—to the north, Union Square, and its big-box consumerism; to the south, the sprawling mosh pit of Washington Square Park—University Place is New York unplugged, downtown with the volume turned down. It is slender as avenues go, a double lane going north, and is largely spared the cab and truck squalor east and west of it. The shops on the street are quaint, if precious, an array of retro jewelers and one-off designers and rococo antique stores. And the buildings that house them are proportionate in size, spruce Tudor limestones and red-brick dowagers that seldom exceed six stories. It is that rare city space in which you don't feel dwarfed, a sweet spot of scale and horizon.

That late January evening, I was keenly aware of the block's amity, perhaps because I was so unsorted. I was on my way to talk business with Dr. Lathon, and felt preposterous, and out of my depth. A post-therapy relationship with your former therapist is always a ticklish thing. There is the vast inequity in power and intimacy, and the sense that you are still, in some ways, a supplicant, the one who does all the talking. Then there is the question of which self to present. Do you show up as the patient, earnest and in-looking, the teller of your own truths and feelings? Or do you show up as the person you are with relative strangers—facile and outgoing, nervously skimming the surface? You shudder to sound false to one who knows you so thoroughly, and yet it is impossible to pretend a deeper acquaintance, knowing next to nothing about this person. It is more complex still if you are in his debt—and to Lathon, I felt I owed everything.

His office was an L-shaped studio apartment in a prewar co-op off University. You walked into a room that broke left at the window and down two steps into a modest half parlor. This smaller space, screened off by a portiere, held two tan suede recliners and ottomans, and was where Lathon did his one-on-one work. Beyond the bronze screen, the larger portion of the room was furnished in a kind of men's club deluxe. There was an assembly of leather armchairs in a cube formation, two on each side of the square. Along the near wall ran a block of burled maple: Lathon's desk and cabinets and a line of low bookcases. On the shelves, side by side with the pharmacology texts and the abstracts on child psychiatry, was a set of boxed editions of Pound and Eliot. And on the walls and credenza and practically every flat surface was art of all manner and provenance. There was a pair of early drawings by Rauschenberg, and a Reinhardt print that was like a hymn to the next galaxy, a lucid set of grids in tones of black. There were Zulu death masks and Russian tramp art and a Chinese wine vessel from the fifth century.

Wherever the eye went, it found something gleaming, from the pickled blond floorboards that gave back the sun, to the bronze and silver swords above the desk. Here, the room announced, was not just a doctor or aesthete but an adept at the pomps of power. The room further declared that life was an art, an art that could be taught, like a tea ceremony. Tastes might differ and aptitudes vary, but anyone could be helped to make dignified choices and craft a self more in line with one's wishes. Last, the room said, this was no place for hushed voices, for the therapy of implication. Rather, it was a theater of action and incident, and anyone seeking caution would be best served elsewhere.

This was to be my third preliminary talk with Lathon. At our first meeting, we had discussed the terms and ground rules. I was to be present, with my notepad and tape recorder, at each of the scheduled sessions. The tape recorder would be placed on a table inside the square, and I some ten feet beyond it. There, I would be able to mark cues and gestures without being in anyone's sightline. In all other ways, I was to be as absent as possible, to merge into the middle distance. The concern the members expressed wasn't about my being present, but of being reminded of it during session. Therefore, no comments or questions at any time, and a minimum of coughing and throat-clearing. Any expression on my part, voluntary or otherwise, would be construed as a comment on the proceedings.

On the subject of side interviews, Lathon was equally firm. I was to see members alone, in the privacy of their own homes, when spouses and children were out. If that was not practicable, I could meet them in public, but without my pad and recorder. At these one-on-one meetings, they would tell me things that they hadn't brought up in group. More, they would ask me questions about each other, and about Lathon himself. I was to respectfully decline and convey none of what I'd heard, either through word or gesture. They had agreed to tell their stories in the hope that they'd be useful, a template for others stuck in suffering. They had also been lured by lesser motives—by exhibitionism, in a couple of cases, and by desperation in some others. In exchange for their participation, they had been moved up on line, a waiting list of a dozen people. The gain was appreciable, particularly to those in crisis; the next group wasn't scheduled until June.

At our second meeting, Lathon explained why *he* had agreed to participate. As a practicing psychiatrist for fifteen years who had run groups for close to eight, he was increasingly convinced that group was the way to effect deep and expedient change. In the form of these six other people in the room, there was a moral force to be harnessed, a power quite apart from his own. Properly utilized, it had the capacity to pierce resistance, enabling him to trim the course of treatment. Where once he viewed group as a genteel marathon, allowing it to keep its own pace for years until it ran out of gas or interest, he'd since redrafted it as a ten-month sprint—twenty sessions, two and a half hours each, over a term of forty weeks.

"What excites me now," he said, "is how quickly I can tap that power. You *don't* have to wait around months for it to develop; you can actually coach it in a matter of weeks. Basically, it's the same thing I taught your group, namely, the practice of 'serious listening.' What I've done is condense it into a set of skills, and teach it to my patients during the one-on-one work. How, for instance, to tell 'pain' that's genuine from 'suffering' that's false and avoidant. How to turn a 'suffering conversation' into an effective and truthful one. And how to break down pain into its particulars, so you can take action to heal the wound."

At those first two meetings, I didn't ask many questions, or press Lathon for further details. The fact is, I was spooked, and brain-locked. However unprepossessing he may be, it is a weirdness of a high order to be addressed by your former therapist as a peer and collaborator. And whatever else one could say about Lathon, he was far from unprepossessing. He was a very large man, an ex–nose tackle in college who at six-two was probably nudging two-seventy. What remained of his blond hair had receded at some point into a patchy widow's peak, making his sizable skull seem that much bigger, and, if possible, more imperial. He had deep-set eyes under a jutting forehead, and they tracked you from a pool of shadow. When you said something that galled him or tried his patience, they glinted like blue steel bearings. Even in neutral, his eyes could dominate a room, presiding with their hawkish intelligence.

Then there was the matter of his attire. Most big men are fashion paupers, resigned to the hand that's dealt them—the broad-in-the-beam suits and blocky sport coats cut like Chrysler K-cars from the eighties. Lathon, on the other hand, dressed like Pat Riley. He had a man down on Mott Street who made him stitch-for-stitch knockoffs of Armani single-breasteds in size fifty. He was partial to banker's colors, a palette of charcoals and navies, but expressed in a range of rich fabrics. For shirts, he favored jewel-toned broadcloths in whitewashed shades of pastel. In a small concession to comfort, he dispensed with a tie and wore his collar open. Nonetheless, he looked like a man with his own Learjet, or the maître d' at a restaurant you couldn't afford.

All things considered, then, what greeted you at the door was a person of outsize presence. Even seated across from him, you had the sensation of looking up, of somehow being smaller than when you entered. As I sat and listened, though, jotting notes to myself, it occurred to me that Lathon had changed. There had always, in his manner, been an odd convergence of severity and flamboyance, a tension between the observer and performer. In the past, he'd resolved it in favor of prudence, saying less instead of more when chance allowed. Now, however, extravagance had the upper hand, and not just in his diction. In his laughter and gestures there was a kind of preening, a projecting to the back of the theater. It was as if, after years of directing, he had decided to act, or, like stars of a certain stature, to do both. And that, I suspected, was why he'd agreed to this book. It enabled him, albeit masked, to take the stage.

Having scarcely said a word, then, in my first two visits, I showed up for the third with a list of questions. It was pushing nine o'clock and Lathon was just knocking off, after a grueling twelve-hour day. He saw me glance at my pad and was eager to get started himself, but wanted to refresh me, first, about "true" and "false" story. We all start out, he said, in other people's stories, a character in a narrative that predates us. From the moment of our birth, the players in that narrative are busy telling us who we are. First, there's our mother, with her lush projections, spooning out a sense of self at every feeding. Next comes the family and its drama-in-progress, in which our part is often scripted before we can talk. Then it's the church, or the school, or the community, muscling in with its demands and judgments, so that by the time we're capable of asking who we are, there are already firm opinions on the subject.

"False story begins in the first year of life, when we learn that doing 'X' gets Mom's attention. It may be smiling up at her, or reaching out to grab her finger, or crying when she goes to answer the phone. We want something from her and don't have words to ask for it, and so we adopt a series of behaviors to try and get it. Soon, though, we discover that there're two kinds of attention—Mom's approval and Mom's disapproval. She likes us when we're quiet and eat all our peach sauce, and allow her to get us changed without a battle. But, oh, she's angry and withdraws her love when we wake her for the fifth night in a row, or hurl that nice, new bowl from Mikasa halfway across the kitchen from our high chair. We desperately crave the nice Mom, and hate and fear the mean one—literally see and think of them as *two different people*—and so we devise new strategies to woo the nice one. In so doing, we begin to learn to work the room, to play to the sensibilities of the audience—"

His phone rang, the fourth time in fifteen minutes. Reaching back for it, he dialed a code in that sent the calls to his service, then continued with his thought.

"Now, so far, no problem, because that's a skill we'll all need, particularly as we enter the world of other people. But what happens if Mom doesn't respond to our ploys? What if she's needy herself, or too young or damaged to react to our cues and give us the attention we need? Or what if Dad dearly wanted a boy, or is working two jobs and weekends besides, and can barely keep his eyes open after dinner? What if, to paraphrase Winnicott, we *don't* get 'good enough' parenting, and have to find new ways to get attention? Become bratty and destructive, say, and do harm to Mommy's things, or withdraw and funnel the anger inward? That's when the ploy becomes false story; when, in our quest for nurture, we corrupt ourselves, and do injury to the truth of who we are."

"So then, is a false story something we tell other people," I asked, "or is it something that's instilled in us? For instance, the mother you just mentioned, whose baby threw the bowl—what if she blew up at him and yelled, 'You *idiot*, how could you? You're a bad, bad, bad little boy'—is that how a false story gets started?"

"Well, no," he said, "not from that one episode. Understand that kids are resilient characters, and can deal with a certain amount of rough handling. But if that's her tone with him, or the one she takes when things go wrong, then, sure, it'll pollute his identity. It'll go down on the master tape in his head, and replay every time he stubs his toe—'You idiot . . . you idiot . . . you idiot . . .' "

He had much more to say on the subject of false story, and would be doing so in the group in weeks to come. For now, though, he wanted to close with two thoughts. First, he said, the false story proceeds from old wounds, and was a strategy to avoid the pain involved. Second, the pain avoided was almost always a sense of shame, which was the most afflictive of the pains to which we're subject.

"One of the things I teach in the first few sessions," he said, "is how to divide pain up into types. There's separation and loss, i.e. the death of a loved one, or the breakup of a family in divorce. There's physical pain, and the psychic kind that goes with feeling impaired. And then there's the pain of shame and humiliation, which stems from being rejected, or, as I call it, annihilated. It's the thousand and one cruelties, both of commission and omission, that tell someone, 'Sorry, not good enough to be loved.' That's the false story I'm trying to dismantle here, and for which a group can be so impactful."

As a therapist alone with a patient, he said, he had only so much leverage at hand. He could correct distortions and make suggestions, point the patient in the direction of what was healthful. What he couldn't do was bring his own story to bear—tell the patient, for instance, that he, too, had crazy parents, and this was what he did to survive them. He couldn't chide patients for wasting his time, or upbraid them for being dishonest. And he couldn't make them heed his prescriptions, because, after all, he was merely the doctor.

A group, however, could do all those things. Run properly, it was part support meeting, part truth squad. It could confront idling members (or "hinderers," as Lathon called them), and tell them to start working or get out. It could draw out the truth by volunteering its own, and disempower shame by doing likewise. And with "ruthless compassion" it could pursue painful feelings whether the sufferer wished to or not. It was under no constraint to mind its manners, to pick its way carefully around a problem.

"You said, I think, at the last meeting, that you couldn't predict who the hinderers would be—that everyone started off on equal footing, and revealed themselves as time went by," I said. "But now I get the feeling that you do know who they are, and purposely put a couple in every group."

Lathon started slightly and raised a cup to his lips, blowing on the coffee to suppress a smile. "Why would I want to do that?"

"As an irritant. A way for you to stir the pot, and keep the others from getting too cozy."

"Well, I mean, there's no way to be sure," he said. "People do surprise you, particularly the ones you know the best. But yes, I do have some inkling beforehand. I haven't spent these years just twiddling my thumbs."

"So then you know in advance who's wasting their time here, or at least have a good idea," I prodded.

He stopped and looked at me in reassessment, a smile still blinking on pause. "Ah, but there, you see, is the surprise," he said. "Some of my biggest success stories have been hinderers. In fact, for every hinderer who walks out angry, there's another one who takes the prize, who leaves here having made the farthest leap, and become a full-fledged, sentient adult."

I thought this over a moment, more than a little skeptical.

"Well, that's nice to know," I said, "although it didn't happen in my group. Our hinderer, Barbara, almost started a riot."

He gave an amused grunt, and drank the last of his coffee. "But it did happen in your group. There were two resisters. You were the other one."

Amused by my stupefaction, he put down his cup, and peered over the rim of imaginary glasses. It was his signature gesture, a rhetorical tweak for taking up his time with nonsense.

"You don't remember?" he said. "You fought me tooth and nail on *everything*. I was 'arrogant,' a 'bully,' I charged 'twice the going rate'—you even gave me hell about the soap in my bathroom. I was too 'cheap' to spring for the liquid kind and forced you to use bar soap, which exposed you all to viruses and bacteria."

I laughed out loud, the details trickling back. "My God," I croaked, "was I that big a dork?"

"Oh, you made quite sure I knew you were out there," he said. "You were clinging to an outdated act from college—the pissed-off writer who was too good for us lowbrows. In short, the very model of false story. And it took us a while to get it across to you that that act wasn't playing real well here. We had to beat it into you that no one cared about your credentials. What we cared about was the guy behind the behavior, and to your credit, you finally got that. Began to fill us in on what it was like as a kid, after your father walked out and left you alone with your mother, who was too depressed and damaged to hold a job. In fact, I remember people in tears here when you talked about being a boy and lying awake listening to her cry in the next room, or how you walked around for years after your father moved out, telling yourself, 'I'm ugly, I'm stupid . . . I'm ugly, I'm stupid.' Those were memorable sessions, and, as I recall, they changed the flow here. Instead of you sitting there, rocking the boat, suddenly, you were up here rowing."

By now, Lathon was fading and in need of refreshment, and I prevailed upon him to grab a bite with me. We went downstairs to the jazz joint Bradley's, and took a booth away from the piano. Ordering a couple of burgers from the cataleptic waiter, we fumbled for the thread of our conversation. There was some ambling chatter about the upcoming Super Bowl, followed by a sidebar about Lathon's practice. It was a relief to both of us when I opened my notepad and proceeded with my questions about his background.

Lathon was born in Tulsa, Oklahoma, and raised in a gulf town in Louisiana. His father worked a shift at a tool plant serving the oil patch; his mother taught art at a junior college. As a teen, Lathon fell in love with football and Kerouac, and aspired to become the first poet to play in a Pro Bowl. However, his father, a former sergeant in the Pacific theater, insisted he join the army and carry a rifle. This was 1966, and Lathon defied him by going to college, where he badly tore a knee playing springtime football. Relieved, at least, not to be eligible for the draft, he buckled down and took a degree at Auburn, then was admitted to medical school at Clemson. It was there, as a student inclined toward pediatrics, that he made a discovery that altered his plans.

"Obviously, this was a very different time and place," he said, "and years before anyone talked about patients' rights, but what I saw really appalled and shocked me, and that was that, almost without exception, doctors didn't listen to patients, and treated with them with all the sympathy of a garage mechanic."

Appalled by a culture of "grandiose deafness," Lathon resolved to become a psychiatrist and make listening the core of his practice. He graduated from medical school in 1976, got a grant to study folk

healing in India for a year, then came to New York to do his residency
in child psychiatry. It was while on a subsequent fellowship at the
Cornell Medical Center that he made a second rude discovery.

"I was working at a nursery downtown," he said, "studying separation issues in kids with working moms, when I learned what people like Margaret Mahler have known for a long time—that a large
percentage of parents don't listen to their children. I mean, here you
had these four-year-olds bursting with the news of the day—how
many blocks they'd managed to stack up, and which one of their
friends they'd decided to murder—and their parents were utterly
indifferent to it, focused on getting the kid into his raincoat. It was
heartbreaking to watch, this pathology in the making—children
coming to bitter terms with themselves because no one gave a damn
about their story."

When he opened his practice, then, in 1981, Lathon devoted it
to the treatment of children. Eventually, he expanded it to include
the parents of his patients, but continued to do postdoctoral training in child psychiatry, and began taking notes toward a book. Originally a disciple of what he calls "Freudian mythology," he found
himself drifting from the transference model, in whose formal re-
straint he saw a certain arrogance.

"At some point, listening is as inhumane as not listening, if that's
all the patient gets from you," he said. "They're in pain and need relief, as well as compassion and guidance, not your two or three in-
terpretive couplets. The sad fact is, a lot of the people I treat are
functionally unparented, and what they want more than anything is
some mentoring. Remedial instruction in how to respect themselves,
and make mature, sensible choices."

And so, after five years in practice, Lathon stepped out from behind the couch, becoming a "hands-on coach in competency," as he
put it. He taught patients how to identify their feelings and voice
them effectively to others. He gave them a practicum on how to
make good decisions and to rein in harmful impulses. He asked

clients to name their goals and interests and assigned tasks in pursuit of these. And he challenged patients when he found them "hugging the shoreline," unable or unwilling to go forward. What fear was keeping them stuck in place, and how credible was that fear, under inspection?

At the same time, something else was happening that would significantly affect Lathon's practice. An early believer in the link between mood disorders and malfunctions in neurochemistry, he tracked the trials of the SSRI drugs, and the reports from doctors using them abroad. Virtually the day they became available for use on these shores, Lathon offered them to his more afflicted adult patients. The results, he said, exceeded his best hopes; in some cases, patients were literally transformed.

"Particularly in people with entrenched depression, what I saw was the emergence of a *soul*," he said. "They'd been trapped for years in an inorganic story, with a mood and a worldview that were alien to them. They weren't morose by nature, or morbidly shy; what they had were flawed neurotransmitters. Now, I'm aware of all the groaning about Prozac, et cetera, and the idea that these drugs are like psychic cheating. And in one sense, the complaint has definite merit—they *have* been wildly overprescribed. They aren't for people with mild depression, or anxiety about taking their law boards. They aren't to be handed out by family doctors whose only knowledge of them is the foldout circular. These are powerful agents with side effects, particularly when taken together. But for someone who's suffering from chronic panic, a drug like Paxil isn't an indulgence; it's the difference between living your life out there and living it in hiding."

At long last, our burgers arrived, after a wait best described as geological. Anxious not to embarrass myself, I cut mine in half, and poured some ketchup on the side. Lathon, on the other hand, slathered it on thick, heaping on pickles and cole slaw for good measure. Tearing at the contraption with prodigious bites, he sat there chewing with his mouth half open, the juices running down his fists. To mask my surprise, I resumed the questioning.

"In broad terms, how many of your patients ask for drugs, and how long do they typically stay on them?"

He dabbed at his chin and forehead with a napkin, sweating from the infusion of food. "It depends," he said, clearing his throat at length. "I've got patients who come for just therapy and get drugs, and patients who come for drugs and get therapy instead. As I said, there's a lot of silliness going on out there, people popping pharmaceuticals like they're antibiotics, and switching on and off at whim. But if you want my general take, here it is. For a small percentage of clients—those with chronic impairment—a serotonin drug is a long-term treatment, like insulin for a diabetic. Very simply, it makes life possible. But for a great majority—and I prescribe for about a third of the people I treat—the SSRIs are a short-term tool, something to help them out of the hole they've fallen into. Whether it's the end of a marriage or the loss of a career, there's a period of paralysis that goes with grief; a time when basic functioning is impaired. But with a short course of Zoloft, they can sort through the pain while they begin to put their life back in order. And that, to me, is the goal of good therapy: to get people better in the shortest time possible, and out living in life instead of in therapy."

This touched on a matter that caused me unease—the reduction of group to twenty sessions from its previously unfixed term. I broached my concern, and he responded with a speech that, for all its vigor, sounded canned. Our time here was short, he said, and meant to be lived with passion. Above all, it was not to be squandered in therapy, lamenting the wasted years and chances. What mattered now was not affixing blame or motives, but making the most of the time that still remained us. To that end, he'd set up a deadline for group, a ticking clock to convey how brief the days were. Since adopting the change, he'd seen marked improvement in the absentee rate, and in the level of intensity in sessions. There was a feeling of sustained purpose, a commitment among the members to put every minute to use.

He explained that he saw patients between three and six months before considering them for group. In private treatment, he established the nature of their pain and brought them through the worst of the presenting crisis. Once they were sufficiently better, he narrowed the bandwidth of treatment, focusing on a chief concern. Exploring that area closely, two themes would emerge: the arcs of true and false story. It was at this point that group became expedient therapy—when the struggle to evolve from false story to true warranted the support and pressure of one's peers.

"Again, if the aim is to get people better fast," he said, "then group can cut the process by half. What might take me two years to get across single-handedly, a group can drive home in one. Of course, it's important that you have the right people in group. Having tried the other ways of putting a group together—choosing people from the same age group or the same social class—I've found that what works best is an equivalency of mind. Choosing people at the same level of talent and intelligence, who can respect the caliber of the person sitting across from them."

"I see," I said, flipping my notepad shut, and pushing away my half-eaten burger. "And how would you rate the caliber of the people in *this* group?"

He sat back and smiled, his gaze straying in the direction of the piano, where the singer was about to resume his set.

"Oh please, I'm no fool," he grunted. "I've stacked the deck good. This is the smartest bunch of people I've ever assembled."

There was one last piece of business to attend to, and for this, we returned to Lathon's office. Putting up his feet on a suede recliner, he gave me a primer on the group. Originally, it had consisted of three men and three women, but in the last week, one of the women had dropped out, having taken a new job that would entail travel. The resulting imbalance concerned him a bit, but he thought it would sort out all right. And given the set of circumstances—a writer in the room, preparing to make the private public—the list of alternates was short. Happily, the new member brought a rich dimension: the complexity of starting over at age sixty.

Here then, at admittedly thumbnail length, are profiles of the group's six members.

Sara, thirty-seven, is the fashion editor of a glamour magazine, having risen through the ranks at Condé Nast. Tall and quite beautiful, she was a model for much of her twenties, laboring in the frenetic and largely anonymous middle rungs of the couture world in Europe. Eventually tiring of the fierce vapidity of the business, and the miracle diet of cocaine and Marlboros, she dropped out and came to New York to finish school, getting a degree from NYU. After several lean years as a freelance journalist, she bowed to necessity and took a job as an editorial assistant. There, her talent attracted notice and marked her out for stardom at the magazine.

"Sara is extremely bright, and locked-in, career-wise," said Lathon. "The twelve-hour workdays, that mix of charm and aggression—at the office, she's one of those people you wouldn't dream of saying no to. But away from there, she's very much a different person. She's depressed and withdrawn, afraid she'll never find a man, or if she does, he'll be cruel to her, like her dad was. And so what you have, really, is *two* Saras, or two sides of a false story. The real Sara is neither as brusque as the one at work or as defeated as the one that's moping at home. She's a bright, stunning woman who could have her pick of admirers, if we can correct some old ideas about herself."

Lathon had seen Sara, on and off, for several months. She was taking no medications as group began.

Rex, thirty-one, ran a risk arbitrage desk at one of the white-shoe banks on Wall Street. A month before group began, he resigned his position, citing a wish to devote more time to his family. His first child, a daughter, had been born on Thanksgiving, and he talked about staying home with her for six months. This would afford him the chance, he said, to reinvent himself, after eight-plus go-go years of acquiring wealth. He had a loft in Soho, a house in the Hamptons, and a cushion of three million in cash and stocks, if he opted out of the money chase for good.

Those, at least, were his stated reasons for quitting. The real reason, said Lathon, was that Rex had crashed and burned after an affair with an exotic dancer. Indeed, while his wife was in her ninth month of pregnancy, Rex was stalking his mistress in Chelsea, whacked on a two-day coke binge. In the course of the affair, he'd put everything he valued at risk—his health, his marriage, even his professional well-being, after a series of accounting errors at work. And though he'd pulled back from the ledge, having broken it off with the dancer and ceased his drug consumption, he was still running around with his Wall Street buddies, behaving as if the blowup were just a glitch.

"Rex is your standard golden boy—the rules simply don't apply to him," said Lathon. "He played hockey at Dartmouth, got A's without trying, and waltzed through Wharton Business School as the youngest in his class. But lurking under the glibness is an angry guy who's acting out all over the place. He grew up in one of those families that never talk about anything—the father obsessed with business and politics, the mother a veritable hive of fake cheer. For all his achievements, Rex never got their attention, much less their rightful applause. And so now he's discovered what a lot of neglected kids know—that you get more attention being a bad boy than a good one. But, of course, it's a false story, and a very dangerous one, too, if he

28

isn't disabused of it fast. The way to get respect isn't to rub people's faces in it, but to open an effective conversation with them."

Lathon had been treating Rex for about six months. He had prescribed Zoloft for depression, but was in the process of weaning him off it.

Dylan, forty-eight, was a former rock-and-roll sideman who in his twenties toured with bands like Yes and Kansas. He had an ear for melodies with pomp and sweep, and at thirty was induced to come down off the road and write theme songs for TV shows. His contact, Greg, was well established in the business, and their partnership was a fine success. The work poured in through their agent, Harold, and the three men became great friends. They were co–best men at one another's weddings, co-godfathers to one another's children, and fellow travelers at AA and rehab, going on and off the wagon more or less in lockstep. Finally, approaching forty, they sobered up for good, and bought houses for their growing families in Montclair.

And then suddenly, the year before, the earth split open. Greg, a reformed smoker who now ran five miles a day, dropped dead of an aneurysm as he sat at his desk. At forty-seven, he was a year younger than Dylan. Three months later, Harold found blood in his urine and was diagnosed with bladder cancer. Though the surgery got most of it, his prognosis was just fair, and he retired to focus on recovery. And in the third of a series of knockout blows, Dylan came home one night and was asked by his wife to move out. Her request wasn't entirely unexpected—they'd been in couples therapy since the spring—but the timing couldn't have been much worse. It was the week before Christmas, and their five-year-old twins were devastated.

"It's like he woke up in a war zone—the bombs just keep on dropping," said Lathon. "My fear with Dylan is he may be in *too* much pain, and overwhelm the group with his heartbreak. But if ever one of my patients needed a place to collapse, Dylan would be it, hands down. His career is a shambles, he misses his girls terribly, and he's living in a dive way over on Tenth Avenue, brooding about what he did to deserve this. I'm seeing him twice a week now, but that's mostly damage control. What this group can do better than I can is grieve with him and help make a new story out of the wreckage. Because the old story—the wife and the beautiful twin daughters, living in a dream house on two-plus acres—that story is gone forever. But when the mourning is over, there's a new story to be written. Dylan's a bright, gifted guy whose only part in all this was staying married to a woman he calls the Ice Maiden. And if we can just get him through the worst of the suffering, he'll find that there's a much better life to be made, for himself as well as his kids."

With and without his wife, Dylan had been in treatment for a year. At the moment, he was taking several medications: Effexor for depression, Ativan for anxiety, and Ambien for severe insomnia.

Lina, forty-five, was the founder and director of a community mental health clinic in Morrisania. An advocate for poor children, she had hand-carried a series of programs into a particularly grim section of the Bronx. As a young case manager in the mid-seventies, she colonized an abandoned building on Southern Boulevard, converting it into a day-care center. She later raised the money to add an after-school program, hiring social workers and reading coaches and art and music teachers. Through years of state budget slashes, she'd somehow grown her clinic, such that she now presided over a staff of thirty, and again that many interns and volunteers.

Her home life, however, was another matter. She was locked into a bitter and, thus far, futile struggle to obtain a divorce from her husband of twenty years. The scion of a wealthy family, Anton was engaged in a stall, the purpose of which was to break Lina financially. As she'd learned in the course of her two-year battle, this was a ploy much in vogue with rich men these days—to inflict huge legal fees on their cash-poor wives through a series of delays and adjournments. Exhausting their funds, and faced with sizable debt, the wives often settled for pennies on the dollar merely to bring the ordeal to a close. Thus far, Lina had refused to crack, but new fault lines were sprouting every day.

"She has two kids at home, a son and daughter," Lathon explained, "and they're getting more freaked out as this drags on. The son, who's fourteen and was an honors student, is running with a real bad crowd in the park, drinking beer and cutting class, and so on. And his sister spends all of her time online, concocting some weird fantasy self in one of those chat rooms. Meanwhile, Lina has dropped thirty pounds, and is prone to bouts of sobbing at her desk. She feels tiny and powerless, thanks to her husband, Anton, who's skillfully wrecked her confidence with years of insults. And one of the things we'll look at is what kept her so long with a man who disrespected her. But first, we need to do some crisis management—relieve her of some of the pain she's in, and help her put out fires at home and work."

Lathon had been treating Lina for nine months. She was taking Serzone for depression, Buspar for anxiety, and Ambien for insomnia.

Peter, thirty-eight, was a senior analyst for one of the Big Five accounting firms. He'd come in the previous spring in a deep depression, after the collapse of his three-year marriage. He was from an old Scots family that traced its roots to the tenth century, and his divorce was the first in the clan's annals. In this and other ways, he felt he'd let down his parents, whose opinion was of the highest importance to him. Owing to his shyness, he was stuck in place on the corporate ladder, despite years of ardent service to his company. He'd made very few friends since his transfer from Boston, and spent most of his evenings alone, watching a ball game. Above all, he felt invisible and weightless, locked out of the life of the city.

"You're not supposed to play favorites in this business, but Peter's someone I root very hard for," said Lathon. "He's a sweet, gentle guy who's basically been ignored by the world, and he's determined to see that attention is paid. To improve his prospects, he went to night school at Fordham and got his MBA with honors last summer. He goes into the office on Saturdays and does *other people's* work, so that management can't help but take notice. And though it took him some time to work up to it here, he finally felt comfortable responding to personal ads, and met a lovely woman in the process. I won't spoil the surprise now, but Peter really hit the jackpot with Kara. He'll be the envy of all the group, when they hear the details."

The upturn in his love life aside, however, Peter had much to work on. He was paralyzed by a fear of being humiliated, which kept him from pursuing a job at another firm. He lay awake worrying about what people thought of him, and kicked himself for his tongue-tied fumbling. And he was loath to make a move without consulting his mother, a matron who presided in stony silence.

"Peter's taken the first steps to becoming his own man," said Lathon. "Now what he needs is a solid push, some pressure from his peers to cut the cord. There *is* such a thing as being *too* good a son. Particularly if he plans on getting remarried."

Peter had been seeing Lathon for eleven months. He had taken Zoloft, then Serzone, for depression, but had been able to cycle off after a six-month course.

Jack, fifty-nine, was a former Broadway producer with almost two dozen shows to his credit. A jut-jawed character with leading-man looks and the kind of charm that opened doors at twenty paces, he had a string of hit musicals in the seventies and eighties, enriching himself and his partner. But by the end of the decade he'd either lost his touch or was hamstrung by addictions to cocaine and alcohol, and began kiting money from his shows. The amounts in question were never substantial, and were replaced as soon as his next profit check came in. Nonetheless, these "loans to himself" were viewed by prosecutors as embezzlement. Through the good offices of his lawyer, Jack managed to avoid jail but agreed, as part of a plea deal, to cease being a producer for seven years.

"When I first started seeing him, I was in fear for his life," said Lathon. "He would hole up for months and not take calls or leave the apartment, other than to go cop drugs. His wife once raced over here in a state of panic, saying she'd found a book on how to kill yourself and make it look like an accident. It wasn't so much the loss of his career that crushed him, though he loved every facet of pro- ducing a show, and from what I gather, was brilliant at it. No, what broke his heart was the loss of his *story*, that tortured set of 'facts' we call identity. He still hasn't recovered from it, though he's been sober for four years, and has worked very hard to get his life back. But what he's up against now is the essential question, and one I'll be putting to each of these people—who *are* you, beyond the job you report to, and the people you share a roof with? What signifies you, what makes you happy? At what are you most completely your- self?"

Jack had seen Lathon, on and off, for five years. He took no medications of any kind.

two
february

It had been, as these things go, a surpassingly mild New York winter. For the latter third of December and all of January, temperatures lolled in the forties and fifties, prompting a rollback in the city's fatalism. There were outbreaks of cruise wear in the bars up Third Avenue, as the young-money crowd mourned the ski season that wasn't with Mai-Tais and Jell-O shots. Schoolkids ran coatless through the playgrounds at lunchtime, cheerfully bruising one another. The trial in Brentwood was at last under way, a Republican broom had swept the halls of Congress, and yet every second conversation you heard concerned the bright side of global warming.

And then, the first week of February, the revels ended. A colossal storm put two feet of snow down, encasing the town in white concrete. For most of three days, nothing moved but the salt trucks, grinding their gears laboriously. Boulder-sized drifts made sidewalks impassable, forcing pedestrians into the middle of the street. A hard, silver light overhung the sky, topping a silence as archaic as horse traffic. More snow was boding, but didn't present. In its place came a punishing freeze.

That Tuesday, the seventh, was one of the coldest in years. Bundled to the eyeballs, people waded against the wind, which seemed to converge from three sides. The few cabs in service crawled ahead at foot speed, unable to stop short on the packed ice. I gave up trying to flag one and walked to Lathon's, ducking into doorways to catch my breath.

In his office, Lathon was apologetic. He'd seesawed all day about canceling the session, but was loath to, given the density of his schedule. At last, he'd called each of the members at work and presented them with the option. None, however, wanted to wait the two weeks, and so, for better or worse, we were on.

It was warm, even sultry, in the larger of the two rooms, as the old radiator hissed like a samovar. The light from the sconces was dialed down, conferring a soft, benedictory glow. In the slim kitchenette, a pot of water was brewing. Grouped beside it sat a cluster of whimsical mugs, each festooned with the caricature of a genius— Michelangelo woozy on his Sistine scaffold, having bumped his head on the ceiling; Thomas Edison, fright-wigged and medium crisp, after sticking his finger in a socket. The inscription below each was identical: NO PAIN, NO GAIN: DULL PLANET.

"They were given me by a former patient," said Lathon. "A very sweet woman, but she made pottery out of all my pet phrases. Nearly put me off of pet phrases forever."

I took my tea in a van Gogh and sat in the chair set apart for me; presently, the wall phone buzzed. Lina and Peter were the first arrivals, entering within moments of each other. Beet-faced and dazed from the assaultive cold, they hung their coats on the rack in the foyer, and warily introduced themselves.

"My God, that *wind*, it's like a tornado," said Lina, rubbing her arms for warmth. "I was afraid it was going to pick me up and throw me across the street. I'm just glad I ate a heavy lunch today."

This last was uttered with an anxious laugh that sounded rather more like a sob, and which quickly established itself as Lina's signature, punctuating much of what she said. She was a tall, gaunt woman with slightly bowed shoulders, as if she had walked a far distance carrying suitcases. Her handsome face had Hellenic lines— a long, thin nose and elliptical mouth, and nut-brown eyes of great expression. Beneath those eyes, though, were the markers of suffering—plump, dark circles that conveyed exhaustion and a surplus of stored-up sadness. She was somberly dressed in a black suit and pale blouse, and wore, by way of adornment, only a plain strap watch.

As would be her way for the next several months, Lina took the chair directly across from Lathon, where she was at all times within his sightline. Peter, on the other hand, chose the seat most obscure to him, two over on the right-hand side. (Tonight, the "circle" of chairs was shaped more like a diamond, with Lathon at home plate along the left-hand wall, and Peter down the line at first base.) Within moments of settling in and shaking off the chill, Peter began to perspire. He dabbed self-consciously at his neck and temples, and wiped both palms on his pant legs. Embarrassed to be seen at it, he stuffed his hands under his thighs, and adopted a queasy smile.

He had a sweet, solicitious face of the sort not seen much in these parts—earnest green eyes; soft, fair cheeks; and a gently rounded forehead that suggested charity. His gray suit and tie seemed deliberately bland, chosen for their indistinguishability from the thousands just like them on Broad Street. So, too, with his glasses, whose thin steel rims shrugged off any pretensions to style. The only trace of vanity could be seen on top of his head, where he'd composed what remained of his baby-fine hair in a plane as thin as spring ice.

At twenty to seven, three of the other members showed up, in more or less lockstep procession. Sara, the former model turned magazine editor, blew in all out of breath but looking radiant. Dressed in a gray cable-knit over velvet stretch pants, she had the sort of effortless, tossed-together glamour of a woman who'd grown up skiing the Alps. She wore no makeup beside a flicker of lip gloss, and had her black hair tied in a knot. And though she'd filled out becomingly since her days in front of the camera, her face had held on to its Modigliani beauty, all length and shadow and oblique angles.

Sara chose the seat located farthest from Lathon, and nudged it another foot closer to the door. Peter, who'd eyed her intently since she entered, saw this retreat and seemed stung by it, as if it were a rebuke to him for staring. Lina also noted the move, and looked to Lathon for reaction. Lathon, however, was on the phone with his service, and gave no sign of having seen it.

Jack, the former producer, was next to arrive, followed close behind by Dylan. They apologized for their lateness, introduced themselves around, and sat in the two chairs to Lina's right. Immediately, everyone began glancing at Jack, a liberty he had the good taste not to notice. Almost sixty, he was improbably striking, with the kind of platinum good looks seen in Cadillac ads: a cleft chin and nautical cheekbones under taut, ruddy skin, and hair the color of sea spray. He even dressed the part of the elegant yachtsman at port, in a blazer with brass buttons and gold Rolex purring away. Only around the mouth was there any evidence of trouble, in the form of a fixed downturn at the corner of the lips, a grimace dug deep, like a trench line.

About Dylan, to the right of Jack, it was hard to draw a sense; he seemed both present and gone in the same breath. He was a tall, trim man with suburban good looks—neat salt-and-pepper hair, the remnants of a tan, and the ease of a loose-fitting life. But behind the bland smile there was something missing, some dimension of affect or spirit. It was evident in his eyes, a kind of deadness or vacancy, as though he'd decided to stay home but sent his body along out of courtesy. While the others kibbitzed, waiting for the sixth to arrive, Dylan stared out the window, tracking the movements of a plane. Occasionally, he turned and followed the chatter, but drifted back to his study of the skyline.

Finally, at ten of seven, Rex showed up. He was profuse with apologies for keeping the group waiting, having badly misjudged the hassle of getting here. "The tow trucks outnumbered the cabs by three to one," he groused. "A little cold snap, and this town just falls apart."

Though he'd come from home (and hadn't worked in six weeks), Rex was dressed in a suit—a three-button Zegna of superior cut, its shoulders pitched perfectly, like a slate roof. The tie I recognized from a stroll through Barney's, where, once a year, they knocked it down to a hundred dollars. And while the others wore snow boots (or, in Peter's case, galoshes), Rex sported a pair of black suede lace-ups, as if the cold were merely a nuisance state of mind. He was of average height but had an athlete's bearing, the loping swagger you see on Big Ten campuses, and the confidence that comes from feats of grace. He had fine blond hair that was just beginning to thin; flushed, pink cheeks exuding boyish vitality, and blue eyes on the prowl for mischief.

Rex plopped down in the chair next to Sara, and, like her, nudged it a foot or two toward the door. Sitting side by side there in their fashionable clothes, at a slight but detectable remove from the group, they looked like they'd wandered in from the theater, in search of a quick drink between acts.

Lathon smiled and looked around with a flourish, welcoming the members to group. He thanked them for trudging over through this "nuclear winter," and was gratified by their eagerness to get started. They were an unusual group, he said, six people of rare aptitude, with wit and accomplishments to spare. All, moreover, were strongly self-willed, having chosen a life that was vastly different from their parents', often at considerable hardship. Of their qualities in common, the most prominent was ambition. They were determined to have the things their hearts required.

For those reasons, he said, a memorable year was in store, a year of leaps and plot turns. Not for this group the modest change by increment; no, this group was shooting for the moon. That was great and he would help them, but it left no time for settling in; for the five or six sessions of getting comfy. Hence, the importance of being on time, and doing all the work that he assigned them. There would be a lot to reflect on, to mull over in the shower, or sitting on the parkway, stuck in traffic. In order to make a new story, they would have to assemble the old one, to bring in the buried pieces of their past. That was a big job, requiring an extensive search, and much of it would be conducted on their own time.

Finally, he said, if hard work was Rule One, then fearless honesty was One-A. The goal here was not to become friends or allies, because allies overlooked things; they equivocated. The goal, rather, was to point one another toward the truth, even if it meant hurt feelings. What they would get in return was worth the discomfort— an unambiguous assessment by their peers. Each should be prepared, then, for the occasional bruise, and to receive it in the spirit of earned wisdom.

Lathon went over some points of order (when to see him about prescriptions; the protocol for schedule changes, etc.), and capped the preliminaries with a smile. "All right, then," he said, "before we push off here, I'd like to invite Rex and Sara to move their chairs in. That way, the rest of us can use our normal voices, instead of resorting to our bullhorns."

There was a smattering of laughter; Lina winked at Peter, vindicated. Sheepishly, Rex and Sara complied, nudging their chairs into alignment with the others. Lathon's smile, welcoming them back into the group, also quietly served notice that very little was going to be lost on him. At the head of the circle, he looked around and deemed it fit, and smiled again to bring the curtain up.

"And so," he said, "who'd like to kick things off for us, by telling us who they are and what brings them here?"

A squirmy silence set in. Group members shrugged at one another and traded shivery grins, like little kids ordered, on the first day of camp, into the deep end of the pool.

"Anyone?"

This time, there was some tentative clearing of throats, though for the most part, the members seemed suddenly captivated by their own feet.

"My God," Lathon said in what remained of his drawl. "Surely, you didn't tramp through two feet of snow just to hang out and pad my bankbook."

This coaxed a couple of laughs from the group, lightening the mood by a quarter turn.

"He's right," Jack nodded. "At a hundred bucks a head, we oughta be killing each other for who goes first."

Squaring his shirt cuffs, Jack volunteered for the honors. He described himself as a fifty-nine-year-old father of four, and the grandfather of nine and counting—"We like to think of ourselves as the Jewish Kennedys," he said. He'd been married twice to Marcia, his "fourth and final wife," for a total of eighteen years now—twelve the first time and six the second, with "a couple of years off for bad behavior." All jokes aside, he felt blessed to have her; she'd been the one person who'd stood with him through the hell years.

Jack paused for a sip of the coffee he'd brought, collecting himself for the next part. "I realize I'm probably telling you about my wonderful wife to try and build up credit for myself. So you'll think, 'Hey, *she's* a great gal, he must be okay, too.' Except that I'm *not* such a great guy, or at least I wasn't for a long time, and I—"

He stopped and looked at Lathon with a plaintive face. "You know, as many times as I've done this at AA meetings, gotten up and said my spiel to a roomful of strangers . . ."

"You're doing fine," Lathon comforted. "Just take your time. If this were easy to tell, none of us would be here."

Jack nodded and eyed his cup, not greatly encouraged. "It's just that, when you're talking to other drunks, you pretty much know where you stand. Whereas here, I might come off sounding like O.J."

"Don't worry," said Lathon, laughing. "There're no saints in this room. Besides which, you drive a Town Car, not a Bronco."

"Yeah, well, not anymore," Jack said amid the laughter. "I let it go last fall. I couldn't afford to keep up the parking."

And with that said, somber but less unnerved, he got on to telling his story. He was an ex-trader on Wall Street who, in mid-career, had chucked it in to become a producer. He'd been stagestruck, he said, since the age of nine, when his mother, a former actress, took him to see *The Pirates of Penzance* at the old Belasco on Broadway. Once a month, they'd dress up and see a matinee together, then afterward, sit in Sardi's and have burgers and Cokes, one booth down from Danny Kaye. When Jack got older, she read lines with him for his school plays, and paid out of her own pocket for his voice and dance lessons. Jack's father, however, who worked the crime beat at the *Mirror*, had little or no taste for such ambitions, and come college, Jack deferred to him and studied finance. He spent the next three decades amassing wealth and ex-wives, and becoming a "full-on, shoot-the-lights-out alcoholic."

"Some people drink because they were abused as children, or because they've got the gene for it, or it helps them relax," he said. "Me, I drank because I flat-out loved it; I loved every single thing that had to do with it. I loved the taste of booze, even if it was third-rate scotch; I could sit there and savor it like old wine. I loved the *smell* of a bar, and just hanging there on a Saturday, nursing a beer and doing some work. I tell you, I got more done in bars than in my office on Wall Street. In fact, at one stretch—"

"Uh, Jack, we could do with less of the Dewar's ad and more of what happened six years ago," said Lathon. "I know I told you to take your time, but do try to stick to the important stuff."

Jack chafed a bit, grousing that this *was* important—at least, it was to him. He was trying to make the point that the drinking was his fault—not his father's, or his mother's, or the bad luck of heredity. Going back to his great-grandparents, in fact, not one person in his family had ever had a problem with booze. And the same thing went for what he'd done *while* drunk—the divorces, the accidents, the embezzlement, and so on. All that was on him and not the addiction, and he wanted that much clear from the outset.

"Uh, well, before we accept your plea," said Lathon, "we *would* sort of like to hear the facts."

The other members laughed at this, but Jack grunted, folding his arms. Already, something was brewing between him and Lathon, a mutual sizing-up and marking of territory. Both were big bulls who were clearly used to primacy, to the deference given men of heft and carriage. Both, moreover, wore their vanity proudly, from the tilt of their jaw to the shine on their boots. Judging by their posture, neither of them liked being pushed. It shaped up to be an interesting undercard.

Jack picked up his story from the point he quit Wall Street, going into production with a partner. Excited by the abundance of new talent downtown—the young Sam Shepard, David Rabe, et al.—they started off bankrolling plays in the East Village. After a couple of bumpy years, they unearthed a writer with a hand for sex farce, and rode him all the way to Broadway. Over the next fifteen years, they brought two dozen shows there, including a number that played profitably on the road. Even in a down year, Jack was clearing two million—and spending whatever he made, plus 10 percent.

He paused here, shaking his head in small circles, as if a minor seismic event were occurring beneath him. Looking at the other members, he seemed to search them for censure. Instead, they looked back at him, murmuring words of recognition, as if this were merely another spin on the tribal story.

"Like I said, Jack, it'll be hard to shock this group," said Lathon. "So just tell it, and don't worry about making enemies. As they say on *The Ricki Lake Show*, 'We can relate, man.'"

Snickering at this stab at hipness, Jack went on. By the middle of the eighties, he was supporting three households and putting four kids through college or prep school. He had also, fatefully, traded in his pot habit for a raging cocaine problem. Initially, this enabled him to drink less and do more, to work a series of twelve-hour days and save the serious bingeing for the weekends. And, for a time, he deluded himself that the switch was healthy; that coke was a functional, even facilitating, drug. But by the end of the decade, he'd burned a hole in his septum, and spent most of his days in a robe and flip-flops, sending out for narcotics and fast food. (This was the two-year period when his wife took off, unwilling to watch him snort himself to death.) Running low on cash, Jack began to "borrow" from his productions, kiting funds off profits earmarked for investors. He repaid the money whenever a check came in, but that didn't suffice to keep a lid on the matter, and in 1989 he was arrested and charged with embezzlement. Thanks to a skillful attorney, he avoided going to jail but was hit with a huge fine and stiff suspension.

"The fine," he said, "ate up most of my assets, and whatever else was left, the IRS grabbed. It seems that, in all my madness, I'd forgotten to file my taxes—for a period of three years running. And so, even though I was still getting checks from shows on tour, the feds took fifty-five percent for back taxes, and then the state and city took theirs. Which is *not* to say that I got a raw deal; far from it, I owed the money, plain and simple. But it did mean feeding my family on a fraction of what I had been, while at the same time being barred from going to work again."

The other members groaned now, not in assent but anguish, shaking their heads in chorus. "How long did they suspend you for?" Sara asked gently.

"Seven years," he said, not looking up at her. "I can apply for reinstatement next April. Though, at sixty, even if they let me back, it's hard to imagine someone wanting to invest their dough with . . ."

He trailed off, exhausted by the rest of the thought. A silence set in, during which Lathon held back, his stillness deterring the others from speaking. For a half minute, the radiator had the floor, harmonizing with the wind that bent the windows.

Finally, Lathon sat up, checking his watch. The session was nearly an hour old. "We're going to have to move on, if we're going to get other people heard tonight. But before we do, Jack, maybe you could tell us what you wanted to work on here."

Jack nodded and cleared his throat, incompletely roused from thought. "Yeah, that's good," he said, rheumily. "I *would* like to do that, thanks." He propped himself up and trimmed the fit of his blazer; there was something almost martial in his physical pride. "Basically, I've spent six years trying to figure out why I did it. Why I went outta my way to ruin this thing that I loved, and that I grew up dreaming of having—a life in the Broadway theater. And after all these years of thinking about it, I still have no idea—but I do know *how* I did it. Because it *wasn't* the wild drinking, or the cocaine years. I know plenty of other people who fucked up big, but came back and started over again.

"No, what did me in was my insanity with money; I was a complete and total sieve financially. I threw gas bills into the garbage because I couldn't be bothered to pay 'em, and—and took five, six people to dinner every night, people I barely knew half the time. Wherever I went, I hadda be the premium player, slipping a fifty to the maitre d' to make sure I got the check, and pitching a holy stink if somebody beat me to it. Never once did I think about saving some dough, because I'd always think the hell with it—*I'll just go out and make more.*"

And so, he said, what he'd come here for was some help in getting to the bottom of it; figuring out why he went through all that money as if he had no right to it. In a way, it was almost moot now, as he'd been broke for five years, and was no sure bet to be flush again soon. But if he could just understand this one compulsion, this crazy impulse to give it all away, then maybe, just maybe, he could get some sleep again. And that would be payoff enough for him.

· · ·

45

Lathon thanked Jack for getting the group started, and applauded his gutsy candor. It was hard enough telling your story to strangers, let alone do so in a way that made sense to them. But beyond that, Jack had told the truth as well as the facts, conveyed a clear understanding of what it was like to be in his skin. That was a lot to ask for, right out of the gate. Archly, Lathon hoped it would inspire the others.

At this, Sara let out a laugh that surprised everyone.

"Um, well, I wouldn't say 'inspire' as much as it scared the hell out of me," she groaned. "I mean, do we *really* have to tell our life story in one sitting? Me, I can't remember *five minutes* ago, let alone five years."

The others responded with laughter, though it wasn't clear Sara was joking. Indeed, judging by her discomfort, it seemed she was merely stating a fact—one offered, perhaps, in hopes of an exemption.

"Don't worry, Sara," said Lathon, "we don't expect a full bio from you. All we want is a sense of who you are, and what pains you."

"Oh," she said, looking neither relieved nor enlightened. "Well, then, could you go around the circle that way, and come back to me next session? By then, I should have something ready to tell you."

Again, the others laughed, this time in cahoots with Sara, not at her. Apparently, she had an arid, time-released wit that played against her wonderful looks. One moment, she was the low-volt, scattershot ditz; the next, she was pulling quarters out of your ear. Even she seemed surprised by the transformation, smiling a beat late at her own remark.

"It's all right, *I'll* go," said Lina, testily. "It's crazy to be wasting time on this stuff."

She sat up and uncrossed her legs, then changed her mind and crossed them back again, trying to come to attention in a chair made for slouching. For the first time, I noticed that she had something in her hand, a strand of black worry beads about the size of her palm. As she spoke, she clenched them tightly, whitening her knuckles.

She described herself as a forty-five-year-old mother of two teenagers, and the director of a mental health clinic in the Bronx. Which, she hastened to add, was just a fancy way of saying that she was a social worker who'd gotten kicked upstairs.

"Ah-ah-ah," said Lathon. "Truth in advertising. You're far more than a drone-bee social worker."

Lina looked pained by this assertion of praise. She cocked her head sternly, inclined to dispute it, then exhaled and let it pass. What she was, she said, was an advocate for poor children, someone who scraped for every last dollar so that kids on East Tremont had a place of refuge. In a so-called "boom year" for the city of New York, the families in Morrisania had never been poorer, and the kinds of abuse that came through the door now were just—ah, well, never mind. She hadn't come here, she said, to whine about her job.

Lina paused, her resolve starting to falter; already, her eyes were wet with forming tears. "You know, I don't even know where to start," she said, forcing a smile. "It's all just this . . . *mess* in my head."

Lathon nodded thoughtfully, mulling it over. "Why not start with what you said when you first came in here?"

"Which was?"

"That you'd been badly betrayed by your husband, Anton, and lost so much weight suffering over it that your kids thought you had cancer."

Lina grunted as if hearing this for the first time. "That's true," she said, bunching her suit jacket, which had a lot of play at the waist. "They're *still* worried about me; they're always on me to eat. My son says I don't get enough junk food in my diet."

Again, her laugh had that odd tremolo of sadness. Unsure how to respond to it, the others fidgeted.

"Anyway . . . yes, my husband, Anton," said Lina, squeezing her

47

worry beads. She took a deep breath and held it in, as if she were about to be made to crawl across a smoke-filled corridor. "You know, on the train coming down here, I made a pact with myself not to cry. I was just going to tell this as if it happened a long time ago, and I was past it and into my new life. Because I really do believe that if I can just get through this—get the court battle over with, and the money straightened out—get *him* and all his dirty tricks out of my life—that I can go back to being the person I used to be. Which was someone that was actually happy with herself, and confident about the future."

Tentatively, then, in a voice that caught but didn't break, Lina told the story of her marriage. At twenty-one, the star of her proud Greek family and the first of its women to go to college, she was on the cusp of graduating from Princeton cum laude when she met Anton at a frat-house mixer. He was tall and quite handsome, if something of a dandy, the oldest son of a wealthy Lebanese builder. He'd read Nabokov in three languages, hiked Tibet and Madagascar, and had a photographic memory for filthy jokes. If you stood next to him at a party, you'd meet everyone in the room. People just naturally gravitated to where he was.

Despite her parents' qualms—they didn't care for Anton's airs, or the nasty tone he took with his own mother—Lina and he were married within the year, and installed in a small apartment in Gramercy Park. The first eruption came ten months later, when Lina dropped out of a clinical psychology program to pursue a master's degree in social work. Anton hit the roof, screaming that it was an insult to him, a wife who chose to wet-nurse pregnant junkies. He was in his second year of law school and already active on the cocktail circuit, making friends and allies that would serve him soon in business. The last thing he needed was a guilt-tripping spouse, one who'd bring nothing to the party but some sob stories.

Nonetheless, Lina persisted in her choice, and after a year or so, Anton got over it. Upon completion of law school, he took a job at his father's firm, and he and Lina settled into their prosperous lives. Three years later, in anticipation of their first child, they were given possession of his parents' co-op on Park Avenue. It was more a compound than an apartment—a library off the parlor, a kitchen big enough to seat ten. At first scandalized by its size (she'd been raised in a Queens row house, sharing a bathroom with her parents and four brothers), Lina soon fell madly for the place, and, perhaps inspired by it, bore two children a year apart. After a couple of years at home, though, her decision to return to work led to a second ugly rift with Anton. He claimed she'd "broken her wedding vow," and preferred looking after black children instead of her own. Again, she stood firm, but some small part of her succumbed, acquiescing to the idea that she was deficient. Eventually, the worst blew over, but Anton's tone had permanently altered; within minutes of praising her to a roomful of people, he was capable of the most cutting cruelty. He called her a "pig" if she had the temerity to gain weight, or "brain-dead" if she said the wrong thing at a party. As their children got older, he tried to enlist them as allies, mocking her and inciting them to laugh along. Now and then, Lina would put her foot down, warning him that this time he had crossed a line. But after a couple of weeks, he'd be right back at it, whittling down the remnants of her dignity.

While Lina was talking, I found myself glancing at Sara, who seemed to be having a hard time sitting still. She kept shifting in her seat, tucking first one leg, then the other, trying, like a restless teen, to contain her energy. When, at last, Lina paused for a sip of water, Sara's hand went straight up in the air.

"Is it okay for us to ask a question now?" she asked.

Lathon checked his watch again, faintly annoyed. "Well, given our time problem, and trying to get one more in tonight—"

"No, no, it's okay, let her ask it," said Lina. "I bet I can probably guess what it is, anyway."

"Well, actually, it's two questions," said Sara. "First off, *how* long did you say you were married to Anton?"

"Twenty-two years," said Lina, smiling defensively. "Actually, twenty of being married to him, and two trying to divorce him. With no end anywhere in sight."

"I see," said Sara, pausing to process this. "Well, if you don't mind my asking, what kept you for twenty years? I mean, after the nastiness started."

Though Lina had, in fact, seen the question coming, she shrank now, losing her moorings. Staring at her hands, she frowned, unable to answer. After several false starts, she looked to Lathon for help, smiling against impending tears.

"What you're hearing from Lina," said Lathon, "and what you're going to hear more of in the weeks to come, is what happens to someone whose story is *hijacked* by another person. For twenty years, Lina forgot who she was, or, more accurately, was seduced, then bullied, out of who she was. In place of her own story, one was plastered on top of it, that of a demeaned and helpless drudge afraid of her husband. Now, why she *let* that happen—well, there are probably a dozen different answers, and we'll pursue them in some detail as we go. But the more relevant question to ask is, how do we undo that? How do we peel back the layers of false story, and restore Lina's sense of who she is? Because the lies Anton fed her go down pretty deep, and are sapping her strength to fight back. And she really needs her strength now, is going to have to fight tooth and nail when this finally gets to court. I'm confident she can do that, make him honor his obligations. But first, it's going to take some shoring up, and we can help with that."

"Oh God, I hope so," said Lina glumly. "Because I feel like this—weakling—against a giant, and he's got a team of lawyers to stomp me out."

"Yes, well, trust me, you'll see," said Lathon, beaming encouragement. "*He's* the one who's weak, and you're the tough guy. After all, which of you's been working in the South Bronx for years, getting gang kids to sweep outside your doorway?"

Lina laughed at this inflation of her power, and proceeded with her story. Three years ago the previous fall, she'd begun seeing changes in Anton. Suddenly, he was spending a lot of time in tanning parlors, and rejuvenating his staid gray wardrobe. At first, Lina chalked it up to middle age, but when he went in for a neck-and-eye job, she confronted him. He insisted he was being faithful, and that this was strictly about business, the necessity of keeping abreast. But on the Upper East Side, a lot gets said by inference, and Lina could read the text of the averted gaze, and the canned joviality of her neighbors. Finally, after months of this, she was at her dentist's getting her teeth cleaned when the hygienist dropped a name, assuming she knew. It turned out that Anton's girlfriend was living a block and a half from them, and that everyone, including her dog walker, had known for months.

"Ucchhhh!" cried Sara, no longer able to contain herself. "What a fucking asshole this guy is!"

For the second time in minutes, she'd taken the room by surprise. Mortified, she clapped a hand over her mouth, and ducked between her shoulders, begging forgiveness.

"Oh God, I'm sorry," she said, "that was so totally uncool, and I apologize for cutting you off. It's just that what you're describing is, like, my absolute nightmare. Being with a guy for all those years and getting totally screwed over, and being the last one in your circle to find out about it."

"Yeah, well, that's what it's been," said Lina. "A complete and total nightmare. And every time I say it can't get worse, it goes and gets worse on me."

She was wearing her sad smile, but had blanched the color of her knuckles. And though she'd refrained from crying, the held-back tears had dissolved her eyeliner, streaking her lower lids like a televangelist's.

"Lina, you look bushed," said Lathon, solicitously. "You want to stop here and pick up next time, or would you rather—"

"No, no, I want to finish," she said, blowing her nose. "I still haven't even gotten to the *problem* yet. These people'll walk out of here thinking I'm all broken up over being dumped for some stupid—hostess."

Lathon assured Lina that no one would be laughing at her, but she insisted on finishing her story. It seemed that, even when finally confronted with the facts, Anton wouldn't come clean. He challenged Lina to produce hard evidence, and—worse—refused to leave. Installing himself in the guest room, he carried on as if nothing had happened, though he would go weeks without speaking to her. Eight months elapsed before she was able to oust him, on the strength of a private detective's snapshots.

But what should have been the end of Lina's problems was, in fact, merely the start of phase two—the International Dodge and Freeze-out, as she called it. Though by now as American as corporate welfare, Anton had preserved his dual citizenship, keeping an apartment in Lebanon. He took refuge there with his laptop and girlfriend, overseeing his father's holdings via satellite. He also placed a freeze on the marital assets, such that Lina couldn't rent their house in Saltaire, or write a check on their joint account. She had some money put away from a small inheritance, but most of that went now to pay her lawyer, and the arrears on the co-op maintenance. Her parents, God love them, had stepped up like champions, scraping together the cash to keep her kids in private school. For all her other needs, though, Lina's salary was no match, and she had long since been dipping into her retirement fund to meet the monthly expenses.

"But I don't understand, how can he just avoid due process?" said Jack. "Believe me, I know the system, I've been divorced four times. If I could've stiffed my second wife by moving to Saint Bart's, I'd probably still be living over there now."

"Yeah, really, Lina, who's your lawyer?" asked Rex. "I know two guys right now who could end this by Friday. Or at least get a check to tide you over."

"People, *please:* Lina's telling her story," said Lathon. "If she wants your advice, she'll ask for it. But just so you know, *therapy's* what we do here. Advice, I leave to Dear Abby."

The others fell silent, stung by his tone. As they were beginning to find out, he was a different kettle of fish here than the Lathon they saw one-on-one. He was something of an enforcer, tough about the rules, and indelicate with people's feelings. His first priority was to protect the narrative, to let the story flow unhindered. To that end, he bit down hard on intrusions, and offered no apologies or explanations.

"Please continue, Lina," he said. "You were telling us about your money problems, and what Anton's tactics have cost you."

Lina paused, getting her bearings again. Though fazed by the interruption, she looked vaguely pleased to have Lathon ride shotgun for her.

"Well, I just want to say that my lawyer's not the problem. What she's dealing with is a guy worth millions of dollars who'll spend any amount to beat me. He hires and fires lawyers, which buys him adjournments, and puts us right back at square one. He appeals every ruling, which is very expensive, but gets him another three months. And twice, before a court date, he's negotiated a deal, then reneged after we called off the hearing. If you're rich, and you get the right judge, you can get away with murder in this state."

"Yes, that's true," said Lathon. "The law in New York is archaic, at least when the case is contested. And for sure, Lina, we sympathize, and feel your frustration, and look forward to hearing this at length. But there's a second issue here that needs our attention, and is perhaps where we can be of more help. And that's the idea that you're a ninety-pound weakling, going against a two-ton giant. Yes, he has money, and no conscience to weigh him down, but he's very, very far from a powerhouse. Whereas you, despite the evidence, are very far from helpless. And *our* job, over the months, is to help correct your vision. To show you what the real picture is, so that you can fight, on equal terms, for what's yours."

And finally, then, there was Peter, who'd been silent since group began. In his chair beside the wall, he'd watched with vigilant eyes that were magnified by his glasses. During a lull in the action, he didn't drift or check his watch, declaring himself by gesture, as the others did. Instead, he took up peering at a colleague across the square, lingering as if in study of some exotic animal.

They'd been in session for two hours and Lathon was looking for a last speaker, albeit one who didn't mind keeping it short. He was apologizing for this, promising that at the next meeting he'd man the clock better, when Peter raised his hand and said he'd do it. It was almost better this way, he said, in his clothespinned voice. Now, he could say his stuff and not feel he *had* to talk for an hour. Because, after listening to Jack and Lina, he was embarrassed at how small his problems were. He'd be lucky just to fill the fifteen minutes.

He began with the rote facts—age, thirty-four; marital status, divorced; occupation, accountant—then got to the matter at hand. He had recently emerged from a long depression, though he couldn't really gauge how long; maybe as far back as childhood. He'd always been one of those kids who was shy and didn't make friends easily, and spent a lot of time alone in his room. Now, after taking Zoloft, he was beginning to wonder if it had always been a chemical thing. . . .

He glanced at Lathon for comment, then thought better of it, remembering the time. In any case, life was a lot better these days than when he first came in for treatment. He had a great new girlfriend, thanks in large part to the doctor, who'd helped him find the courage to go out looking again. And he was pretty much over the throes of the divorce, which had hurt him very badly and made him leery of a repeat. Things were happening fast with Kara—in fact, he was set to move in with her next week, after knowing her for only five months—and suddenly, his nerves were acting up again. He was waking bolt upright at three in the morning, his palms sweating like a pair of—

He stopped and looked at his hands, which were toweling themselves on the armrests.

"See?" he groaned. "I don't even know I'm doing it half the time. This is exactly how it was as a kid."

Mortified, he shoved his hands under his thighs, where they remained in detention for ten minutes. Changing tack, he talked about his other concern—getting his career out of the ditch it had fallen into. For eight years, he'd worked at one of the Big Five accounting firms, where he'd been repeatedly passed over for promotions. It was really starting to eat at him, pulling sixty-hour weeks—going in on weekends to clean up *other people's* workloads, and earning first-rate yearly reviews at bonus time—only to watch someone else make partner because he had his nose up the Big Man's butt. To be sure, Peter conceded, he was a lousy politician. He froze up around the watercooler, and didn't fare well at the corporate picnics, where he was all left feet in the three-legged races. He wasn't an ex-jock or a born self-promoter, one of those cigar-smoking twits who knew how to order a martini. He was just a quiet, steady guy who broke his tail for the firm, and it was high time they showed some respect for that.

He finished with a scowl and clamped his teeth shut for emphasis, aroused by his own warm rhetoric. His voice, normally a monotone, rose by a full note before cracking at the end for lack of air. Even his feet came to life, drumming in place on the floorboards, working off his ginned-up animus.

There was a moment's pause before Rex put his hand up. "Could *I* ask a question now?"

"Uhhh . . ." Lathon grimaced, clearly disinclined. "Is it answerable in twenty words or less?"

"Well, I can *ask* it in twenty or less," said Rex, flashing his showy smile. Turning to Peter, he said, "You know, I hear what you're saying about being hacked off. I mean, if *I* worked somewhere and didn't make partner in eight years, I'd be up there with a shotgun and a ski mask. So my question is why haven't you gone somewhere else? It must be so beat, getting up and going in each morning."

"Ah, good *question*," said Lathon. "Concise, and on the mark. How about it, Peter? You want to take a whack at it in these last minutes?"

"Ummm . . . sure," said Peter, though he seemed suddenly back on his heels. "I suppose I would say it's because . . . uh, I'm not really sure, to be honest. In fact, I—I haven't even sent out my résumé yet. I was waiting to see how my review would go, and then have a talk with the department VP, but I guess I . . ."

He gazed at the floor, his forehead glossed by a light sweat. "I don't really know," he said.

"Well, hey, you're probably focusing on the move to your girlfriend's," said Rex, trying to fill some dead air.

"Um, yeah, I guess so," said Peter, grateful for the help. "Except that, actually, I wasn't. In fact, that was one of my reasons for *changing* jobs. You see, my girlfriend does very well financially, and it's kind of . . . embarrassing to make so much less than her. And so I really wanted to find something, or get a raise where I am, before we moved in together. That way, I could sort of hold my own, and not feel like a gold digger around her. . . ."

He resumed his inspection of the floor. The silence stretched out: ten seconds; twenty. And then, about the time it became intolerable, a noise came to the rescue. It was the sound, reasonably enough, of someone giggling.

"I'm sorry," Sara gasped. "I just got this picture of Peter as a gold digger, and I couldn't stop myself from . . ."

Again, she started laughing, inspiring peals of it from her neighbors. Even Peter fell in with it, tossing his head back and howling, a high, adenoidal groan. Far from sustaining insult, he seemed jolly about it, even flattered, as if it was heady to be thought of *at all* by a woman like her.

"Actually, folks," said Lathon, "you shouldn't be so quick to laugh. Why don't you tell them, Peter, what Kara's worth."

Peter laughed again, being the willing good sport, though this time, stifled a grimace as he did so.

"Um, well, it's hard to really say, because some of it's tied up with family money. But if I had to make a guess, I'd probably put it around . . . eight million."

There were whoops and gasps now from the other members. A couple gaped at Peter disbelievingly, as if he'd hiked up his shirt to reveal abs of steel.

"But wait, it gets better," said Lathon. "Tell them the story of how you met Kara."

At the mention of her name in this more tender context, Peter broke out in a smile. He sat up straight, composing his knobby shoulders, and seemed, almost, for a moment, to preen.

"Um, well, that *was* sort of weird, how that happened," he said, laughing. "Let's see, about five, six months ago, at Dr. Lathon's suggestion, I answered some personal ads in *New York* magazine. As you can probably imagine, it wasn't the sort of thing I usually do; in fact, I had to take an Ativan just to dial the phone. And I still wouldn't've done it, but it'd been a year since my divorce, and almost two years since I had . . .

"Well, anyway, the first one to call back—in fact, the only one who called me back—was Kara. Her ad had read, 'In search of Pavarotti,' i.e. big, first-tenor types. Well, *I'm* sort of big, at least compared to most women, and I do like opera enough to listen to QXR, when there isn't a game on TV. Anyway, I showed up with flowers and said, 'Pavarotti couldn't make it tonight—he had to go in for a tummy tuck—and asked me to pinch-hit for him.' Well, under the heading of 'go figure,' she went for it—"

But here it became impossible to hear what he was saying, because the group erupted in laughter. They had just got the joke that this pale accountant could be funny, and responded with almost patronizing glee. So grateful were they for a sign that they weren't going to be bored senseless by him for a year that several actually broke out in applause.

Surprised to find himself the life of the party, Peter looked around him warily. It was clear he'd told this before to less gut-busting effect, and mistrusted the reaction it evoked now. Checking Lathon for a read, he saw that he, too, was laughing. Baffled, Peter shrugged and waited it out.

When the hilarity died down, Sara asked about his girlfriend. Who *was* this fabulous heiress with the eight million dollars, and why, of all places, was she cruising the personals?

"Yes, by all means, tell," said Lathon, with proprietary pride. "But that, I'm sorry to say, will be the last of the questions. If you want to know more, check back next session."

Peter mulled the question, choosing his words with care. "Well, first of all, Kara's *not* some fabulous heiress. She's just a nice, normal person who buys her clothes on sale and drives a Camry 'cause it's good on gas. Which is not to say she's stingy; if anything, she's too generous. With the last guy she was with, she offered to bankroll his microbrewery. And she was crazy to do it, because the guy was a real dirtbag; he kept pushing back their wedding at the last second. In fact, the week they were supposed to get married—in some big ceremony at the Royalton—he called her from the Bahamas and said it was over. Now, how anyone could do that completely escapes me, because, besides being a sweetheart, Kara has all this money, and would spend it in a minute to make you happy. She's already hinted that if we do get married, I'll never have to work a day if I don't want to. Which, of course, I'd never take her up on," he said. "I wouldn't want her thinking I'm a gold digger."

The group broke out in its biggest hurrah, much taken now with Peter and his improbable good luck. Dylan leaned over, saying he needed to talk to him about a loan. Rex was eyeing him with new-found respect, and more than a smidgen of envy.

"So when's the wedding?" cried Jack. "They've got planes to Vegas every hour."

"Yeah, my God, what're you doing in *therapy?*" wondered Sara. "Shouldn't you be out shopping for a red Ferrari, or whatever men buy when they hit the jackpot?"

But here Lathon stepped in and cut them off, saying that all would be revealed in time. As Peter was trying to tell them, you can't buy a story with money. Even renting one will cost more than you've got.

three

february

It was the better part of a week before New York emerged from tundra. Snow was still piled on the edges of sidewalks, like barricades set out before a parade. Cars were buried under their parcel of permafrost, costing the city millions in unwritable tickets. What whimsy the blizzard inspired had long since turned to mush, and the town settled down to its late-winter sulk, cursing the wind in its face.

That Wednesday, the twenty-second, checked in surly, and the mood in group wasn't much better. The compromise start time—six-thirty—was unpopular, chosen for the sake of those with kids to care for. For other members, though, it meant an hour in limbo, or a mad dash home to feed the dog and then hurry over. As such, it was one more stressor in a day chock-full of them, and it showed in the frowns and slouches around the square.

If it was incumbent on someone, then, to goose the air in the room, Rex was nicely suited to the job. He'd shown up for the session clad not in Zegna or Zileri, but dressed like his other couture avatar, Dennis Rodman. He had on a leather vest that zipped like a wet suit, and a pair of jeans torn at knee and thigh. His arms were huge, and articulated in sections: the deltoids rounded like ball-bearing joints; the biceps cut big, on a half-moon bias. Somehow, he was tan, or, more like it, *burnt*, his cheeks raw pink and peeling. In a bid for further attention, he was wearing his showy grin, and toting a stack of photos of his baby daughter.

"These were taken last week in South Beach," he said, passing them out. "An old teammate of mine from Dartmouth just opened a club down there, and my Marisa was the belle of the beach. Only five months old, and already a supermodel. These little boys were crawling over to her and *flexing.*"

The group, as per the law in these things, made a fuss over the pictures. As it happened, Rex's wife appeared in some of the pictures, and her own beauty did not go unremarked. In a high-on-the-hip two-piece, Claudia was tall and dark, baring the ropy muscles of a runner. She was a producer, said Rex, for one of the network newsmags, but with her precision-cut bangs and Revlon smile, she could have been mistaken for on-air talent.

"Well," said Lathon, "since you brought in show-and-tell tonight, how 'bout kicking things off for us?"

Rex rolled his eyes as if he'd been asked to scrub toilets, but no one was fooled for a minute. Having been silent for most of the first session, his desire to take the stage now couldn't have been clearer if he'd arrived in greasepaint. He pushed himself up in his seat and flashed his trademark grin, a confection of snarky charm and self-rapture.

"Well, first of all, emotionally, I'm as high as a kite," he said. "I've got this little cherub who just makes me *laugh* like a hit of nitrous. Hanging out with her all day, and rolling around on her play mat—it really doesn't get any better than that. I was sure I would get bored of it, but if anything, it's the opposite—I can't get enough of her. Even my wife is starting to look at me like, 'Honey, you need to get out more. What happened to all those strip clubs you used to go to?'"

Lathon met this last line with a caustic laugh. "Nooo, I don't think she said *that.*"

Rex granted the point, giving his stagy grin. "Yeah, you're right," he said. "If anything, it's, 'Go out and get a *job*, so we can pay off your *old* strip club bills.'"

After foot-dragging a bit longer—and being tweaked for it by Lathon—Rex proceeded with his story. Roughly a year and a half before, he walked into his building one evening and saw the doorman chatting with a young woman. She was "off-the-hook gorgeous," a honey blonde with green eyes, and "one of those slow, Southern accents that curl your ear hairs." He flirted with her a while, then said good night and didn't think of it again. After all, why should he? He was in love with his wife, and had the world "by the ball-sack," in his phrase. All of thirty-one, he was a vice president at a front-line bank, and had built enough capital to get out for good already, although he'd decided to "hedge retirement till thirty-five." He owned a loft in Soho, a house in Amagansett, and some acreage in "horse country" that he planned to build on. When you're on that kind of roll, he said, you don't want to push your luck. And yet, over the course of the next year, that was precisely what he did.

Rex had a crew of players that he ran with after work—strapping, thirtysomething traders, most of them ex-jocks like himself, who talked numbers over dinner and then hit the strip clubs in force. Now, you had to understand something about the culture he swam in: strip clubs were where the bond market did its bonding. You took a client to Scores, let your hair down and played some grab-ass, and by the end of the night had a new best friend, a guy you could do big deals with over the phone. Officially, the firms frowned on this, didn't want their key men being seen there, what with coke all over the scene and the mafia in effect. But the dirty little down-low was that Wall Street made its bones there. In fact, compared to what his company was earning at Scores, the Gotti mob was working for bus fare.

During the course of Rex's speech, the others looked him over with a mixture of contempt and bemusement. Adopting the cross-armed posture of skeptics at a car lot, they squinted and cocked their ears, as if they couldn't credit what they were hearing. Whatever their take, though, they were clearly intrigued by him, sampling his jock-dude parlance, with its hip-hop shadings, and his preening good humor and energy. Here, apparently, was one bad boy who didn't mind letting you in on it, who took a sort of glee in courting outrage. It was all part of the package, a test of his prickly charm, to see how far he could put you off while keeping you on the string.

Already, though, one of the other members decided he'd heard enough. "You know," said Jack peevishly, "I've still got friends on Wall Street. One's a senior partner at a white-shoe firm; another's a VP who sits on all sorts of boards. And I feel confident in telling you that not a single one of them has ever set foot in a strip joint. I mean, it's preposterous to say that people do deals there—and then get up at five in the morning to go to work!"

"Yeah, I gotta say, that's the thing that struck me, too," said Peter. "To go out partying all night, with the booze and cigar smoke, and still be able to function at a high level the next day . . . I don't know. I can't imagine doing it *one* night, let alone regularly."

"And can I ask where your wife was when you were out doing this?" said Lina. "Did *she* know where you were conducting— business—and if so, why didn't she put a stop to it?"

Rex scrunched around, looking over at Lathon. "Man, they're already up in arms, and I just *started*," he teased. "Now I'm starting to wonder if I should go on with it."

"No, no, do," cried Sara, missing his coy inflection. "I've always wondered how guys like you operate."

Lina chimed in that she was thinking the same thing; it might shed some light on what made her own husband tick. And then Dylan spoke up, saying that he, too, was curious, and in short order, the whole group had taken the bait.

Rex thought it over a moment, consulting his nails. "Guys like me?" He smiled, arching an eyebrow rhetorically. "And what kind of guy would that be?"

Sara checked her own nails, standing firm. "You said it yourself:

you're a player who hangs with strippers. And from what I'm hearing, you're not exactly embarrassed about it."

"Hell, he's proud of it," Jack said. "Look at the smile on his face. He's gonna make some divorce lawyer very happy."

The others, Rex included, laughed at this, dispersing some of the tension. And then, one by one, he took them on, in an even but forceful tone. First of all, his marriage, he said, had never been better. He had done some dumb things that had hurt his wife, but was busy making it up to her. His decision to quit his job and be the stay-home parent was one way of renewing faith with her. Another was reducing his boys' nights out, and keeping a far distance from places like Scores. These and other changes had been warmly welcomed by Claudia, whose opinion, he added, was the only one that counted.

As for Jack and his old cronies who'd never set foot in a strip club—well, no offense meant, but the key word there was *old*. A new generation had taken over on Wall Street, and had its own way of greasing the wheels. Morally, you could quibble, but you couldn't ignore the numbers—the first sustained bull market since the eighties. In short, it was one of those things it didn't pay to pass judgment on. There were facts of life you dealt with, and that was that.

Rex was explaining why Claudia had been okay with this when Lathon stepped in, preaching brevity. "I want to avoid what happened last session, and give Sara and Dylan their full turn. So how about skipping to the part about Erika, and we'll come back to this other stuff at a later date."

Rex was about to say something but stopped himself, the first twinge of unease crossing his face. "It's just, I'm trying to give a context, so they'll understand why this went down. What I'm saying is, it didn't happen in a vacuum."

"Point taken," said Lathon. "And there were other factors, too, like a bout with drugs and alcohol."

"That's right," said Rex proudly. "I haven't had a toot in five months, and they've been the best five months of my life."

He looked around the circle, evincing pride in this change. Still uneasy about going on, though, he fell back upon himself, picking his words with effort. He began by apologizing, saying he was "uncool" with what he'd done. When you were married to a winner like Claudia, you didn't put her through "such drama." What you did was go to church and thank God for His generosity, which was something he'd done a lot of lately. Somehow, he'd slacked off there the last five years, and he knew now that was part of the problem. Because church, for him, was like going to AA; it centered him, and cooled the turmoil in his head, that churning feeling that there was something better in the next room, something hot, something exciting that he couldn't afford to miss, and that everybody else was in on but him. . . .

Rex paused, taking a breath before resuming. He'd seen Erika again at Goldfingers, where she was dancing to pay the rent. An actress with a couple of small parts in indie films, she said that stripping let her keep her days free for auditions. Rex talked with her for hours, feeding her twenties to keep her next to him, paying her, in effect, to leave her clothes on. Despite her vocation, there was something different about Erika, a softness and lack of guile that was out of place there. He went back a couple of times, found it painful to watch her work, and asked a friend who owned a restaurant to give her a job. Shortly thereafter, a guy at his firm moved to Washington, and Rex grabbed his apartment for Erika. He was careful to pay the rent in traveler's checks, and to give her cash for things like the utilities.

And so matters proceeded for several months. Rex's wife was off on assignment a lot, and when in town often worked till late at night. This afforded Rex the luxury of long weekends with Erika, and trips together to Brussels and Amsterdam. He found, however, that the more he saw her, the more he *had* to see her, developing an attachment that had only partly to do with sex. She had this intangible . . .

something, he said; it was in her voice, her scent. Whenever they were apart for more than a couple of days, he'd start fiending for it like a cracked-out junkie. And then Claudia announced that she was six weeks pregnant, and he tried to do the right thing and break it off with Erika. But after a month of staying away from her, he got drunk at a party and wound up banging on her door, sobbing declarations through the keyhole.

The next five months were like a fog, a brain fever. He'd end it again with Erika, then wake up trembling at three in the morning, unable to catch his breath or slow his heart down. Finally, she called it quits and fled the city. But still he couldn't drop it, actually tracked her back to Charleston, where she'd gone to get her head straight at her parents'. Abandoning all shame, he caught a flight down there, and staked out her family's ranch house. He tailed Erika to a mall, begging her to please just listen to him—

"What!" cried Sara. "Are you saying you *stalked* this woman?"

Rex glanced over at her, then looked away. "Well, I mean, no, not literally. It was more just trying to talk to her. I only wanted to tell her that I—"

Again Rex ducked, avoiding her gaze. He scratched at his tricep, raising a port-wine splotch. "I—I guess, technically, yeah, I did," he murmured.

A silence set up, abuzz with small sounds. From afar came the gossip of Broadway traffic: car horns and brake squeals, the evening threnody. Closer to hand was a thump from the apartment above us, and the radiator's cranky respiration.

"Well, I, for one, don't get it. Why didn't your wife just shoot you?" Lina seethed.

The remark was out of her mouth before she knew she'd said it. Rex started, but gave no reply.

"Actually, I'll take a stab at that, if I might."

Rex looked over in Lathon's direction. The doctor had been listening in perfect stillness, only his eyes moving from speaker to speaker. When he sat up and resettled his bulk, it was as if some balance had shifted, a tilt in the room's ecology.

"For the first three months that Rex came here," he said, "I saw him and Claudia together, on the side. And in case you were wondering, she's very far from stupid; she knows her wayward husband back and forth. When I asked why she stayed with him, she said that there were *two* Rex Dimauros, and she was still in love with one of them. Not the one we've met tonight, obviously, with his show-off muscles, and his smarmy bragging about strippers; that Rex, she said, showed up several years ago, after he made his first killing on Wall Street. And even then, she only saw it when he was around his buddies; at home, or with her friends, he was still the guy she'd married. And *that* Rex, she said, was really a very dear guy. He loved to cook a meal for her, complete with candles and opera music, and make a big deal on their anniversary, whisking her away to some fabulous inn for the weekend. Or there was the time she was in an accident and he was wonderfully tender, taking two weeks off to stay home with her, instead of leaving her with a private nurse. That guy, she said, any woman could love, and she was willing to give it a shot to get him back.

"And so the question I put to you is which of these two people is he? Yes, it's true he's been on his best behavior lately, but his language tells a different story. It says that, underneath the piety, he's got a foot in each camp, and is having a hard time making a choice. So over these next months, I want you to press him on it, and don't let up till you've got an answer. Because either way it goes, that answer's going to mean a lot to the pretty little girl in those snapshots."

Rex affected injured righteousness, but his heart wasn't really in it. In fact, behind the scowl, he seemed almost relieved, having eluded, at least for the moment, the wrath of the mob. And then Lathon checked his watch and turned the stage over to Sara, who looked both eager and spooked in equal measure. She smiled and made a joke about having crammed all week for this, but the hand carrying the pint of water to her lips was visibly trembling. She had her hair down tonight, and some of it spilled over her eyes. She kept pulling it back with her free hand, which seemed to soothe her.

Sara began by bemoaning her rotten luck, having to take the floor after Rex. My God, a story like that, full of sex and obsession—how could she possibly compete? All she had to offer was her boring old life, full of work, work, work, and more work. She apologized in advance for the lack of soap opera, but then again, that was pretty much why she'd come here. To shake her out of this . . . daze she was in, where all she seemed to want was sleep and junk food.

Again, she flicked a hand through her hair, pulling on the ends like buggy reins. Though she wore a minimum of makeup, her face was opaque, the expression emanating chiefly from her eyes. Even when she smiled, it seemed a rhetorical gesture, a way of setting a phrase apart in quotes. The effect on the surface was coy detachment, an ironic remove from life's vaudeville. But just behind the skin, one sensed a different tone, the thrum of something volatile kept in check.

"Basically," she said, "I'm here not because of something that's happened to me, but more because of something that hasn't. I'm thirty-seven years old, I have a great job and wonderful friends, and I'd like very much to be married and have kids—preferably by Friday, if possible. What makes that hard is that not only am I not pregnant or engaged, I haven't got a boyfriend at the moment. In fact, I haven't dated anyone I'd even *think* of having kids with since . . . well, let's just say it's been a while."

Sara paused for a sip of water, smoothed the placket of her blouse, then outlined some of the difficulties. As the fashion editor of a glossy women's mag, she worked a madman's schedule: up at seven, in the office by nine, rarely home before ten at night. Then there was her round of peripheral duties: the dinners, location shoots, fashion shows, and launch parties. To be sure, she met the occasional man at these things, but they mostly fell into two categories: the downtown artist who never seemed to actually *paint* anything, and the "entitled, prince of Wall Street type." These were men who liked sleeping with her, and taking her skiing in Colorado, but who were holding out for a younger model. Literally: they were constantly on the lookout for a model, age twenty, whom they could marry and make babies with.

"Now, I'm not one of those women," she added, "who jump up and down that there are no good men in this town. Believe me, I know there're good men, I meet them on airplanes and at dinner parties, and they all have one thing in common: they're *married.* In fact, my cousin, who I'm very close to, is married to such a sweet, funny guy that I have this dream where she comes down with a"— Sara coughed comedically over the phrase "rare illness"—"and I run away with him and their daughter to Barcelona."

The others broke out in laughter at this. In fact, as Sara told her story, tossing in grace notes of wit, you could see them sitting up at attention. They smiled as they listened, nodding in recognition, as if this were a species of nineties comedy: the droll, self-mocking aria of complaint, with a half note of sadness behind it. It only sweetened the irony that this tale of true woe came from such a beautiful, well-dressed woman.

"And so, the question," Sara concluded, "is not whether it can be done, but can it be done by me? Is there something I'm doing, without being aware of it, that's keeping the good men away? Because, as much as it hurts to say, I'm going to be thirty-eight years old soon, and I really feel like time is running out on me."

There was a moment of silence, and then Lathon broke it, holding out his arms and applauding. "Bravo!" he called, to the surprise of the others. "Bravo, and two gold stars, Sara. Did everyone hear her, because that was a model of clarity: 'This is what hurts, and what I need help with.' "

Sara colored, not quite sure how to take this. "Uh, well, there was one thing I wanted to add," she said.

"Yes, do," said Lathon. "I didn't mean to throw you. It's just that when someone comes in and nails a triple axel, I can't help but applaud."

"Right," said Sara, still perturbed by the fanfare. "Well, anyway, there's this fear I've been having, related to getting older. In the fashion world, there's a certain kind of woman who goes to all the shows and after-parties. They're in their fifties or sixties, wear gobs of red lipstick, and dress from head to toe in black, usually Chanel. We call them 'couture spinsters,' because they've never been married, and their whole life is the buzz about the next season. And when I see them now, I get chills down my spine, thinking that could be *me* in twenty years!"

Sara's voice, normally a pear-toned thing, rose by a sharp when she said this. And her eyes, the keepers of explicit feeling, grew wide for a moment in panic.

"That's also well put, Sara, and very useful to hear," said Lathon. "We now know a little about what *scares* you, as well as what pains you. Once we know those things, we can follow them down. Tend the wound at the level of deep tissue. So, as you listen to your peers, gathering the facts of their cases, ask yourselves two questions: What is the nature of the pain I'm hearing, and what is this person afraid of?"

Sensing she was done, Sara slumped in her seat, looking like the first to put her pen down after an exam. Possibly, Lathon saw this, and thought she'd kept something back. Or perhaps he had some internal meter gauging the amount of disclosure required. Whatever the case, he returned to Sara, asking her to tell about her father. We needn't hear the whole story, he said; that could wait until later.

What we wanted was just a sense of the tension between them, as a backdrop on her dealings with men.

"Aiigh, do I really have to?" she groaned.

She slunk still further down the spine of her chair, so that she now looked less like a woman near forty than a balky, hemmed-in teenager. "I was hoping to get through at least one session of this without having to talk about him."

Lathon seemed amused by her reticence. "Would you rather we talk about your mother, instead?"

"*No,*" said Sara. "I'd rather we didn't talk about *either* of them."

She chafed a bit longer, carping that *no one else* had discussed their parents yet. Moreover, if she had to make a list of her problems, her folks would be way far down the page. Giving in, she described her father as a wealthy Swiss merchant who exported fine leather goods. Through cunning and tirelessness, he'd lifted a small family firm into the ranks of premium brand name. Those qualities, however, that made him formidable in business were less attractive at home. He was cool and peremptory with his two young daughters, running the household like a shipping plant. All aspects of their lives were regimented, from the time alloted for bathing in the morning to the duration of their bedtime prayers. What tenderness he showed them came across as generosity, in the form of cash and trips and playthings deluxe, such that their dolls were better dressed than some of their classmates.

Toward their mother, however, there was no compensating kindness. He took every chance to shame her in front of the children. She was *fat, ugly, stupid, an embarrassment*—though in fact, she was none of these things. She was a taciturn beauty from Keokuk, Iowa, who had met him while modeling in Paris. Married at a young age, and hopelessly isolated in Zurich, she'd never developed an adult life of her own, focusing instead on her daughters. She baked them fabulous cakes, and drove them to ice rinks and dance classes, installing them in a kind of gingerbread day-world. And then at night her bilious husband came home, and she reverted to mute passivity.

"It was not—a nice thing, to watch him treat her like that; in fact, it was pretty horrible," said Sara. "I don't remember much from that period, but I remember how tense it was. We'd be sitting at the dinner table, eating in silence, and I'd be *praying* to get through it without an eruption."

The others looked on, absorbing this information and weighing it against her even tone. It was as though the events described belonged to someone else's life, a life Sara found hard to imagine.

"Are they still together, your mom and dad?" Jack asked.

"No, they got divorced about twenty years ago," she said. "Though even that was totally strange. I was in my last year at college when I got a letter from my father, asking what I wanted for graduation. He recommended a Volvo, and listed the reasons against an Alfa—too light and unreliable; impossible to get parts for. And then, somewhere on page two, he says, purely in passing, 'Oh, and your mother and I are no longer married.' I thought, my God, what a ludicrous way to tell me. Could you possibly have been more impersonal?"

"And how did you respond?" asked Jack. "Were you very surprised?"

Sara pursed her lips, thinking it over dispassionately. "No, I wouldn't say I was surprised. I mean, they hadn't been happy for a long time. In fact, one of my few childhood memories was being called downstairs and having my father announce he was getting a divorce. And then, the very next morning, he called us back downstairs and announced they were staying together. It was like, 'Ignore my previous memo, and go on about your business.' So, no, I wouldn't say I was shocked."

This answer, and its lack of affect, seemed to stymie Jack. He frowned and cocked his head, shaking it in sad circles.

"Well, I know one thing for sure: you aren't Jewish," he said. "Because when *we* get divorced, we don't sit and write a letter. In the time it took to get there, it'd be all over town."

"Good point," said Lathon. "What do you make of the way he told told her?"

"Well, come on, isn't it obvious?" he scowled. "It was cold and heartless. I've seen stock charts with more feeling than that."

"Exactly," said Lathon. "And therein lies our task: to connect Sara to her feelings about her family. Because as bright as she is, and as keenly self-aware, she's adopted the family style when it comes to emotions. In a word, I would call it *disembodied*—a short between her cortex and limbic system. Now, structurally, there's nothing wrong there; Sara's capable of feeling her feelings, at least as they apply to other people. But when it comes to her father, those feelings are so painful that they had to be put in a box and hidden away.

"Now, someone might ask, why open that box? If those feelings are so hurtful, why expose her to them? Well, the fact of the matter is, there's more in that box than just feelings; there's a major chunk of Sara's story. There're all her memories from birth to age twelve, of which she has almost no recall now. And, more important, there's the self she left behind, the girl she detached from to escape. And until we can get her out, Sara, and listen to her story, I think that men are going to find it hard to get close to you."

Sara crooked her brow, betraying the first sign of temper. "What does one thing have to do with the other?"

Lathon sat up, unable to restrain a smile. He seemed to enjoy being challenged, even courted it with such pronouncements.

"As this group will see for itself," he said, "this is a pretty tough customer we're hearing from. Sara's a businesswoman who takes crap from no one, and who can scream with the best of them when someone crosses her. But beneath that toughness is a lot of pain that's gone untended. We don't know if Dad was abusive of her or her sister. But we know he abused the mother who loved them, and that it was excruciating to watch. And we also know that Sara's never been married, or met anyone she'd 'dream' of having kids with. Off those two facts alone, it's fair to deduce that you're terrified of being hurt again by a man. And until you resolve some of the pain he caused you, it's going to be hard work to earn your trust."

Sprawled in her seat, Sara took this in, crumpling the sides of a plastic bottle.

"How often do you speak to your father?" Jack asked.

Sara shrugged, not looking up. "He calls about once a week, from Zurich."

"And do you ever see him at all?"

"As little as possible," she grunted. "Although he keeps hocking me to go over there. Spend my vacation with him."

"Which brings us to your second line of defense—avoidance," said Lathon. "Sara lives six thousand miles from her dad, and if she could, it'd be twelve thousand, or twenty. Even on the phone with him, she's gnashing her teeth; she can't get off the line fast enough. But in order to make a new story with a man, she has to first come to terms with the old one. And that's going to require confronting her dad—either the one who lives in Zurich, or in that lockbox."

For most of two sessions now, Dylan had occupied his own orbit, lost in space by the window. He looked on from his club chair, occasionally nodding or smiling, but he might as well have been watching via satellite. There was a thick sheet of numbness that separated him from the others, a malaise that was all but dimensional. He could hear what was being said, and grasp the sense of it well enough, but the life the words described seemed largely wasted on him.

Tonight, he was wearing what, in the months to follow, would become his standard outfit—khakis, deck shoes, oxford and pullover, of which he had a collection. His black hair and beard were neatly trimmed and flecked with gray and silver. He was the kind of man who was unembarrassed about getting a manicure, and who brushed after eating even when dining out. For all his care, though, there was something unkempt about him, a seediness around the eyes and nose. You had the intimation that, grooming aside, this was someone who was beginning to let things go.

He introduced himself with the quotidian facts—he was fifty years old, wrote music for TV shows, and was newly separated from the mother of his twin daughters. But as he delved into the particulars of his "year from hell"—the death of his partner and best friend in March; the cancer-induced retirement of his agent in June; and the sudden collapse of his marriage in November—his voice faded in and out. He would begin a sentence audibly or heed a request to speak louder. By the end of the thought, though, he'd revert to a mumble, as if reminding himself of an errand. This only deepened his dislocation from the group, as the others craned forward, struggling to hear.

Finally, Peter, at the far end of the circle, raised his hand. "I don't mean to be rude, Dylan, but I haven't heard two words since you started talking."

"Yeah, me either," said Rex, one chair over from Peter. "It's like that episode of *Seinfeld*, the one with the 'low talker,' where Jerry's with this woman and can't hear a word she's saying and nods at her to be polite, and winds up having to wear this puffy shirt on the *Today* show with Bryant—"

"Uh, thanks, Rex, we can do without the plot summary," said Lathon. Glancing at Dylan, he added, "Rex is very big on *Seinfeld*, you know; he thinks it's a documentary about his *own* life. Even though he's Italian, and comes from Cleveland."

Dylan smiled wanly, drawn out of himself a moment. "Yeah, well, me, I never watch it; I'm the last of the holdouts. That bass riff between scene changes drives me crazy."

He opined that theme music should always be hummable, a

hook at the base of your ear. Even if the show died, its song could live on, become a permanent part of the culture. Take, for example, a show like *Cheers* or *Taxi*—their tunes were on the soundtrack of our generation. The problem these days was that the theme music was being written by kids. They were all twenty-four-year-old geeks who composed on laptops and had never done a day's apprenticeship in their—

"Whoa," he said, hearing himself. "That was a pure geezer moment. I sounded like an old man on a park bench."

"Hey, that's okay," said Lathon. "At least we could *hear* you. Your voice came in loud and clear."

The others laughed at this, welcoming Dylan aboard, or at any rate acknowledging him in a less arm's-length way. Sara asked what he'd written, and he ticked off a list that included two or three series everyone had heard of. Rex broke out in one of the theme songs, garbling the few words he knew, and some of the others chimed in, correcting him.

"People, if we *can* . . . " said Lathon, restoring order. Turning to Dylan, he apologized sheepishly.

"That's all right," said Dylan. "Those songs are paying my bills. I've been living on royalties since the summer."

In a voice that, though tentative, was audible to all, he told what the year had cost him. In Greg, his partner of nineteen years, he'd lost more than a lyricist and best friend. Greg was the schmoozer, the guy who handled the studios, flying out to L.A. every couple of weeks. Though Harold was their agent, many of the jobs came through Greg, who knew everybody on both coasts and was loved by all. When he died at his desk of a massive stroke last spring, it both broke Dylan's heart and stemmed the work flow, sending projects they'd normally get to other people. And then Harold got sick, and things dried up completely, such that Dylan hadn't had a gig since the fall. Luckily, he still had stuff in syndication, which helped to soften the blow financially. But if nothing broke for him in the next couple of months, he was going to have to start unloading some of his assets—beginning with the "dream house" in Montclair.

"It's probably lost to me, anyway—I won't be back there regardless, unless Jeannie and I work things out," he said. "But I really did want my kids to grow up there, and hand it over to their own kids when the time came. . . ." He trailed off, a bitter smile crooking his lips. "Man, I never knew you could have such strong feelings for a *house*. . . ."

"Ah, but you can," said Lathon. "Particularly if that house says something about you, like who you are and how far you've come."

Dylan took a breath and held it close, as if it were a life preserver in deep water.

"Yeah, it did," he said gloomily. "I mean, I got *sober* in that house. I stopped drinking, and became a father, and a human being."

"How old are your daughters?" asked Sara gently.

"The twins'll be six in April," he said, brightening at the mention of them. "They're five and five-sixths, as they like to tell people."

"And are they with you or their mother most of the time?"

Dylan's face dimmed as quickly as it had lit. "Um, well, the place I've got now, it's not really suitable," he said. "It isn't the greatest area, and the apartment is pretty cramped. . . ."

He paused again, fingering the top of his mustache. "Ah, who'm I bullshitting? The place is a dump, and I'm ashamed to be seen there."

He explained that he'd bought the house in Montclair in the eighties, when interest rates were locked in the teens. And though he'd later refinanced at a less punitive rate, he was still carrying a heavy debt load—seven thousand dollars just to start the month. That left very little over for additional rent, and so he was back in his old studio in Hell's Kitchen. It was a place he'd been holding on to since his bachelor days, subletting it to a series of grad students. Though he hadn't actually lived there in more than a decade, it retained a lot of bad memories for him—the weeklong coke binges with hookers and bar girls, and the evil smell of those morning afters.

"Are you in The Program?" asked Jack, with a peremptory frown.

"Ah, um, well, I *used* to be," said Dylan. "For seven and a half years, in fact."

"But you aren't anymore?"

Again, Dylan dithered, casting a look at Lathon. "Actually, that was something we fought about," he said. "My wife's an AA fanatic who goes to two meetings a day, and associates pretty much only with people in The Program. Whereas for me, after seven years, it was enough, already. I wanted to be with people who had *other* things to talk about. And it became this big rift, with her accusing me of betraying her, and putting our whole family in jeopardy. And I understood what she was afraid of, but I'd been sober for a long time, and I went on *being* sober until a minor slip last spring. And so, while I've thought about going to a meeting, it's just so . . . tainted for me now. So wrapped up with her twelve-stepping bullshit."

Jack grunted as he heard this, struggling to hold his peace. In the silence that set up, he looked from face to face, as if attempting to beam his thoughts into someone else. Finally, he couldn't take it anymore.

"You know, I've only been in The Program since May of ninety," he said, "but in that four and a half years, I've probably heard a thousand excuses. 'Oh, I can't make a meeting, it's supposed to pour tonight,' or 'I hate going to that one, there's no Starbucks nearby.' In fact, I've heard more excuses now than I've heard reasons to drink. And you know what my favorite was? 'Aw, I can't go today—it's *Tuesday.*' "

There was some scattered laughter among the other members,

but Jack wasn't trying to entertain. He fixed his high-watt glare on Dylan, who stared back, then broke it off.

"Have you managed to not drink, since that time last year?" asked Lina.

Dylan nodded, keeping his eyes where they were. "I've been clean and sober for eleven months now."

"And how long do you think you're gonna stay that way, holing up on your own?" Jack asked.

"Now *look*," said Dylan, coming forward in his seat, "I don't want this to be a gang bang about AA. I've got bigger things to deal with now. Like how I'm going to make a living, and feed my kids."

He glared at Lathon, looking wounded and feral, while the others withdrew to their thoughts.

"Look, Dylan, don't misunderstand what I'm saying," said Jack. "I'm not trying to bust your balls about AA. It's just that with all of this . . . stuff that's landed on top of you, it'd be easy to crawl off and hide. I remember when I lost *my* ticket, I hid out for two years. And all I did, besides double my intake, was think up ways to die and make it look like an accident, so my kids could collect the insurance."

Dylan glanced up at him, marking this information. "Yeah, well, that's what I've been doing," he muttered. "Crawling into my hole. But I haven't had a drink, and I don't intend to."

An awkward pause ensued, thick with strains of the unsaid. Rex folded his arms, bored and dismissive of what he was hearing. Lina, by contrast, was close to tears, eyeing Dylan as if he were a child in a wheelchair. Rex aside, in fact, *all* the members seemed in the grip of strong feelings, and to be wrestling with the protocol of voicing them. They glanced at Lathon, or at Dylan, then Lathon, importuning him with their eyes to please say something. Lathon sat silently, though, with his chin on his thumbs. A half minute passed in this fashion.

Finally, Lathon stirred, hitching himself up in his seat. He rubbed his face with both hands, then pinched the crease of his trousers, the latter act a sure precursor to a monologue.

"Last session, if you'll remember, we talked about shame, and the ways it can wound and distort you," he began. "Tonight, what I'm hearing is the pain of *loss*, so let's stop for a minute and examine it. When you lose someone dear to you, or for that matter, some-*thing*—a marriage or a career or the house of your dreams—the pain that comes along is very complicated. The grief alone is crushing, and can make its own complications—illness, depression, sleep disorder, what have you. But underneath the grief are pains like guilt and recrimination—*What did* I *do to bring this on, and who could ever love such a person?* Loss, in other words, can do harm to your identity, and breed fear for what lies ahead—a life of poverty, say, or of growing old alone. And that fear of future pain can really lock you down, keep you from doing things that're healing. Spending time, for instance, with loved ones, or getting back to the work you care about.

"Let me restate this, because it's very important. There's the pain itself, which is acute but temporary, and then there's the fear of the pain, which I call 'suffering.' And the more we suffer—i.e., avoid the pain involved—the more entrenched it becomes. Sara, as we heard, tuned out the pain her dad caused her, and has been suffering with manlessness ever since. And Dylan, who got hit with the triple whammy this year, has dealt with it by basically shutting down. He's retreated to his cave, not seeing his two girls, or going to AA, where they really know from loss. For him, it was just too much pain all at once—the loss of his two best friends and partners, his marriage and dream house—I mean, with a year like that, your only job is to *survive* it, and Dylan's still here to tell his story.

"And so *our* job now is to help him rebuild. Help save what's fixable, like his relationship with his kids, and to make new where the old is beyond fixing. And what we ask in kind, Dylan, is that you show up with your pain, and let us help sort it out. You can endure some of that pain now; it's the suffering that's so dangerous. The hiding out and brooding—that's risky stuff for a guy like you. As Jack, with a similar history, reminds us."

Slumped in his seat, Dylan stared out the window, his eyes gone as flat as the roofline. With a thumb and forefinger, he plucked at his beard, vacantly browsing its curve.

"I mean, I hear what you're saying," he murmured. "There're friends who've called to see me—asked me to their house for a week in Sea Bright. And I could see my daughters more, but it would mean staying in Montclair, with Jeannie and I under the same roof. . . ."

"Then, is it possible," Jack asked, "that she could sleep at a girlfriend's, and lend you the place for a weekend?"

Dylan's gaze sharpened, considering this. "Yeah, I could ask her, I guess; her best friend's right across the street. Although things're so tense now, we can't even talk without fighting, which is why I've kept my distance. But, like I said, I could try that, and also try getting out more. It's really been—"

"Uh-uh, don't try," said Lathon. "Trying implies failure. What I preach, instead, is *practice.* Practice is the path to competence in this world. And from competence comes a life of your own making."

four

They'd recently changed the name from Hell's Kitchen to Clinton, and the neighborhood seemed much the better for it. The drug trade had been strong-armed off of Theater Row, and prostitution and its ills driven south and west, to the badlands along the river. Blocks of old brownstones had been gutted and reborn, home to the new winners in mergers and acquisitions. Even the cuisine, once inedible to all but tourists, had begun, by any measure, to improve. Gone were the ziti mills and hash joints of yore, replaced by a province of hybrid bistros serving the cuisine of the New World Order— duck ravioli by way of Thailand, with a raspberry pilsner from Norway.

So pervasive was this crawl of prosperity, in fact, that only a couple of buildings on West Forty-fifth Street had staved it off. One of them was the yellow tenement that Dylan lived in. Old men with cranky dogs stood guard in front of it, reciting the kvetch of the day to each other. Inside, an indifferent porter was sitting at a bridge table, engrossed in a Spanish sex mag. I mentioned Dylan's name to him and he waved me along. Even the lone elevator was in a foul mood, inching up the shaft like an arthritic butler and lurching to a halt on five.

I stepped out of the elevator into a mix of odors: boiled cabbage and pork pierogies, fresh garbage in the chute, and a deep and possibly septic unhappiness through the soot-colored walls and moldings. The numbers on the doors had been painted over, making it necessary to stop at each of them and squint. Through a doorsill came the strains of a Caribbean talk show; through another, the drone and thrash of Black Sabbath. Through Dylan's door, once located, came a handsome tenor, singing a sad ballad by Neil Young. There was a flub on the piano, but the singer played through it, completing the verse in stride before starting over. I listened for several minutes before I knocked.

"Eh, I was just trying to get loose," said Dylan, deflecting my praise at the door. "I haven't been playing much, and my hands are stiff. One of these days, I ought to use them to try writing something."

I stepped into the apartment and was shown around, a tour that didn't take very long. The place consisted of two rooms, each the size of a small maid's quarters, mediated by a narrow bathroom. The bedroom was taken up with Dylan's equipment—a piano, synthesizer, and a stand of expensive guitars. On the walls were framed pictures of Dylan with assorted rock stars, in varying degrees of inebriation. In one, a black-and-white shot, he was slung across a couch, clinking beer bottles with Duane Allman. In another, tilting perilously back on a barstool, he was raising a toast to Joey and Dee Dee Ramone. Even allowing for the changes in hair and weight, the man depicted was unrecognizable as the one beside me. There was a wildness and avidity in those red-rimmed eyes, the leer of a guy who stood up on roller coasters, mocking the laws of gravity. By contrast, the Dylan who'd returned to these rooms seemed landlocked, pinned to the ground. He clicked off the piano, folded his sheet music carefully, and asked if I'd like some coffee.

The front room was marginally the less bleak of the two. There was a black leather sofa with faded scroll arms that looked better for the wear and tear. The walls were a pleasant Wedgwood blue, with white moldings and crown intaglio. However, the seats of the cane armchairs sported large holes, as did the stools underneath the kitchen pass-through. One stool was reupholstered with a picture book on gardening, the other with a carving board.

"I apologize for the place; as you see, I haven't done much with it," he said. "I've actually got some okay pieces in storage, from before when I bought the house. But every time I think of moving them over here, I get this . . . pain going across my chest. It's like, if I bring that stuff over, it means I actually *live* here. That this is my home, and I'm accepting it."

On the table in front of us stood a cluster of photos in a three-sided acrylic frame. The picture that faced us was an eight-by-ten blowup of Dylan and his family on their patio. The two little girls were sitting on his lap, gap-toothed and adorable in velveteen jumpers. Cinching them in his arms, Dylan glowed for the camera, the handsome, prosperous father with his treasure. Jeannie, on the other hand, sat well apart from them, as if posing for her own formal portrait. She was a tall, stylish redhead with Princess Di bangs and intelligent, convivial eyes. Serene in a silk blouse and man-tailored blazer, she looked like the kind of woman you would buy a house from, perhaps even something out of your price range.

"When was this taken?" I asked.

"Last summer," he said. "Father's Day. Might've been the one day all year we weren't arguing."

He thought back on the occasion, a wistful barbecue with his dead partner's widow and children. The mood had been somber, the adults talking in low voices, tiptoeing around Greg's absence. And then one of the twins, Olivia, who had a crush on Greg's youngest, began chasing him around with a plastic hatchet, and pelting him with kisses. Everyone laughed, especially when Olivia got up and announced she was having a baby.

"She just has this way of saying things from another planet." Dylan grinned. "I've no idea where she gets it from. And her sister, you know, is the straight man of the act. If Olivia says, 'Let's go make Kool-Aid in the tub,' Rebecca'll say, 'Grape or cherry?' "

As he talked about the girls, some of his deadness dropped away. He was seeing them this weekend, having taken the group's counsel and put in a call to Jeannie. To his surprise, she was glad to lend him the house; it would be her first night out since the separation. More, she was amenable to trying it twice a month. She had a girlfriend in Bloomfield with an extra bedroom.

"Hey, well, great," I said. "You can see your kids regularly, and do it up there, where they're more comfortable."

Dylan gave a nod, looking past me to the next thought. "Actually," he mused, "it was probably our best talk in a long time. Both of us were cordial, no one raising their voice, or trying to get a lick in edgewise. She even asked how I was holding up, living alone. In fact, it almost sounded like she was . . . feeling me out. Maybe sending a signal that the door was still open."

"And is that something you'd respond to?" I asked. "In group, it kind of sounded like you'd closed the book."

"Did it?" he murmured, looking out his gray window at a covey of pigeons across the air shaft. They had gathered on the cornice of a low-lying rooftop, bickering and preening like chess hustlers. Every couple of minutes, a noise would rout them, scattering them in six directions. Moments later, though, they would reconvene on the cornice, picking up their thoughts in mid-squawk. "I'm sorry, what was the question?"

"How you felt about getting back with Jeannie."

"Right," he muttered, frowning in self-reproach. "Right, right, right, right, right." He took a deep breath, collecting himself. "I don't know, man; it's complicated. The last five years, all we did, really, was fight. I'd come back from the store with the wrong kind of skim milk, or the girls would be slow getting dressed in the morning, and *wham*, the screaming would start. And I'd say, 'Jeannie, calm down,' or 'Can we not do this in front of the kids?' and that'd just wind her up more. It got so tense, I dreaded getting on the train at night, knowing what was in store for me at home. And whenever I'd try to talk about it—rationally, just the two of us—she'd either go into her happy mode—'*Problems?* We have no problems'—or tell me that I knew what the matter was, and blow right out of the room. Even when we saw Lathon and got something worked out, it seemed like two days later, she'd be back in a snit—and I'd be back in the guest room."

"Whose idea was it to see Lathon?" I asked. "From the sound of it, I'm guessing it was yours."

"Actually, no, it was hers, and I thought that was big. That she cared enough to take the initiative. But when he tried to pin her down about what she was so angry about, it'd be a different reason each time. Same thing when he asked if she would do what's necessary to preserve the partnership—she gave the most bozart non-answer you've ever heard. If I'd had half a brain, I'd've walked out right there. But, of course, I didn't."

"And why do you suppose that is?"

Dylan made a snuffling noise and turned away. It was the closest he'd come to laughing since we started.

"Well, I could lie and tell you it was for *their* sake," he said, nodding at his children in the picture. "They didn't need me there— not with all that screaming. One of us had to go, and *she* wasn't budging. So, even though they miss me, and I'm on the phone with them twice a day, they're much less freaked now than they were."

As he spoke, a virulent quarrel broke out in the apartment above us. Most of it was conducted in keening Spanglish, and though the text was unclear to us, its tenor was not—they could have been standing in Dylan's bedroom with the door open.

"My God," I said. "How often does that go on?"

He glared at the ceiling. "You see why I can't have my kids here? If they're not brawling up there, they're having a fuckfest, or drinking with their faggot boyfriends—"

He reached over, plucked a paperback off the table, and slung it, spine up, at the ceiling. "Shut that fucking racket!" he yelled.

There was a pause before the quarrel resumed, in something like a shrill whisper. Dylan shook his head and sat down again, kneading his forehead with his knuckles.

I held off a moment, then returned to my inquiry. If he hadn't stayed on for the sake of his daughters, then what had kept him from leaving?

"You mean, other than the thought of moving here?" he snorted.

He crossed his arms, and resumed his study of the pigeons. "Well, I mean, our first five years together were probably the happiest of my life. We went on safari for a month, which had been a dream of mine since childhood. And we loved to jump in the car and drive to Maine or somewhere, or play Monopoly, naked, for two days straight, and eating nothing but peanut M&M's. I mean, yeah, there were arguments, but we just had so much fun—the kind of boy-girl fun I'd never had as a kid. And plus, for the first time, I actually confided in someone. Told her what it was like, as the oldest son, to have to deal with my mother when she was drunk. You know, my father couldn't be bothered, he worked all hours of the day and night. And so it was on me to see that the dinner got cooked, and that my brothers went to bed at a decent hour, instead of staying up watching *Outer Limits.* And Jeannie could relate to that because her dad was a lush, and she'd had major, mega-weirdness to deal with. Physical abuse, step-moms, moving from town to town—she'd lived in six different states before high school.

"And so, there was all this . . . stuff that we had in common; it was almost like we'd grown up together. And then the twins came along and I was so excited. I thought, wow, a whole family in one shot. But instead of being psyched, Jeannie started to stress out. She was like, 'My life is over before it even started.' And I said to her, 'Look, we'll get through this. We'll get a woman in here to help you—you can go back to work in six months.' But from the day the kids got here, she was like a different person. It was like I'd tricked her or something, gotten her pregnant behind her back. And that's when the fights started, not later, when I stopped going to meetings. She begrudged me for having 'stolen' her chance for stardom."

We sat there a while, listening to the rooting of the pigeons, and the amplifying tensions above us.

"Why would you consider going back, then?" I asked. "Are you hoping that after a couple of months off from each other it can be more like those first five years?"

Dylan snuffled again, laughing through his sinuses. "Nah, no chance of that happening. There's too much stuff she holds against me."

"Then, forgive me for seeming stupid, but what is it that makes you want to . . . ?"

He looked at me with a kind of pleading candor. "Is it that hard to see? It's because I *love* her, man. Why else would I be waiting in this dump?"

five

march

There are a couple of months a year that hike anxieties in New York, shading it with a grim neuralgia. November is one such month, bearing troughs of cold air, portents of the seasonal lockdown to come. March is another, with its procession of gray days, and the long wait for reliable signs of life. The mornings are warmer but rarely warm, the rain snarls traffic and backs up basements and makes mold the first bloom of spring. And right behind a mild stretch is a reprise of winter, the blizzard that catches everyone unawares. It is a wonderful time to take sick for ten days or to surprise your aging parents in Florida.

When Dylan didn't show for the start of the third session, then, it was casually assumed that he was under the weather, or detained by the daylong downpour. Lathon said nothing about it, waiting on Sara and Lina, who had phoned ahead to say they were running late. When the women arrived, though, and had taken their seats, Lathon made an announcement. He said that he had gotten a call from Dylan Sunday night, confessing, in AA parlance, that he had "gone out again." The details were sketchy, but apparently it had begun the prior weekend, when he drove over to the house to see his kids. A fight ensued with his wife, the exact nature of which was unclear, but he'd bought a six-pack on the way home. As night follows day, this sparked a full-on binge—a week of round-the-clock drinking and drugging.

Now, the good news, said Lathon, looking around the circle,

was that Dylan had come back down. As was the case last year, when he'd had a brief relapse, he had agreed to do an in-home detox. It wasn't the perfect solution—a month at a clinic would have been the first choice. But given Dylan's money problems, and his animus against rehab centers, whose paper-slippers protocol he detested, the in-home regimen was about the best alternative. There was also the matter of his divorce proceedings, which promised to be lengthy and bitter. If Jeannie found out that he had had another slip, it would be a major chit for her in court. Luckily, they hadn't spoken since the fight, so it was safe to assume she didn't know.

"Now, I know this is disturbing, and I'll hear your feelings on it in a second," said Lathon. "But first, let me remind you that this is an illness, and as such, deserves our sympathy. If Dylan was a cancer survivor and had suffered a relapse, we wouldn't hold his tumor against him. We would send him our prayers for a speedy recovery, and assure him we were keeping a place here."

The five members stared at him, flushed and tongue-tied, thrown back on their thoughts. The air in the room felt clammy and inert, like the ambience in a snake house. Outside, the rain fell in silver arcs, spattering the window with fat droplets.

"What does this home thing involve?" asked Sara. "And do you think that this slip, or whatever you call it, will change his mind about AA?"

Taking her first question first, Lathon said that a home detox was no picnic. Under a nurse's supervision, it was five days of misery, with fevers, dry heaves, and night sweats. High doses of Librium made it marginally more tolerable, but for someone like Dylan, who drank beer by the caseload, there was no such thing as a soft withdrawal. However, he had come through it last year with good success, and had agreed to go back into addictions counseling. But as for AA—well, he was still divided on that. He said he'd see what he would see when he got sober.

Now, suddenly, the questions came all at once. Would Dylan be on his feet again in time for the next session, and if so, in what kind of shape? What should they say to him, either through Lathon as proxy, or in the flesh whenever he showed up? And what if he got sober and then relapsed again—was there a limit on the number of slips allowed?

"Whoa," said Lathon, holding his hands up for quiet. "Everyone form a straight line."

He said that, yes, he hoped Dylan would be back for the next session, so that he didn't fall too far behind. As for his frame of mind, that was harder to predict. For sure, he'd be ashamed, since shame was a given; it was what kept addicts in traction, feeling hopeless. But it was also possible that this stumble would scare him, rouse him out of his self-pity. Because while it was true that he still had the house in Montclair and a marketable skill to purvey, it was also true that he was in open free fall, and in very real danger of losing everything. As he'd said himself, it had been a while since he'd written anything—and in show biz, they weren't much in the habit of keeping a seat warm for fifty-year-old men.

After a long pause, Peter raised his hand, saying he felt somehow responsible. He'd been very worried about Dylan, thinking about him between sessions, and wondering if they just should focus on him for a while, at least till he was out of the woods. But he hadn't brought it up for fear of embarrassing Dylan, and now he was kicking himself for it.

"Well, but I reached out to him," Jack harrumphed. "I talked to him good and straight after the last session. I could see he was on the ledge there, not going to meetings, and bad-mouthing The Program left and right, and so I asked him to call me if he was in trouble. But he didn't, and I'm sad about that, because I think I could've helped him, and told him I would meet him halfway. I can only conclude, then, that he wanted to pick up again, and nothing anyone did was going to stop him. And as for these home detoxes, let's just say I'm highly skeptical. You want to stop drinking, you start making some meetings. It's no more complicated than that."

"Except that, obviously, it *is* more complicated than that," said Sara. "Otherwise, he'd have done it." Turning to Lathon, she said, "My question is, isn't there some cheaper form of rehab, where he could go and get the help he needs? You say he's done this home thing before, but if it worked so well, why's he drinking again? I just want to see him get this squared away, so we don't go round and round with it all year."

Lathon allowed himself an opaque smile. "Well, I, too, would like it wrapped up neat and tidy. Unfortunately, it doesn't work that way. And even if there were some quick-stop treatment place, I couldn't force him to go there. If he was out running around, being a menace to others, then, yes, I could call the cops on him. But failing that, there isn't a lot else I can do. I'm his therapist, you know, not his parole officer."

And with that, he tapped his watch and suggested they get down to business. This was an important session, not that any of them were trivial, but tonight they'd begin the process called "serious listening." He laid out the format, describing a series of interviews to be conducted one-on-one in the "hot seats." By these, he was referring to the two black club chairs directly across from him in the square. From here on in, he would appoint two members to interview each other for twenty minutes. When that was over, he'd open the floor to the others, who would make assessments of what they'd heard. The first goal, he said, was to learn to "hear down" to the truth, to the pain and fear underlying the story. The second was to be able to distinguish it from "suffering," or behavior that distracted you from your real pain.

Looking around the room, he selected Lina to be interviewed and Jack to be her interrogator. There was a bit of horseplay as Jack and Rex switched seats, each giving the other a couple of feints before going around him. Lina, meanwhile, remained where she was, clenching her worry beads. The rain had wilted her fine black hair, matting it against her forehead. Under the amber light, her face was severe, engulfed in slanting shadows.

Lathon was coaching Jack on what line to pursue when Sara put her hand up vexedly. "I'm sorry," she said, "but something's still bothering me about Dylan. What if, after he detoxes, he comes back for a while and then starts drinking again, and becomes, like, this ongoing distraction?"

There was some scattered grumbling from the other members, but Lathon put his hand up for patience. "No, no, I'm glad Sara asked, because this is bothering her, and it allows me to define a new term. For Sara, and maybe some others of you, as well, Dylan's relapse is a *suffering invitation*. That is, it's a chance to worry about some pain in the future, instead of dealing with the one at hand. *Will* Dylan's drinking become a hassle here, and prevent us from doing our work? I doubt it, though there is that possibility, if we don't take steps if the need arises. But as you can tell by the number of 'ifs' in that sentence, this is a purely hypothetical problem. What isn't hypothetical, Sara, is the pain you came in with. That's as real as the chair you're sitting on."

Sara's gaze dropped to the lid of her coffee cup, which she was perforating with a thumb and forefinger. "Well, I do see your point about worrying about the future. That's something I do a lot and need to stop doing, because it winds me up for no reason. Like, out of nowhere, I'll suddenly think, what if my best photographer left and went to some other magazine? Or what if I wound up sick in the hospital and none of my friends came to visit me? I mean, it's ridiculous and I know that, and yet, you can't just *stop* worrying, because there're some things you *should* be worried about. Like, what if your car breaks down on a dark road, and—"

"Hey, hey, slow down," said Lathon, grinning. "I can hear you revving from over here."

There was a clatter of laughter from the other members. Sara glanced up with an astringent smile.

"Let me offer you a rule of thumb about worrying," said Lathon. "If a sentence starts out with the words, 'What if,' you can be pretty sure that what follows is a suffering invitation. So listen for that phrase, and pay attention to your response to it—the butterflies in the stomach, the sweaty palms and racing thoughts. There's a biochemistry of suffering that I want you all to get acquainted with. Because once you're on to it, you can dismantle it before it starts. And stop living from one state of crisis to another."

He talked a bit more about the brain's false alarms, and how they rob you of time and adrenaline. And then, after Sara acknowledged that that was helpful, he turned to the evening's theme. Tonight, he wanted to talk about family history, calling it the "template of all false stories." In the interviews, the questioner's job was to learn as much as possible about the subject's childhood. What was it like to be a kid in her house? How did her parents relate to each other, and what dreams did they have for their children? What, in short, was the culture of this family, and what imprint did it leave on its members?

Lina, who'd been waiting impatiently to get going, sighed and folded her arms. Clearly, she'd come in with more pressing concerns, and had little or no interest in discussing her past. Indeed, as Jack started on his line of questioning, she kept working in the subject of her marriage. She'd grown up, she said, in a loving family in Queens, on a block literally teeming with friends and relatives. Her parents were Greek immigrants who wanted better for their four children, and worked long days in their Astoria men's shop to send them all to college. Of course, there *had* been the occasional fight and flare-up—try living with five people in a cramped three-bedroom, sharing a single bathroom, without fighting! But on the whole, her family was warm and protective, and unfailingly proud of its children. That was why Anton had caught her off guard; she had never been exposed to such lies and insults.

"I know this sounds strange, coming from a native New Yorker," she said, "but I was raised to see the good in people. When a person says he loves you and truly values your character, I stupidly believed he meant it. Obviously, I was naïve, but that was my upbringing— to trust what was in someone's heart. And also, I was influenced by my parents' relationship. I mean, it wasn't all wine and roses every minute, but there was love that you could see and feel between them, and they've been together now for fifty-one years. Whereas, with *his* parents, it was like a war all the time. The cursing, the screaming—they went at it like crazy people. I kept waiting to read in the *Post* that they'd killed each other."

As Jack's Q-and-A with Lina progressed, however, two things became apparent: one, that he'd missed out on a great career as a trial lawyer, and two, that Lina's childhood was more complex than stated. Asking a series of questions to which he seemed to know the answers beforehand, Jack drew out some troubling details. Though the only girl in her family and, as such, much pampered, Lina was told, in a variety of ways, that less was expected of her than her brothers. From an early age, she was an exceptional student, representing her grade in spelling bees, and winning the school science fair two years running. But far from reveling in his daughter's success, her father tartly referred to her as "the brain," and "the grim reader," even telling her, at one point, that she was hurting her chances at marrying well. And though he later made sacrifices to send her to Princeton, it was long since clear that his hopes lay elsewhere, in the person of her oldest brother, Teddy.

"Hunh," said Jack, scratching his nose contemplatively. "Sounds like your husband wasn't the first guy to disrespect you."

A murmur of grunts went up around the circle, registering agreement.

"I—I'm sorry, what?" said Lina, looking up from her memories. "I didn't quite catch that last part."

"What he said—and by the way, Jack, splendid work on the interview—was that he thought he heard an echo," said Lathon. "That what your father said to you about being studious sounded a lot like Anton's insults."

Lina said nothing for a moment, her brow knit in bafflement. She gazed at Lathon with her mouth half open, as if he'd sprung a cheap surprise. "I don't see how you can make—I mean, yes, he said some things, but there's no way he'd hurt me like—"

She sputtered to a stop, and took a short breath. Tears stood out on her lashes. "I'm telling you, he's been *wonderful* to me, especially this last year or two. I could never've gotten through it without him."

"To be sure," said Lathon. "And no one's saying otherwise. His love and support for you are very real. But thirty or forty years ago, when you were fashioning your true self—winning spelling bees and science fairs, pursuing a life of the mind—what you got from him was some pretty major dissonance. He *didn't* call the neighbors, bragging on your test scores, or gloat about his daughter, the whiz kid. Instead, he tried to shame you out of being yourself, to dissuade you from trusting your talent. And that's the paradigm, the blueprint, of false story: an attempt to impose a narrative on you, to define you by his prerogatives."

Again, there was a quorum of grunts from the others, uttered in assent or recognition. Lina, meanwhile, had been studying her nail beds, pushing back the cuticles with her thumb.

"Well, but what I'm saying is, he's from *such* a different era," she said. "In his day, you know, they didn't push girls for the professions. And he really didn't get it that this was a whole new ball game and that nobody was playing by those rules here. And you should also understand that . . . there was something else going on . . . a thing my mother had done that really—hurt him. It wasn't really an affair, per se; it was more of, like, an infatuation . . . an in-

98

terlude between her and one of the sales reps. I'm not sure, even, if they ever had sex, though my father claimed that they—God, I can't believe I'm even talking about this—!"

She cupped her brow as if she had a headache, kneading the edge of her hair line. With her legs crossed twice, at the knees and ankles, and her free arm cinching her waist, she looked like a length of tightly wound cable, energy trapped between points.

Sara, who'd been watching intently, raised her hand to be called on. Lathon nodded, saying he would take questions from the floor now, starting clockwise from Sara.

"Well, I was curious about how your father treated your mother," she said. "Did he say stuff to her like he did to you, and if so, what did she say back to him?"

"Ah, good question," said Lathon. "How was this family on women *in general*, and how did they respond?"

Lina returned to her nails. She was a private person, measured in her responses, and answering these questions pained her. For others, perhaps, this was a less grueling proposition, a chance, even, to preen, to hold the stage. But for Lina, there was no pleasure in self-exposure, only the shame of having come to such a pass.

"Well, they—they fought," she murmured. "There were a lot of . . . things said both ways. But my mother was *not* the kind to sit back and take it. If anything, she was the aggressor."

"Really? How so?" asked Sara, her interest perking.

Lina colored, the blood mantling her cheeks. "He, I guess, also had his little—venture. Sort of like revenge for what she did. And when my mom found out about it, he tried to say, "Well, this makes us even," but she got nuts about it. For the next year, year-and-a-half, she was vicious to him, constantly throwing it back at him. It was a really bad time, not just for him but for all of us. I was convinced they were going to break up."

"And was that when he started making those comments to you?" asked Rex.

Lina nodded, blushing to her hairline. "I was about nine when it happened, and the whole atmosphere just changed. When I think back to that time, it's like it was always dusk out, and I'm home by myself in the dark."

The room went silent for several moments, as a tinge of that melancholy set in. The light in the room was pearlescent, a shade between gray and yellow. You could hear the faint *plink* of raindrops ticking metal, and the footfalls of the children playing above us. It was as if, by some trick of mood, we'd been transported to the house in Queens, where we and Lina waited in the gloaming.

Finally, Lathon ended the silence, talking about the resonances of the past. Old pains, he said, often come cloaked in new ones, and make our grief a kind of double labor. Hence, the sheer volume of Lina's sadness: she wasn't mourning the failure of one family but two, feeling her parents' suffering as well as her own. What they had experienced was a kind of minor death: the loss of their dreams and innocence. So, too, had she been cheated by Anton, robbed of her dreams of happiness. In spite of his falseness, she had made this true thing—a family that prized its two children. And now he had ruptured it, bringing pain to its members, and she grieved for her children's loss more than her own. Because, at the end of the day, that was who she was—not a social worker or an administrator, but a mother to her children. And they were what mattered to her.

"Yes, that's true," said Lina, giving in to tears. "I love them both very, very much."

And then, for what seemed like a very long time, no one said anything else. The others looked on as Lina wept, several near tears themselves, caught in the bind of being a witness to grief and unable to do much about it. Finally, Lina's sobs abated, and Lathon cleared his throat and sat up.

"It took your father a long time to see how strong you are, in part because you were afraid to show him. And the same thing goes for your husband, Anton: you rarely showed up as yourself with him, a person of bearing and courage. But, boy, is he going to find out what the real Lina's like. Especially when you whip him in court."

"You really think so?" she croaked, wiping her eyes with a tissue.

"Oh, I know so," said Lathon. "Five, six months from now, he's going to look over at you in court and say, 'Who *is* this person, and where's she *been* the last twenty years?' "

six

march

There was no sign of Dylan at the fourth session, either, though the news about him was better this time. He had completed the home detox without a hitch and had been in to see Lathon several times. Further, he was in daily contact with his addictions counselor and had agreed to a regimen of Antabuse, a drug that, combined with alcohol, turned the drinker violently ill. He had also gone to see an arbitrator with his wife, in hopes of reaching an amicable split. Both now saw that a pitched battle would be madness, given their dwindling assets. Alas, the strain of these last weeks had taken a toll, and at the moment Dylan was laid up with the flu.

"He asked me to tell you, though, that he was okay, and would be back for sure next session," said Lathon. "He also said to thank you for bearing with him, and that he was touched by your thoughts and wishes."

The others said nothing for several moments, conferring with oblique glances.

"And what do *you* think?" asked Sara, cocking an eyebrow. "Do you think he means it about staying sober?"

"Uh, yes, I do," said Lathon, "although I also believe my eyes. I saw him as recently as Friday, and he looked determined to move his life forward. He sees now that he'd been nursing a pipe dream about Jeannie, waiting for her to take him back. And she'd encouraged it, frankly, in a variety of ways, making noises about missing him, too. But after that weekend in Montclair, when they couldn't go an hour without fighting, he finally understood that there was no hope, and decided to pick up and move on. Now, is that a guarantee that he'll stick to the plan, and get through this patch of rough sledding? No, obviously not, and I'd be lying if I said otherwise. But today—right now—I like his chances, and look forward to having him back."

"Even though he still hasn't agreed to go to meetings," Jack huffed.

"Yeah, I mean, what's *that* about?" said Rex. "If you admit you're a drunk and are powerless to stop, why wouldn't you go where there's help?"

Lathon cleared his throat, betraying impatience. "Look, recovery is a *process*, and the steps aren't always big ones. But I assure you that his chances are better with this group than they would be if we pushed him out now."

The members conferred with sidelong looks, staking out a position. "Is that an option?" asked Sara, coolly sipping her coffee.

Lathon glanced away, choosing his words with care.

"It's early in the day to be talking about that," he said. "If, somewhere down the road, this becomes disruptive, then, yes, I'll ask him to leave. But I think the best thing now, for Dylan and his girls, is to support him in the process. That's the side I've appealed to directly—the loving dad who wants to get well again for their sake. When someone's drowning, you look for any line you can throw him—and right now, his daughters are about all there is."

A prickly gloom settled over the group. "You know, you almost make it sound like this is life or death," said Sara.

"I'd say that, yes, if he doesn't unload that heartbreak, the odds of something bad happening are fairly high. He's got chronic health problems associated with drinking, and I worry, frankly, if he can survive a prolonged binge. And this is also a guy who, when he's drinking again, climbs into his car and drives to Montclair with twenty beers in his system."

"What!" cried Lina. "How can he even think of such a —"

"*This* is what I'm talking about," Sara bristled. "This is the kind of person who flips his car, and kills some poor, innocent family on vacation."

Jack, chagrined, recalled his own history of drunk driving. A teetotaler all day, he'd make up for it at sundown, bolting three or four doubles before dinner. Shortly after midnight, he'd catch a cab to Penn Station and "sober up" on the last train to Roslyn. He only lived a mile or so from the station, and at that hour, there weren't many cars on the road. He managed, however, to hit more than a few parked cars, and fell asleep one night with a quart of Stoli in his system and "wiped out some poor bastard's front porch."

This report did nothing to lift the group's spirits. Sara urged Lathon to *do* something about this, to force Dylan to start going to meetings right now, or, failing that, to rip up his driver's license. But again, Lathon pleaded powerlessness. Even if they posted Dylan's picture at tollbooths, it still wouldn't stop him from driving while drunk. After that first cold beer, his brain was running on dopamine, and nothing but an act of God would short those circuits.

And with that, he moved that they get under way, inveighing against the trap of suffering invitations. This was one such instance, though, that was clearly of his own making. In authorizing its worst-case fears about Dylan, Lathon had turned him into a ward of the group. The members couldn't be expected now to treat him with rigor, to insist he be held to the standard of ruthless compassion. No, taken all around, it was a bad call by Lathon that soon enough would become bad policy. For now, it merely cast the first doubt on him, complicating the group's view of its therapist.

The theme of tonight's interviews was a holdover from the last session—the scope and nature of family history. Sara was picked to sit in the hot seat, and Peter to do the questioning. Before they got started, though, Sara raised her hand; she wanted to correct a false impression. Far from being aloof, or, in Lathon's word, disembodied, she was constantly at the mercy of her emotions. She was hell on cab drivers who made a wrong turn, and blew up at least once a day at the production people, raking them over the coals for minor errors. This embarrassed her to no end, and she was trying to put a stop to it, but invariably things would happen that seemed *designed* to set her off, and—wham—she was gone before she knew it. She also had stretches where she was horribly depressed, and went home at night and wept at the sheer hopelessness of it all. So if she'd given anyone the idea that she was numb and detached, the truth was, she was exactly the opposite.

Lathon thanked her for setting them straight. "What Sara is telling us is she does feel her feelings—only, they're often the wrong feelings or directed at the wrong people. Instead of telling her father how angry she is at him, she's giving it to some cab driver or the guy who does her dry cleaning. Not only does that make her feel crummy about herself, it also leaves the original pain untouched. She's still angry at her father, and suffering its side effects—a sense of shame, and an inability to change."

Sara thought for a moment, running a hand through her hair. "Sometimes, I really feel that, like it's impossible to change, and that you just are who you are, so why fight it?"

"Oh, come on," said Jack, with a peremptory frown. "Surely you don't believe that, or you wouldn't be paying *El Jefe* here a hundred bucks a pop for group. Not to mention the one-seventy-five for private sessions."

There was a sudden, collective intake of breath. Everything seemed to come to a stop, including the mayhem of the children upstairs.

Lathon blinked, wheeling his head around like a turret. "You know, that's the second time you've said that, Jack. I'm beginning to get the feeling that you have a problem with my fee."

"Well, they *are* a bit on the high side, don't you think? About double the going rate, if I'm not mistaken."

Rex let out a chortle, then caught himself, as if he'd just gotten a kick under the table. The others looked on, though, in consternation, as the first test of Lathon's authority unfolded. Perhaps sensing this, the doctor weighed his answer carefully, picking at a thread in his sock.

"Yes, you're right, Jack," he said finally. "I do charge more than some other therapists. That's because I do good work, and I do it quickly—I get people out of here fast, and back into their lives. You, for instance, I've worked with around your recovery, and I think you generally found me effective, no?"

Jack smiled down at his plaited fingers. "I'll grant you're good at your job."

"Then why, after six years, would you raise this now? I wasn't charging cut rates *then.*"

Jack, who kept a handsome, year-round tan, darkened to the color of new bricks. "Didn't you tell us not to use the word 'why?' "

He was referring to one of Lathon's rules of interviewing: an injunction against questions that began with *why.* They were too broad to be answered usefully, and were less effective than *how* or *when* questions, which called for concrete information.

"Yes, well, *I'm* allowed to ask it," said Lathon flatly. "I never claimed to be running a democracy."

The tide was going against Jack and the others picked up on it, bringing their chilly gaze to bear upon him. In this test of strength between two alpha characters, it was clear where their sympathies lay. They seemed to understand, in their mute support of Lathon, that a therapist whose will is mocked is all but lost. If he cannot draw a line and hold it fast, then nothing else he says can be taken seriously.

"Eh, you're probably right," Jack allowed. "It wasn't the best time to make a joke. Although I still stand by my point that I don't believe Sara when she says that she can't change."

"Me either," said Lina, eager to change the subject. "That'd be like me saying, 'I'm forty-four years old and my marriage died, so my life is basically over.' It's not true and I don't believe it, or I wouldn't be coming here. There's always hope, as long as you keep trying."

"That's right," said Lathon. "There *is* always hope—though, again, I'd change the word 'trying' to 'practicing.' Life is a craft whose skills can be mastered, if only you'll put in the practice. But let's get back to Sara, and put the question to her. Does she really think it's useless to try and change?"

All eyes turned to Sara, who smiled her Noh-mask smile. Despite her sharp edges, there was something girlish about her, a surprising lack of artifice or guile. "No, I don't think it's pointless," she said. "At least, not for other people. But for me, I don't know; this is my third go in therapy, and the other two had next to no effect. And so, I guess I'm sort of coming to this with lowered expectations. If it helps and I meet somebody—wonderful; great. But if it doesn't and I'm alone still . . . I'm okay with that. I've got a job that totally absorbs me, and a circle of friends I'm very close to, and my cousin and her family, who I love dearly. Maybe that isn't the best possible life, and it doesn't come close to my fantasy, but I know a lot of women in the same boat."

The others fell silent a moment, mulling this over.

"I don't know," said Peter, to no one in particular. "I just don't understand it."

"What don't you understand?" Lathon asked.

Peter was bent forward, his hands on his knees, examining the grain of the floorboards. When he spoke, he only looked up fractionally, as if it pained him to meet Sara's gaze.

"I just don't understand how a person with such—advantages

could settle for a life like that. I-I mean, you're smart, Sara, you're beautiful, you've got all these connections. . . . How could you even *think* of giving up?"

Sara's brow arched in surprise, then amusement. Aside, perhaps, from a stalled subway car, it was hard to imagine where else in New York two such unlikely characters could be seen talking— she, the very glass of style, and he, the born equivalent of beige.

"Well, um, *thank* you, Peter," she said, "that's very kind of you to say, but the fact is, I don't *feel* very beautiful. In fact, I feel just the opposite, like I'm ugly and fat, and that my thighs squish together when I walk."

Peter's eyes bulged. He looked back at Lathon, as if to confirm the sense of what he'd heard. "Are you serious?" he gawked. "You're saying *you're* fat and ugly? B-boy, if *that's* true, what does that make me?"

There was an outburst of laughter, to which even Sara joined in. In his unthreatening way, with his high, cracked cadences, Peter was quietly marking out a place here. He was someone who dependably asked the right questions, and was a resource of sturdy, good sense.

"Well, I feel stupid for even talking about this—I mean, aren't I a little old to be worried about looks?—but I *do* feel unattractive, and even thought so when I was modeling," said Sara. "And it sure doesn't help to be working around scarecrows, the Christy Turlingtons and Kate Mosses—who, by the way, isn't *all* that thin. And what's making it even worse is my appetite these days. I am just ravenous all the time, yearning for cookies and ice cream, and eating off of other people's plates in restaurants. It's like an addiction all of a sudden; I manage to be good for most of the day, but then I go home at nine o'clock and just eat till I'm ready to pass out. And then, I don't run or go to the gym for five days, and I feel *hideous*, and ashamed to be seen."

Still crouched over his knees, Peter took this in, his right foot going like a jackhammer. "You were talking last time about how your father treated your mother, calling her 'fat' and 'ugly.' Did he ever call you those names?"

"Good, Peter," said Lathon. "Go for the history. What's the *root system* of this story?"

Sara's eyes flared in mild impatience. "Well, but there we go again, with the problem of my memory. I hate to repeat myself, but I basically remember nothing from that period. In fact, here, right now, are my two memories from childhood. The first I already told you, about being called in by my father, who announced he was getting a divorce, et cetera. Number two was much earlier—I was maybe four at the time—when he picked up a knife and threw it across the kitchen at my mother. Other than that, I'm sorry, I really can't help you; it's all just snippets and vague impressions."

"Wait a second," said Peter. "Your father threw a *knife* at your mother, and you mention that just in passing?"

The others chimed in their agreement. Jack said it chilled him to hear such things told in a free and easy tone.

Sara smoothed the front of her shantung blouse; as usual, she was in black from head to toe. "Well, I mean, it happened so long ago, and I *have* told this story before. And by the way, you know, he missed."

"Yeah, well, I was *wondering*," said Peter. "You sort of left that part out, you know."

The others, including Sara, cracked up at this. One of this group's gifts was the capacity to tweak itself, to head off gathering tensions with humor. Now and then, the tactic worked against them, and a useful confrontation was defused. But for the most part, the group was well served by its wit. It allowed them to go far at their own speed.

Resuming the interview, Peter fumbled a bit, unsure how to proceed. Lathon cut in, reminding him that there was a question on the table: Had Sara's father talked to her the way he did to her mother?

Sara took a breath and let it out, a moody, restive sigh. Clearly, it pained her to cover this ground, if only because she recalled so little of it. A woman of powers, it galled her to apologize, to plead again this dreary amnesia.

"Well, as best I recall," she said, "I don't *think* he took that tone with me. If anything, I was probably his favorite. He always took an interest in how I did at school, and pushed me to work harder as I got older. For some reason, he thought I'd be a big success some day."

"And he was right,' said Lathon. "In business, you *are* your father's daughter: smart and tenacious, a star with a big future. But then the question is, if you weren't a target—if, in fact, you were Daddy's favorite—then how did it feel being exempt from his rage, and watching your mother take the brunt of it?"

Sara picked at the rim of her cup. For the first time, there was a trace of moisture in her eyes—not tears but a sort of preliminary sadness.

"It was terrible," she said. "I used to excuse myself from the table, so I didn't have to watch it go on. And the more he did it to her, the worse she got—ditzier and more tongue-tied, just a nervous wreck around him. . . . You know, I was going through some things this weekend, and I found a batch of pictures. Nothing special, really, just some early snapshots, from when we had the house in Zurich. But I couldn't help noticing how stunning my mom was, with these long legs and complexion like Ingrid Bergman, so pale and shimmery. And in most of the pictures, she was taking us places—to the park for a picnic, or ice-skating with our friends. And I thought, God, she really did try to make this a family. To see that we had fun as kids, and weren't just sitting home, watching TV. I mean, in spite of her—flakiness—she really was very sweet to us, and I just wish that . . ."

She paused, inspecting her deconstruction of the cup.

"Did you know that, at age sixty, she's still a perfect size six? In fact, whenever she comes to visit, people mistake us for sisters. Which galls me no end, by the way."

"Why?" asked Peter. "I would think that you'd be—"

He stopped, backed up, and rephrased it in the approved way. "What is it about her looks that annoys you?"

"Well—" she grimaced, flicking her hair back brusquely. "I mean, isn't it kind of ridiculous to be in the gym at sixty, taking step classes with twenty-year-olds? And then to get involved with these ludicrous men, who always break her heart and leave her ten grand poorer? It's like she's learned *nothing* all these years. Like she's the same helpless ditz, always calling me to complain how miserable she is. . . ."

Peter frowned at the floor in concentration. "Are you afraid she won't find someone, and you'll have to take care of her one day?"

"No, it's not that so much as—well, yeah, I am, a little. I mean, I worry *right now* that she's going to move to New York to try and be closer to me."

"And would it be so bad if she did?"

"Oh God, *please*, my life is hard enough as it is. I go nuts just seeing her twice a year."

"Why, what happens when you—"

Peter stopped again, flustered. "That's not an easy word to avoid."

"Don't worry, you're doing fine," said Lathon. "Just follow the fear. What *pain* is Sara trying to avoid?"

Peter turned to look at her in his diffident way. "Are you afraid, when you get together with her, of being reminded of old times? Like, when you were a kid and he was mean to her, and you couldn't do much to stop it?"

Sara took a breath, eager to be done with this. "No, I . . . I mean, no, I don't think about it. In fact, most of the time I'm with her, I'm on the phone to other people—talking to my office, or to people on location."

"In other words, avoiding her."

Sara pushed her shiny bangs out of her eyes. "Well, yeah, I suppose so."

Peter pressed on, asking the same question in different ways. New facts emerged concerning her father's harshness, and her mother's limp response to it. But each time Peter probed the matter of her own feelings, Sara grew vague and elusive. No, she didn't fear meeting someone like her dad, because after the first cruel word, she'd be gone. And it didn't really sadden her to be detached from her parents; maybe it did in her teens, but she'd long since come to terms with it. After all, *most* families were screwy in some way or other, so why should hers be any different?

Finally, Lathon turned it over to the others. Rex asked about old boyfriends, and what Sara was doing to find a new one. Jack wanted to know if she actually talked to her mother, or just hustled her off the phone like she did her father. And then it was Lina's turn to ask a question, and suddenly, things got interesting. She began by asking if Sara was ashamed of her mother, and if so, what was most embarrassing about her.

"You mean, *aside from* her kookiness and taste in men?" She picked at the coffee cup, fluting its creases. "I—I don't know, it's just like she's so damn . . . *needy*. Like she can't take control of her life."

"You mean, she won't settle down with a man her age, and stop hanging around in a leotard?"

"Yeah, I'm saying, it's just so—desperate-seeming. Why can't she behave with more dignity?"

"But as you were saying, she lives in San Diego, so how does that reflect on you?"

"Ah, good question," said Lathon. "You're right on the pain."

Lina ignored this, her gaze fixed on Sara. "What do you think your mom's behavior says about you?"

"Bingo," said Lathon.

Sara stared away, her eyes dampening again. "I just wish she could act like a *normal* person. Like a normal *mother*. That's all I ask."

"Do you ever worry you'll end up like her? Alone, with no one who loves you?"

Sara let out a grunt that was both a sob and laughter. "Do I *ever* worry about it? Yeah, I'd say it comes up. Like, basically, Monday through Sunday."

seven

The rich are, indeed, different from you and me: they build the kinds of kitchens you and I could live in. Rex's was so big, I half expected a man to burst in, shouting, "Where the hell's that veal chop for table twelve?" The room had taken its styling cues from retro steakhouse culture: a quilted steel door with diamond-shaped portals; black-and-white box tiles on the walls and backsplash; and an eight-burner oven with crimson knobs and handles. The centerpiece was an oblong cooking island made of fruitwood and charcoal granite. Twin Sub-Zeros were sunk into the near wall, one reserved for beer and soft drinks. And on pegs by the door hung a change of white chef's jackets. *Rex* was the name stitched above the breast.

It was a little after eight on a cold spring evening, and the dogwoods were stirring against the window. The apartment, a duplex loft, faced north, affording a view of the moon. Rex's wife, Claudia, was out of town on a story, and but for the baby upstairs and her nanny down the hall, the two of us had the place to ourselves. Rex had been chopping bok choy and onions, only pausing to sear the skin of a pair of tuna steaks. Now, he was adroitly carmelizing the onions, giving the pan a flick of the wrist to turn them over. It was a show-off performance—three burners going at once, the tuna steaks blackened but pink on the inside. For all its bravura, though, there was something endearing about the show—the look of boyish absorption on Rex's face, and his transparent eagerness to please.

115

Cooking was a skill I wouldn't have figured him for, in part because he hadn't bragged about it. His greatness at snowboarding and timing the bond market—these and other gifts he touted freely. That he was reticent about this one talent made me curious. I asked him if he was a closet chef.

He let out a peal of his firecracker laugh, and poured us more Chardonnay. "Dude, there's a *lot* that you don't know about me. In my spare time, for instance, I'm a feminist."

This occasioned another cackle, and a toast to "the sisterhood." He was one of those jolly Republicans who loved to do battle, shocking you with his robust antipathies. It wasn't so much a politics as a brand of insult shtick, Don Rickles meets P. J. O'Rourke. What he really got off on was getting you going, winding up the stem of your righteousness. If you stiffened or went back at him, he would grind you all night. I inquired again about his cooking.

He parried a bit longer, then answered the question. His grandfather had come over by himself from Genoa, with a fifth-grade education and a stutter. After years of grim struggle, he opened a restaurant in Ohio, just a place off I-80 decorated with Christmas lights. But such was the food that came out of his kitchen that, by the time Rex was born, his grandfather had relocated to Cleveland, and bought a house for the family in Shaker Heights. Most of the clan worked for him, including Rex's father, who'd been drafted out of college to run the bar. Though he had a knack for management that bolstered the operation, he hated the food trade and regretted capitulating to his father. He told Rex, in sharp terms, to avoid the business, drumming it into his head to select a profession.

"The thing of it is, though, I always loved to cook, and it totally cooled me out; just this zoned-in, Zen type of deal," he said. "And if things had gone differently, I could've seen myself doing this. I think I could've held my own at it."

"Did you ever think about chucking it and going to cooking school?"

"Hell, I think about it *now*, though I can't afford to. My little daddy-sabbatical's almost over."

"Really? Are you going back to work soon?"

"Yo, I gots to, son. Them bills be high, as the girls from the projects say."

"Somehow, I had the idea that you were set for a while. That you could afford to take a year off, if you wanted."

"Not if I want to live in *this* style, I can't. It costs money to be the king of New York, dude."

He laid out, in broad terms, his monthly expenses, a figure that popped my eardrums. But this topic (like the next one, the paltriness of a million dollars now) was essentially a diversion. It ducked the question of family and vocation, which had apparently cut too close.

"What do you think your dad would've said if you'd become a chef?" I asked.

He pushed around his wineglass in short, slow circles, holding it between a pinkie and ring finger. "Immaterial," he said. "I never would've done it, so the subject would never've come up."

"Well, but humor me a second. How do you think he would've reacted if you'd said, 'Dad, I'm not going to business school?'"

He laughed indulgently, dismissing air through his nostrils.

"Dude, he and my mom are, like, *so* in my corner. Anything I go with, they are most definitely on board for."

"Is that true?" I asked. "Anything?"

"Sure," he said. "As long as I'm not led away in handcuffs."

"And how did they handle your affair with that stripper? Assuming, of course, you told them."

Rex tossed back his head and let out a grunt. "Yeah, like I didn't see *that* one marching up Broadway."

He explained that he had, of course, told his parents, and that they were furious at him. They loved his wife, Claudia, and had been eagerly awaiting their first grandchild when he broke the news to them the previous summer. His mother was especially hurt; she had no clue about his "dark side." She'd still thought of him as the straight-arrow kid she raised: the one who honed his wrist shot on the wall of their garage, and who dutifully ran errands for her when he got his driver's license. She didn't know, and he never told her, what sort of changes he'd undergone since heading off to college. There was no hint of the debaucheries that began during pledge year, when he discovered a taste for alcohol in large quantities, and the sex perks accruing to star athletes. Nor did she think to question him closely when, as a junior, he drove home in a BMW. He told her that a teammate's dad owned a dealership, and had given him a sweetheart loan. In fact, he'd paid for the car in cash, laundering his profits from the coke trade. His frat house, the jock dorm, was a kind of preppie cartel, booking bets and selling drugs and even dabbling in light loan-sharking. Rex, good at numbers, was the house accountant, though for the rush of it, he rode along on drug buys. That feeling, he said, that "balls-in-your-throat speed-jam, when you copped a couple of bricks from the wiseguys"—it was a high that was even better than scoring a goal. It beat anything he'd ever felt, aside from seeing his child born.

"So what you're saying, if I hear you, is that you were a good, clean kid, until Dartmouth made you a gangster."

"Pretty much," he said. "Or let me take that back. I was a gangster who didn't know it till I got to Dartmouth."

"And did you continue being a gangster when you went to Wharton, or did—"

"Oh, hell yeah, son. In fact, worse than ever. I was the biggest little hood in Philadelphia."

He began to tell me stories attesting to his badness. One involved a "throwdown" with a drug gang in west Philly. Another had to do with converting his fellow business students into full-blown gamblaholics. But after a couple of these tales I managed to nudge us back to the subject of his transformation. What, given his happy childhood in the suburbs, had disposed him to become a hood in college, and later, to risk his marriage with a stripper?

He shrugged and put his feet up on the dining table, still not taking me seriously. Indeed, judging from what I'd seen tonight and in group, it was hard to imagine what he did take seriously.

"I guess there're just some things you can't explain," he joshed. "My own theory is, I'm a child of Satan."

And from there on in, he boxed me to a standstill as I tried to draw him out about his home life. Relations between his parents had been "first-rate," "world-class"; on the scale of wedded bliss, they were "off the charts." So, too, with the bond between him and his younger brother, who was "basically a junior me, with a smaller penis." They played Peewee hockey together, and Pop Warner football, and owned their own Sno-Cats at fourteen and twelve, proof definitive of an ideal boyhood. I kept poking at his story, testing its gee-whiz kitsch, but would have been better off culling stock tips from the SEC. Rex reveled in the divide between his badness and his parents' goodness. In fact, as he toasted their virtues, I thought I detected a whiff of condescension, and was about to take this up with him when we heard a cry. What with the tenor of our conversation and the bottle of wine we'd had to drink, it took me a moment to connect the noise with a baby. But in that flashbulb instant, Rex was up and out of his chair and halfway across the dining room to the stairs.

His daughter's room was the first one off the landing. The walls were flocked with Winnie the Pooh characters: Piglet cavorting with Kanga and Roo; Pooh Bear blissed beside a jar of honey. Massed upon the shelves and sundry flat surfaces was a menagerie of new stuffed animals, from Curious George to the whole cast of *The Lion King*. Clearly, I'd landed in baby heaven, a retail Xanadu not of Kubla Khan's making, but that of his spiritual heir, Walt Disney.

In a crib by the window was the object of all this splendor: the plump little pink-thighed Marisa. Katja, the fiftyish Slavic nanny, had just picked her up when we entered.

"Here, I'll take her," said Rex, with surprising softness. He bundled his daughter against his shoulder, and rocked her in place where he stood. While Katja fixed a bottle, he sang, in a tuneless whisper, the chorus of "Love Me Do." Swaying by the window, he repeated the verse, then started in on "Till There Was You." By then, though, the nanny had come and gone, and so, shortly thereafter, did I, given another in a series of firm rebukes about the complexity of the human heart.

eight
april

For a variety of reasons—not least of them the schedule, with its two-week lag between meetings—this group seemed to find it hard to form attachments. You could sense it before sessions, a kind of tetchy shyness, as if the members were being introduced again as strangers. After the first ten minutes, that stiffness would pass, and they would warm to the particulars of one another's stories. But when the two hours were up, they went their own ways, and the emotional amnesia returned. There was no exchange of phone numbers, as there had been in my group, or postgame analyses at a diner. For us, the session was often merely a prelude to a raucous confab after hours, at which we schmoozed and cajoled and hand-held each other on the unmarked path to progress. This group, by contrast, was composed of people who were intent on traveling alone. It seemed an odd and needless disadvantage.

In private, though, when I asked the members about one another, one name kept coming up. All were deeply concerned about Dylan, and the impact of his drinking on the group. It was a great relief to everyone, then, when Dylan showed up for the fifth session. He was carrying a paunch from his ten-day spree, and limped on an ankle that was tender from a spill he'd taken. In spite of that, he looked invigorated, as if the blowout had been somehow cathartic. His eyes were brighter and more engaged than they had been in earlier meetings. He had a modest tan, having spent several days at his brother's place on the shore. Most of all, his manner was different by kind. Where once he'd seemed vacant, an emotional cipher, now he was warmly and attractively present, eager to make a connection. As the first on hand, he stood to greet the others as they came through the door one by one. When everyone was seated, he led off the session with a long and trenchant apology.

"And so, again, I'm sorry," he said, "for putting you all out, and giving you *another* thing to worry about. It's not like you don't have enough on your plate without me adding to it. But like I say, I let myself get buried under, and when I do that, I'm in danger of picking up again. This was a big reminder that I can't let myself isolate. That even if I'm miserable, I've got to go and be with people; with the friends and family who care about me. And I do have those people, I have some wonderful friends, and my brother and his wife and, of course, my two girls, who're right there for me always. And I also have you guys, and I'm grateful for that, and I really want to put this to use."

The others received his speech with goodwill, clapping when he announced a month's sobriety. He was seeing his counselor regularly and felt great about that, like there was a real affinity there. And he was also going ahead with the mediation process, getting closer to a divorce deal with Jeannie. There were still a few sticking points, like her strong sense of entitlement to half his retirement fund. But soon enough, he thought, she'd come to her senses and sign an agreement that was fair to all. As for things between them otherwise—well, something had happened over the weekend that really sent him for a loop. But that would keep, he said, until his turn came to talk. For now, he just wanted to listen.

"Terrific," said Lathon, who was delighted to see him, and perhaps a bit vindicated, too. He assured Dylan that he would, in fact, be heard from at length tonight; there was a lot to catch up on there. But first, Jack was directed to go sit in the hot seat, and be interviewed about his family story. This being the fifth of their twenty sessions, they had reached the quarter turn, said Lathon. After tonight, the focus would be on current events—the pains and fears that had brought them here. So if any of them felt that they had left something out, now was the time to raise it. It needn't be earthshaking; it might only be a detail, but one that put things in clearer focus.

The members changed seats to accommodate Jack, as well as Sara, his interviewer. But as Jack took her questions, he seemed off somehow, dissociated from his usual sharpness. Sure enough, after several minutes, he turned to Lathon and said that he was too distracted to go on. An old, dear friend had died that morning and he was in a great deal of pain about it, in part because he had turned his back on the man. Lathon nodded and bid him, by all means, to talk about it, saying that they'd deal with the family stuff later. Jack thanked him and paused to gird himself, his tan face puffy with sadness.

Earl, he began, had been a columnist at one of the dailies, a guy who'd started out working off the police scanner, and who'd gone on to a career of distinction. Besides being a hard charger, Earl was also a hard drinker, and he and Jack closed down a lot of bars together, toasting their rise to the top of their respective heaps. Somewhere along the way, Earl taught Jack to fly-fish, and how to bluff at high-stakes Hold 'Em. In return, Jack invited Earl to his glitzy parties, introducing him to showgirls and congressmen. Thus grounded in male privilege, the friendship had bridged much of their adult lives, and could be fairly said to have had more invested in it than several of their early marriages.

"We'd stayed buddies and seen each other through all sorts of drama," Jack said. "Earl's two serious heart attacks, and the death of his baby daughter—and me, of course, and my fuckups with wives one through three. But then, all of a sudden, I got busted for embezzlement, and for some reason, I stopped taking his phone calls. I mean, not just his, of course—I stopped talking to *everyone*—but Earl kept trying to reach me. He was one of several people who really wanted to help me, but I was so furious and self-hating that I never returned his phone calls, and after a while, I guess, he stopped trying. And just like that, I let the friendship die; let this dear, sweet guy go out of my life, and now, I just feel sick about it."

Jack's eyes brimmed, and his cheeks hung slack, drooping like veal off the bone. For the first time, he looked not like a chief executive but an old man alone at a diner.

Sara tried tactfully to pursue the matter, inquiring about the details of the friendship. But Jack backpedaled, lapsing into boilerplate about his lifelong aversion to intimacy. He'd always been great, he said, in a roomful of people, telling stories and jokes until they yelled out last call. Rarely, though, did he get up close and personal with people, preferring the company of six or eight buddies to an evening alone with any one of them. Even in sobriety, he'd kept the world at arm's length, and couldn't think of anyone he felt obliged to talk to now, aside from his wife and children.

"Well, that's strange," said Sara, wrinkling her nose. "I've never thought of friendship as an obligation. For me, it's been the one great pleasure in life, having friends I can share my time with. How odd that you'd find that a burden, instead of—"

"Sara, let me remind you that you're gathering facts, not rendering opinions," said Lathon. "To do that, you have to ask Jack a question, like, 'What does it *feel* like when people get close to you?' Or, 'Is it scary when someone says they enjoy spending time with you, and that you've meant a lot to them?' "

"Good question," Jack grunted. "I guess I'd tell you that I don't believe them."

"Ah," said Lathon. "Now, we're getting somewhere. Ask him how long he's felt that, Sara."

"Pretty much ever since I can remember," he said. "As far back as childhood, I didn't have many friends, and spent most of my time alone reading spy novels. On weekends, I loved to go in and see a show, and couldn't always get my mom to take me. So, on Saturday afternoons, I took the train in from Harrison and paid two bucks to see a matinee, standing room. I suppose that sounds strange now, a young kid spending his allowance to catch a play by himself. But that's how I was, and it never felt odd to me. I was just always more comfortable being alone."

Sara picked up there, asking about Earl, and about the shame that had kept Jack from calling him. But his answers, though candid, broke no ground on his decision to end the friendship. So, too, with his feelings about friendship in general, about which he was neither evasive nor enlightening. Yes, he'd been close to Earl for a long time, but some of that was booze-related. In a sense, liquor was the excuse for getting together—drinks after work, a bottle of wine with dinner, or a nightcap at Gallagher's with their cronies. It wasn't the basis of the friendship, but it certainly greased the rails, making everyone in their crowd funnier and better looking. And then he got busted, and two years later got sober, and . . . well, obviously, that wasn't the place for someone nursing a cup of coffee.

After five or ten minutes, Lathon took questions from the group. Lina was the first to raise her hand.

"Well, I don't have a question as much as a comment," she said. "You know, as you were talking, Jack, I got this picture of you in my mind. Not as you are now, but as a twelve-year-old boy, acting all grown-up and taking the train in by yourself. And for some reason, it just felt really sad to me, like a kid who gives a party and nobody comes. Maybe it had to do with it being on Saturdays, when all the other kids were out playing somewhere, or going to some dopey movie together. And I found myself thinking how lonely that must've been, and that maybe some of your grief now is for yourself as a kid. When, deep down, it must've hurt to be left out."

Jack looked away, the blood congregating in his cheeks. "You know, I've often wondered why it was so hard for me back then. I mean, I'm a personable enough guy, I've made lots of friends since then—you can't be a producer without being a schmoozer and a *tummeler.* So what was so different that I couldn't get started, and even kept to myself in those summers on the Vineyard . . . ?"

The question curled away from him and lingered awhile, pluming above him like smoke. Jack stared off in the direction of the foyer, where the overcoats hung in thick shadows.

"Well, I hope this doesn't come out the wrong way," said Rex, "but maybe it's because you *weren't* a producer then. I mean, as incredible as it may seem, I wasn't a popular kid, either"—he flashed his deadpan wink—"and didn't become cool until I made the varsity as a junior. I'm saying, sometimes you don't become *you*, per se, until you've got a gold star to show."

"Actually, that's very well put," said Lathon. "Who *was* Jack, before the résumé? It sounds like he was a pretty lonely kid, with a strong inclination to withdraw. What else do we know about Jack, pre-résumé? Well, he told us before that he was an only child, and that his parents were in their thirties when he came along. He also told us that his dad was a reporter, and worked long hours covering a story. Using those facts, let's see what else you can learn, and how it links up to his feelings about his friend."

Peter asked Jack about his childhood, homing in on his mother and father. But Jack robustly defended his parents, calling them lovely people. Maybe his dad was a "touch" less attentive than others, but his mom had more than made up for it. A former dancer and actress, she read lines with him for his school plays, and sat out back with him on sunny afternoons, playing Yahtzee and teaching him swing steps. She always treated him like a peer, regaling him with stories about her life, particularly her exploits in vaudeville. Probably, he should've spent more time with other kids, but it was so much fun hanging out with her, and he wouldn't have traded a second of it for anything.

Going nowhere fast, Peter turned to Lathon, who was about to render a summation. But Sara raised her hand, getting permission for a last question.

"Well, this is maybe a little off the subject," she said, "but something just clicked in my head. I was thinking of what you said, about not trusting people who liked you, and it reminded me of when you said you always grabbed the check at dinner. And I started to wonder if that was sort of like a bribe. A reward to all these people for hanging out with you."

Jack frowned, and made a production out of clearing his throat. "Well, no," he said, "it just gave me pleasure to do that. In fact, I used to tip the waiter to *make sure* I got the check; that's how much it meant to me. I figured, what the hell, you know, I make a lot of money—and if I ever run out of it, I'll just go and make more."

"But after you got arrested and people like Earl tried to help you—what, was your money no good anymore?" asked Lathon.

Jack slumped at the mention of his old friend's name. His breathing became heavy and sonorous, as if sorrow had converted air to vapor. "I—I don't know what to say. It was a very bad time for me; such terrible shame and remorse . . . I mean, it wasn't just my livelihood but my *life* they took away from me. And without it, I—I had no . . ."

"Story," said Lathon, softly.

Jack nodded and closed his eyes. Lathon let the silence ride for several moments, then reached behind him for a pad. "Any comment on what you're hearing from Jack, aside from guilt and regret?"

The others shrugged, consulting the floor. After a pause, Lina offered, "Self-loathing?"

Lathon nodded, sketching something on the pad. "Other ideas?"

When no answer came back, Lathon held up the pad. On it was written FEAR in block letters.

"Anyone know what this refers to?" he asked.

The others eyed the floor again, clearly stumped.

"Ever since Sartre first posed the question," said Lathon, "philosophers have been in open debate: Who *are* we, if we're not just this thing that we do? We're no longer identified by our relation to God, or by any root connection to the place we live. And as for our families, most of us can't detach fast enough. In every other movie and sitcom now, the family's a joke, the butt of our mass-pop sarcasm.

"So where does that leave us, at the end of the day? Well, if you're Jack, and you've just lost this thing that defined you, where you are is a scary place. You're alone, and feeling empty and unreal to yourself, wondering what the last forty years have come to. That's the real terror of losing your job—sitting home alone at ten in the morning, with the Big Questions circling around you. Who have I loved and mattered to, and have I done them more harm than good? What have I made of any lasting value, if not to someone else, then myself? Those are hairy things to be confronted with, all of a sudden—particularly if you're sixty, and feeling like time is running out on you."

Lathon stopped for a sip of spring water, letting the sense of this resonate. He had, as noted before, a quick ear for silence, for the pause that deepens and ramifies. On occasion, he overplayed it to underline the trivial or puff a well-turned phrase into bombast. But here, his instinct was right on point, producing a passage of reflection among the members.

"Now, as I've said before," he resumed, "Jack isn't the only one in this fix. After the crash of '87, I was overrun for a while with Wall Street executives who'd lost their jobs. And what I found with so many of them wasn't that they'd lost their story, but that they had no story beside their job. They thought that an identity came with the MBA, and that all the other appurtenances followed—the wife and three kids, the big house in Connecticut. But that isn't an identity, it's a *portfolio*, a list of tangible assets. And like all such things, it can be taken away—with or without due cause."

He stopped again for a sip of water, a short pause, the length of a comma. By now, the members were pinned to their seats, alone with their lengthening thoughts.

"So then, what do you do about it?" Jack asked, coming out of himself.

"Ah, that's the million-dollar question," said Lathon. "What do you do when you've got no story?"

The group heard from Lina next on the subject of her divorce troubles. She recounted, in shorthand, the medley of blocks that her husband had placed in her path—the delays, the appeals, the motions, the set-asides—and the barrels of money spent by both sides. The upshot was that, after two years of wrangling, she still didn't have a separation agreement. Without one, she couldn't establish a fair rate of child support, which allowed Anton to pay the bare minimum. He was also supposed to pay her co-op bill and the children's school tuition, but these he sent along as the mood arose—or, for months at a time, not at all. When Lina went to court to press him for payment, the judge chided her for her "shopping habits." It turned out that he was an old friend of Anton's father, a fact he didn't acknowledge until it was discovered by Lina's lawyer. Therewith, he promptly recused himself, putting the case right back at the starting line.

"I am just so *furious* at the whole, damn system," she seethed. "The judges in divorce court are rotten, old hacks, or are in outright cahoots with the lawyers. And divorce lawyers—forget about it, they're the worst of the worst. They just suck you till you're dry, then dump you flat. I've spent all of my savings now, and some of parents' savings, too, and what have I got for it? Nothing!"

She railed a while longer about her hatred of lawyers, and the unfairness of divorce law in New York. Nowhere else in the country did you have to "prove" a charge like adultery to end a lousy marriage, or pay money to a private detective to dig up evidence. And nowhere else were courts as lax about enforcing their own rulings, letting creeps like Anton duck and dodge for years. You didn't stand a chance if you were the spouse without deep pockets, she said. She'd gotten so down, in fact, she'd actually thought about leaving the state. But she couldn't, of course; it would mean moving her kids, and pulling them out of school, where they were happy.

The interview ended soon, per Lina's wish; she wanted to save some time for Dylan's turn. Besides, she didn't want to take questions tonight; what mattered more was the chance to vent. These last couple of years, she'd felt like she was drowning in her own feelings, just dizzy with fear and anger. Those feelings were so strong sometimes that she couldn't find words for them, and thought her head would split open. There were middle-of-the-night panic attacks, and break-downs in her office, bursting into tears at her desk. So, even if she wasn't saying the exact right words, it still felt good to get them out.

Lathon praised her for speaking her heart, calling it a model performance. Without preliminaries, she had gotten right to the pain, describing its effects in her body. That, he said, was the antidote for pain—finding words for it and saying them to other people. Doing so had proven clinical benefits, such as raising circulation to the heart and lungs, and spiking the brain's supply of dopamine. In time, it also created a kind of psychic clearing, a place from which to plan effective action. But that was step two in the process of heal-ing, and for now, he wanted to focus on step one, which was telling your own story and naming your pain. And with that, he turned the floor over to Dylan.

Dylan got up and sat in the hot seat, beside Rex, who did the questioning. He led off by talking about the weekend of his "slip," when he'd driven to the house in Montclair with high hopes. He and Jeannie had been chummy on the phone, chatting about how beau-tiful their girls were getting, and cackling about Olivia's latest brain-storm. There had been plans for the four of them to have brunch on Sunday, and maybe, if it was nice out, to go to the zoo. But an hour after Dylan got there, she was in one of her states, screaming at the girls to go put their shoes on, and flitting from room to room, leaving him hanging in midsentence. He could feel it all starting again, the pressure behind his eyes, and the tightness in his gut and bowels. They never even made it to dinner that night, a fight erupting over a dress that Jeannie had bought and then decided she didn't like. She had closets full of clothes with the tags still on them, stuff from three and four seasons ago. When he asked her about her Visa bill, she stormed out of the house and didn't call him from her girl-friend's until Sunday.

"Boy, I felt like a jerk, like she'd got me again; one more twist of the knife," he said. "*Of course*, there was no chance of us patching it up, but I let her suck me back in. And that's what started me drinking: not the sadness of it being over, but anger at playing her dummy again. I thought, 'Damn you, you putz, how weak can you be? Don't you have any pride at all?' "

At Rex's prodding, Dylan backtracked a bit, describing the last years of his marriage. Jeannie had always been the high-strung sort, but in the beginning, that was part of her charm. She had boundless energy, and was constantly in motion, pushing him to do things and go places. In their first four years together, he'd had more new experiences than in the previous forty combined. Life with her wasn't always peaceful, but, on the other hand, it was never dull, and Dylan often thought to himself, So *this* is it. This is what it feels like to be happy.

But after the twins were born in 1989, a series of changes came over Jeannie. Once vivacious, she was now restless and irritable, like a tiger in a cage that was too small for her. The girls, who had her temperament, would have been a handful for anyone, but in Jeannie triggered a state of hysteria. She was always chasing after them, scolding them like rogue employees, bemoaning the things they did to "ruin her life." This horrified Dylan, for whom the girls could do no wrong. By way of amends, he spoiled them rotten, and told them, in so many words, to ignore their mother. Loud fights ensued between him and Jeannie, usually within minutes of his coming home.

They stopped doing their once-a-week "date night" on Fridays, partly out of fear of making a scene, but largely because they were exhausted from quarreling. And, most painfully for Dylan, the sex between them ceased, or occurred so seldom as to salt the wound. No matter their difficulties, he was strongly attracted to Jeannie, and her refusal to sleep with him hurt him terribly.

"I'll admit that that—area wasn't so fabulous for us," he said. "It was clear right away that she wasn't the most sexual person, and even in the beginning, she was pretty . . . wooden. But I know I enjoyed it, and put in a lot of—effort there, to try and make it better. And when it dropped off—going from twice a week, steady, to every three months or an anniversary—I started to obsess about her . . . you know, with other men. I mean, I knew that she wasn't, or at least—well, she was home with me at night, though, during the day, when I was gone, she could've . . ."

He stopped and rubbed his stomach, wincing as he pressed the abdomen. "Man, every time I think about it, I get this pain right *here . . .*"

"Why don't you see me after session," said Lathon. "I'll listen with my doctor's cap on. In the meantime, please go on."

"Mmmph," Dylan grunted, holding his gut. "It's like there's someone in there with a cocktail sword, and he keeps making the sign of the Zee. . . ." Laughing feebly at his own joke, he peeled off a Tums from a roll he kept in his shirt pocket. "At any rate, even though I didn't suspect her, I kept getting these . . . images in my head. Thoughts of her having sex with some other guy, and . . . really getting off on it. And it became this sort of—torture, seeing that expression on her face, like she'd finally found a guy who could . . . who—"

He looked down, pressing a fist to his lips. It was clenched so tight, you could see striations in his forearm, the muscles bunching under the vein. He went on staring straight down at his knuckles, waiting for the squall to pass. One of his eyelids began to flutter, sending out its own bleak semaphore.

"Anyway," he said, regaining his voice, "I went up there again on Saturday. No contact this time; no palsy-walsy; just me and the twins for the weekend. As I pulled into the drive, she was coming out the door, carrying her gym stuff and a suitcase. I said hi, and was very civil, talked about the girls' birthday next Friday. And then she took off, said she had an AA meeting before she went to her friend Kaitlin's in Bloomfield.

"So, anyway, I go in, and play with the girls for an hour, and then we head out for lunch. Well, as I'm driving around the mall there, looking for a spot, what do I see but *Jeannie's car*, a blue wagon with Maryland plates. I thought, whoa, that's weird, she doesn't miss many meetings; maybe it broke up early. So we go in and have a bite at the pizza place, and when we come out, there's this BMW by her car. So, now I'm *real* curious, and as we walk past the Beemer, I crane my head to look in. Well, lo and behold, it's Jeannie and this guy, necking like a couple of teenagers. And suddenly, she sees me and ducks down in her seat, and the guy starts the car and peels out so fast he almost causes an accident. And I . . . I just kinda stood there, frozen, for a while. With my kids tugging on my sleeves, going, 'Wasn't that *Mommy's* car?'"

The others let out a groan, grasping the measure of his humiliation. Lina reached over and touched his arm, murmuring something of comfort. Even Rex, normally the soul of snappy sangfroid, seemed thrown for a loss of words. He gaped at Dylan, as at a wounded dog, the blood going out of his face.

"Do you think there's any chance that your daughters saw her?" asked Sara.

"I . . . I don't know," said Dylan, with lowered gaze. "I—I was in such a state of shock, I didn't think to ask, or—or to make up some story about—"

"Don't worry," said Lathon. "It's not important. Just tell us what happened next."

"Well . . ." said Dylan, struggling to regain focus. "My heart just started crashing, going 'boom-boom-BOOM!' and my arms were covered in this heavy sweat, and I tore home to have it out with her. Except that, of course, she didn't go home, and I had to wait till Sunday, and by then, I was about ready to *break her.* And, sure enough, she comes in there, all speedy-jumpy, like, 'What did *you* do this weekend?' And the first thing out of the twins was, 'We saw your car!' 'Oh, yeah? Where?' 'At the mall, silly.' And she's all, 'Oh, yeah, I went there after my meeting. Me and Kaitlin had a lot to talk about.'

"Well, that was about all I could stand. I grabbed her by the arm and dragged her upstairs, saying, 'It's time for you to stop *lying.*' And she got scared and started talking a mile a minute, saying the guy was just a friend from AA and all, and that they'd been having a cup of coffee after meetings and so forth, but that there was really nothing happening between them. And as I stood there listening to just *obvious* lies, for some reason or other, the rage went out of me. I don't know how to say it, but it felt . . . good to watch her squirm, to have her be the bad guy for once in her life. Ever since I've known her, she's pointed the finger at me, making me out the bad guy, and I let her. Well, now it was her turn and I really *liked* it—although, a half hour later, I was so sick to my stomach that I hadda pull over and throw up. . . ." He stopped again, clutching his abdomen.

"Did she ever come clean about the guy in the car?" asked Peter.

Wincing, Dylan let out a gaseous sigh. "Yeah, finally, she admitted what was up there. She said he was married, and had a kid himself, so it was hard for them to find time to be together, and so that was why we had seen them at the mall on—"

"What!" Rex cried. "They were having a hard time *getting their schedules together?* What kept you from whaling her right there?"

"Hey, wait a minute," said Lina. "You've got *no* business giving advice here."

"Yeah, really," said Jack. "That's not funny to even joke about. Besides, if anyone should be getting whaled, it's you."

Rex peeled off one of his snarky smiles. "Yo, what*ever*. All I'm saying is, she dogged him out, and then she did it again by saying that."

"And that part's well taken," said Lathon, making peace. "How does it *feel* to catch your wife red-handed, and then be patronized after the fact?"

Dylan squinted and thought this over, as if he'd been asked to name the square root of x. On the one hand, he was furious, after his worst nightmare had come true. On the other hand, he did feel a little . . . phony, having slept with an old girlfriend during his relapse. In fact, to be honest, there'd been a couple of others, too—nothing serious, just a friendly face at a bar. Someone to feel less lonely with for a night—

"Group," said Lathon, cutting him off, "what are you feeling as you listen to this?"

"Um, sort of confused," said Sara, wrinkling her nose.

"Oh God, just really, really sad," said Lina.

"Well then, *tell* Dylan that, because he needs to hear it," said Lathon. "With all these bombs dropping, he's in a state of shock. So convey your sympathy, and help him separate the wounds. Say, 'Dylan, I can hear how badly you're hurting. What did it *feel* like when you saw your wife there?'"

"Oh, boy," said Dylan in a quavery whisper. "Oh, boy, would I crave some of *that*. . . . See, the thing that always killed me is I could never get her to listen. If, just once, she'd had the guts to stop lying for two seconds and admit what I could see plain as day, that she was having an affair and trying not to hurt me with it. God, what I would've given for a moment like that. It would've hurt me so much less if she'd just been straight. . . ."

He stopped and put his fists to his lips, using short breaths to stave off tears. His eyes bulged slightly and his shoulders arched, as if they were holding up a wall of water. The others drew off, giving him room to weep. But, teetering at the edge, Dylan pulled back slowly, and sat there with his eyes shut, breathing fast.

"I talked before about the body in pain, and the effects of having that pain heard," said Lathon, softly. "One of those effects is a rise in body temperature—the body literally gets warmer when it's listened to. By the same token, we talk about 'warm' and 'cold' families, i.e., families that pay attention to their members, and families that tune out emotionally. And what Dylan is telling us is that it was cold in his house, and that the whole family suffered for it."

Dylan stared off at a point out the window, his eyes still glassy with tears. "Yeah, well, I *tried* talking to her—I spent *eight years* trying to do that. But every time I did, she'd switch the subject on me. Jump to some total non sequitur."

"Yeah, but did you tell her *this* time how much she'd hurt you?" asked Jack. "That it really tore you up to see her with him?"

Dylan glanced over at him, then looked away. "Um, well . . . no, not really," he murmured. "But, I mean, she had to know that. . . ." He eyed the floor sullenly. "No. I said nothing again. As usual."

"Precisely," said Lathon, "and there's the rub. You and Jeannie were *masters* at saying nothing. Rather than discuss things that hurt you, you communicated in slips. Slip number one, Jeannie had her relapse three years ago, getting drunk again to say that she was miserable. Slip number two, you went off the wagon last winter, saying, 'Well, that goes double over here.' And so on and so forth in this deaf-mute fencing match—both of you in pain and both of you *inflicting* pain, trading places as the virgin and the vampire. Misery, you see, grows beautifully in silence; it's the ideal media for suffering.

"Now, the second thing about suffering is that it's *progressive.* The longer the underlying wound goes untended, the worse the symptoms and outlook. If you deal with it straight on, it heals and that's the end of it. But if you don't and it festers, it'll kill everything that matters to you. Whether it's Jack's career, or Sara's relations with her father, or your marriage and dream house in Montclair."

"Which, by the way, is going up for sale," Dylan muttered.

"Oh no, really?" said Lathon. "I was speaking figuratively. I didn't know things were moving that fast."

"Yeah, well, the work's dried up for me, as I figured it would, and my monthly nut is a killer—we bought at the very height of the market." He shrugged. "But boy, I really loved that house. It's the first place I felt proud to come home to."

Most of the others grunted or shook their heads, unsure how to respond. But Jack sat by with his jaw on his fist, X-raying Dylan with a stare.

"Man, I've gotta say that I'm baffled," he said.

"By what?" asked Lathon.

Jack frowned at what he took to be willful obtuseness. "His wife's got the kids, she's getting laid on the side, and now his house is up for sale. My question is where's the rage?"

"Hunh," grunted Lathon, immoderately pleased. "Or to put it more usefully: Dylan, if you were to tell Jeannie how angry you are— freely and unedited, with no fear of reprisal, how do you think it'd sound?"

As before, Dylan paused and thought it over, studious of giving the right answer. And then, without warning, he tilted his head back and emitted the most heart-stopping scream I have ever heard. It was a shriek from the monkey house, wild and piercing, a cry like a cornered animal makes to announce it will fight to the death. It came and kept coming, doubling back on itself, two ends of the same sword stabbing our ears. Even after it had stopped, the others sat with their mouths open, unable to respond in word or gesture.

"*That's* what it would sound like," said Dylan quietly. "Like that until my throat started bleeding."

nine

A week or so later, Peter and I met for a beer at a pub near his apartment on Thirtieth Street. The place was one of those melds of sports bar and singles joint that you find in working neighborhoods like Kips Bay. At tables near the door, shouting over concussive lite rock, sat the men and women of the para-professions— big-haired legal secretaries, jangling their bracelets as they talked, and goateed assistant buyers clinking longnecks of Bud. Meanwhile, in the back, under fourth-rate jock kitsch—the team photos of clubs that never won anything, and the jerseys of players inducted into no one's Hall of Fame—slumped a motley of older men watching ball games. It was the third week of April, and nothing of interest was on—an early-season sleepwalk between the Mets and Expos, and an even duller (if possible) affair involving the Rangers and Nordiques.

Peter showed up a few minutes late, still dressed in his suit and tie. He apologized for the venue, saying it was the only place he knew of, having just moved in with Kara the month before. As great as her place was, he didn't care much for the neighborhood; it was all just noodle joints, and white-brick buildings. As soon as they got married, he was going to lobby her for the Village—or maybe, if he could get his nerve up, Central Park West.

Before I could ask him how it was going with her, he harked back to Dylan's scream. "That was the most amazing thing I've ever heard," he marveled. "I thought an *alien* was going to pop out of his chest."

A waitress came by to take our order. "You know, I really wish I'd told Dylan that, hey, there's life after divorce," he resumed. "Because two years ago—really, as recently as *last* year—that would have been me doing the screaming."

He paused a moment to consider the sound of that. "Well, maybe not screaming," he said, and laughed.

In fact, as he subsequently described his divorce, it seemed to have taken him unawares. Without warning one day, he broke down at the office, sobbing in front of his bosses. Though everyone was very nice about it, his humiliation was extreme. This was, after all, a Fortune 500 company, where tearful paroxysms were about as welcome as cross-dressing, and just about as helpful to one's prospects. Moreover, crying was so out of character, he said. When it came to things like feelings, he was every inch a McKeon: repressed like nobody's business. That was probably the reason he'd lost it at work—he hadn't talked to *anyone* about his problems. He couldn't tell his parents, who, in *their* prim dispassion, made him look like Sally Struthers. Nor was there anyone in his corporate circle that he felt comfortable opening up to. And so, with great unease, he picked Lathon out of the phone book, and became the first person in the thousand-year annals of the McKeons to seek professional help.

"It turns out I'd been probably been depressed for years," he said. "We talked about these symptoms I'd had as a kid—severe insomnia, an inability to focus on schoolwork, and just a feeling of hopelessness about the future. It was like this dark cloud was hanging over me—not sadness so much as a feeling of doom. And the first time I ever really stopped feeling that was after I started the Zoloft."

Though the depression lifted, his sense of failure was less tractable. In the rich and rarefied history of the McKeons, there had never, to Peter's knowledge, been a single divorce recorded, a fact that, like a good deal else about his family, conspired to shame and daunt him. There was the example of his parents, who after forty years together seemed the model of wedded amity. He, by contrast, had married a "nut job," a realtor who behaved like a rational person until the day of the actual ceremony. On their honeymoon, though, she confessed an interest in paganism and the practice of "earth-friendly" witchcraft. She staged rituals at their bedside, invoking the blessing of the four winds, and confided, while astride him, a "thing for bondage."

"I—I practically fell off the bed," he said, giggling. "Here I am, with this supposed good girl from Roslyn, and she's scaring the crap out of me. I said, "Couldn't you have brought this up a little sooner— like, say, *two and a half years ago?* She said, 'Well, I didn't want to rush you. Besides, my psychic said you'd be into it!' "

He sank back with a grin on his face, agog at the thought of it even now. Witchcraft, bondage, psychic advisers—it was like a joke played upon him by coworkers. Nor did it help when Amanda opened their house to some of her "white witch" friends. They hung out after dinner, drinking coffee and cognac, gabbing about the politics of fetish wear. After six or eight months of this, Peter was sleeping on the couch. After twelve, he filed for divorce. He'd tried to make a go of it, to meet Amanda halfway. But in the end, he felt duped, a hostage in some "Stevie Nicks video." And to make matters worse, his mom had been right about her all along.

"She picked up on it straight off, said, 'There is something wrong with that woman,' but like an idiot, I didn't listen to her. And the thing of it is, I *always* listen to her, even when she doesn't say anything. I just *know* what she's thinking, I can read it in her eyes. But this time . . . well, I was determined to be married. I had this crazy idea about it—I thought it changed your life, and filled it up with parties and all. You know, sometimes I go out for a drink with Kara and see these mobs of people hanging out, like ten or twenty at a shot. And I'll think, man, I haven't had that many friends my entire *life*. And, like last night, I lay awake worrying about getting married and having no one to invite besides my family. I know that's what Lathon calls a suffering conversation, but it bothers me that I don't have more friends."

He explained that he'd always been reclusive, a "cocooner," especially as a kid in Buffalo. Although the oldest of two children, he felt outmatched by his younger sister, who had sailed first through high school, then MIT, and was off blazing a trail now in virology. *That* was the kind of résumé befitting a McKeon, not his lackluster showing at a state school. And though his parents, both doctors, never disparaged him, he was sure he heard disappointment in their silence. On the walls of their dining room hung the portraits of the forebears, among them Edmund McKeon, for whom they'd named a street in Glasgow, and Gerald McKeon, who'd brought down three of Hitler's fighters in the climactic Battle of Britain. Ever since he could remember, Peter had felt their eyes on his back, monitoring and bemoaning his every misstep. It was bad enough that he hadn't been a credit to his parents, that he was living a small life in a family of big shoes. But to have brought dishonor on them with this laughable marriage—!

"Even though they were supportive of me, I felt like a complete embarrassment," he said. "You know, you want so much to make 'em proud of you, to talk you up to their friends instead of just sitting there with their mouths shut. And sometimes, you wonder if you should just . . ."

He shook his head forlornly, insensible of the clamor around us. The place had filled up in the last half hour, pushing the bar crowd back to us. At the table to our right, three women were discussing domestic arrangements in a fetching Queens patois ("So I goes to him, I go, 'Where do you get the *stones* to be talkin' shit to me at Donna's wedding?'") Two tables over, a herd of rhinos in hockey jerseys were watching the Rangers and Nordiques, yelling, *"Hit* 'em, Beukeboom, ya stupid fuck! Nail his *ass-bone* to the boards!"

"You were saying, you wonder if you should just . . . ?"

He shrugged and shook his head, gazing into his beer. "All I know is, thank God for Dr. Lathon. He said that anyone can make a mistake and be fooled by someone else, and that the real failure would've been staying in that marriage. He's also helping me relax about the family thing. He says, you are who you are and you do the best you can—and if that's not good enough for 'em, tough. And above all, I really do thank him for the Zoloft. I mean, a week after I started on it, I was back to being myself again, especially so at work. I had gone into a tailspin, having panic attacks at my desk, and not being able to make basic decisions. As far as I'm concerned, Dr. Lathon can do no wrong. Even if this group is a wash for me."

"Is that what it's been?" I asked, mindful of how little we'd heard from him in session.

"Oh no, I'm getting something out of it, although I do have to speak up more. It's just that things are going so well right now, I'm almost afraid to say something. Like there's someone up there listening, waiting to stick a fork in it. I mean, Kara and I are pinching ourselves, living in this great apartment of hers, the *bedroom* of which is bigger than my last place. I can't explain it, we just love *being* with each other, even if we're only hanging out reading the paper on Sunday, or playing Scrabble, which she slays me at. It's just, you know, I don't get it, she's all you ask for in a woman: sweet, and—and pretty, with a great sense of humor. Why was someone like her running a personal ad?"

"I don't know," I said. "I guess she could ask why you were *answering* one."

"*Wellll* . . . " He laughed, "I doubt we're *exactly* comparable. But the thing of it is, I responded to six ads, and none of the others called back. So now, I'm waking up with a millionaire, and she's looking at me like, 'Well, slugger? When're you gonna step to the plate and pop the question?' "

"And?"

"Hey, I'll get there, don't worry—I'm swinging a bat in the on-deck circle," he said, cackling. "It's just that I take this marriage stuff very seriously. Those aren't just words out of the side of your mouth; you're supposed to really *live* by them. And right now, I've got some things I need to do. Like, for one, I want a job that's worthy of me, of this person I'm starting to become. All my life, I've lived according to my mom, who told me not to call attention to myself. Well, I'm sorry, but's that's *over*; I want some respect and—and some acknowledgment, and if I can't get it at Arthur Anderson, then I'll go down the street to Price Waterhouse.

"Second, I need to start widening my circle. I know I'm never going to be Mr. Popularity, with the phone ringing off the hook and people on call-waiting. But I'd love to just have, like, a handful of friends, guys I can maybe go to a Mets game with, or knock off early and shoot a round of golf with. Basically, in other words, it's time to come out of *hiding*. It's not selfish to want a little happiness, is it? I—I mean, I *know* it's not, but something keeps . . . gnawing at me. It's almost like there's someone in the next room talking about you, but you can't quite hear what they're saying."

Peter checked his watch, looking around for the waitress. He and Kara had to get up early the next morning, as they were driving to his folks' place upstate. She had met his parents before, but this was the first time they would be spending the weekend.

"Well, that should be interesting," I said. "What do they think of her?"

"Actually, they love her," he said. "In fact, they like her more than me, I think. Though they're worried that she has a little *too* much money."

He laughed out loud at this and rapped the table, attracting the notice of our neighbors. But as quickly as it had cleared, his mood darkened again, his brows scudding together over his glasses.

"What is it?" I asked him, chasing the cloud.

"Nah, you know, it's just . . ."

He looked down, jiggling the last of his beer. "You know, if I get nothing else out of being in this group, I'll settle for not caring what my mom and dad think."

ten

april

Back in the fifth session, Lathon had assigned the group some house-keeping. In our daily lives, he said, there are four areas of potential suffering: relationships, career, identity, and environment. In addition, there are three broad categories of pain: shame and humiliation; separation and loss; and physical pain, or tissue damage. He urged the members to learn these distinctions, and to practice them in session—to declare, in the first ten minutes of each meeting, what area most concerned them tonight. That way, if there were two people with relationship problems, he could match them up as interview partners, and get at the story more expediently. So, too, with pain: the sooner they could identify its nature, the sooner they could get help for it here.

Quite apart from any value of the above as taxonomy, it was instructive to watch the group come to terms with Lathon's argot. Lina and Peter picked up on it right away, jotting notes at home and using the words in session, naming their pain and suffering with growing confidence. Jack, for his part, fought the language to a draw, grasping it well enough but declining to utter it himself, as if afraid that Lathon would bill him for user fees. And Rex and Sara evinced no interest whatsoever, comporting themselves like fashion victims trapped inside a Sears store. In their louche indifference, they seemed to be saying, 'Look, it's bad enough that we're *here*, all right? Don't make this any harder by asking us to try the stuff on.'

At the start of the seventh session, it took everyone by surprise, then, when Sara announced she had "a concern in the relationship domain." She began by apologizing for not bringing it up sooner; it was just that—well, being with this person was so weirdly vague, it almost felt like it hadn't happened at all.

She paused, pulling her hair back with a nervous tug. Clearly, she'd been dreading this occasion. "In any case, it's been twelve weeks tomorrow since Gary and I met, but, hey, who's counting, right? He was this handsome and seemingly nice-guy lawyer who I liked right away and who seemed to like me back, and for a month or two, we got along great. We had some wonderful nights together, and late mornings in bed, and went away for a week to Colorado, where he has a time-share at a ski resort. And then, all of a sudden, my phone stopped ringing, or he'd call me at work and we'd have these nothing conversations—'Hello, how are you, let's get together sometime.' In short, the Chinese water torture.

"Well, anyway, we went on seeing each other in this half-baked way—a night or two here, a weekend there, but no real flow or connection. Then, one night, as we're lying in bed, he says, appropos of nothing, 'God, you're always such an optimist about things.' And I said, *'What?* Who are you *talking* to? I never think *anything'll* work out.' And something about that got me started crying, and he just lay there like a log and didn't comfort me. Anyhow, fast-forward to last Sunday morning, when we woke up together and it was gorgeous outside. He jumped out of bed and said, 'Great! I'm going Rollerblading,' and I said, 'Hey, can I come with you?' Well, he gives me this look like, 'Is there *no* getting rid of you?' and I got up with my heart pounding and went home.

"Anyway, I guess he felt guilty or something, because he called later on and asked if I wanted to have dinner with him. But I said no, I don't think so, I'm very depressed right now, after three months on this roller coaster with you. And he tried to talk around it but finally admitted that I was right, that he wasn't, quote-unquote, 'engaging with me.' And he *was* very decent about it, taking all the blame, and telling me how great I am and how the loss is all his, and so on. But then today, I get a letter, repeating all that nice-guy bullshit—'I so enjoyed my time with you, and really hope we can stay friends, et cetera'—and I just thought, ugh, what a patronizing jerk! I mean, here I was, crying my eyes out all weekend, not because I loved him, but just out of utter hopelessness. I mean, it *could've* worked out with him, but for, like, the hundredth time in a row, it didn't, and I just sat there asking myself, 'Why, why, why—"

"And there, in three words, is the essential suffering conversation: why, why, why," said Lathon. "It's bottomless and circular, and we could pursue it all day. But I think the better thing is to pursue the *pain* you're feeling. Group, what were you hearing as you listened to Sara—a relationship pain, or something disguised as such?"

Lina was the first one with her hand up. "Well, I wasn't hearing 'Why?' so much as 'Why *me?* What is it about *me* that's causing these problems, and how do I get it to stop?' "

"Excellent," said Lathon. "Right on point. Yes, it hurts when someone dumps you, then sends an emotional form letter. But beyond that, what we're hearing is suffering—suffering about who you are. Who is this person that's driving men off—a hundred times in a row, by your account?"

Sara frowned, plucking a thread off her shoulder. "Well, but I *was* being myself—just relaxed and having fun, not putting any pressure on him. But every time I think I've got something going, it collapses after three or four weeks."

After several moments of silence, Peter raised his hand. "Frankly, I'm a little confused, Sara," he said. "You came here saying you wanted to get married, and needed help figuring out what you were doing wrong. Except that *now* we find out you've been seeing someone for three months, and that it's just a relaxed and casual deal, nothing serious. I mean, I'm not trying to bust you, but how could that not come up here? And if you meant it about getting married, then why waste three months on *this* guy, who obviously didn't share your intentions?"

Sara shrank back, evading his gaze. "Well, like I said, you know, this wasn't a full-on thing, so it didn't seem crucial to mention it. And also, you know, I *was* still looking around, so—"

"Yeah, but c'mon, Sara, you know what he's talking about," Jack huffed. "Are you really serious about finding a guy, or are you just jerking yourself?"

"Yes, of *course*, I'm serious—why else would I come here? I want it more than anything in the world."

"By a show of hands, how many of you are convinced of that?" asked Lathon.

None of the members raised an arm.

"But it's true," cried Sara. "It's all I *think* about most of the time. You know, maybe I don't hang a sign out the window, but believe me, it's my top priority."

The others began to fidget, increasingly vexed with Sara.

"What, you think I *enjoy* being lonely? That I *like* going home to an empty apartment, and spending weekends alone, reading copy? I *hate* it, it's the worst, but what do I do? I can't make a man out of thin air."

Lathon grunted, not looking up from his notepad. "How many think the problem is a shortage of men?"

Again, the absence of hands was unanimous.

"Um, can I jump in here?" asked Dylan, shyly. "I know I've missed some sessions, so I haven't got the whole picture, but I was wondering if maybe I could—"

"Yes, by all means," said Lathon. "You know the basic outline of Sara's story."

Dylan scooted his chair forward a couple of inches, so that he could see around Rex to Sara. "Well, again, I'm catching up, Sara, so forgive me if you've said this. But was there a time where you really got burned by some guy and said to yourself, 'That's it?' "

Sara gave a groan, rolling her eyes at the ceiling. "What, you want just one, or should I list them alphabetically? Yeah, there were a few—crushers in there, especially when I was modeling. But for the last whatever, at least since I started editing, it's been mostly short, insubstantial things."

"Because I thought if there was some lingering heartbreak or something, maybe we could help get a fix on it and—"

"Nope, nothing," she said. "At least, not that I can put a finger on. When it comes to heartbreak, I've been relatively unscathed late—"

She stopped there, drawn up short by a memory. "Actually, there *was* one guy who did a number on me, though it was five or six years ago. He was this British journalist on assignment over here, and for a while, I thought we were going places. But he got a job in L.A. and broke up with me over the phone, and it totally bummed me out."

Rex, who was Sara's interviewer, picked up from there, asking about the extent of the damage. But this inquiry went nowhere and the group was back where it started, bored and impatient with Sara. A couple of members glanced in Lathon's direction, curious as to what he was doodling. For the last several minutes, he'd been engrossed in his notepad, sketching with long, slow strokes. Now, feeling their stares, he looked up with a start, as if surprised to find he had company.

"As I was listening to Sara," he said, putting down the pad, "two things struck me as interesting. One, that this vibrant, beautiful woman has never been engaged to be married. Two, she said something at our very first session that I thought was rather revealing. If you'll recall, Lina was talking about her husband, Anton, and how he'd betrayed her after twenty years. And then Sara cut in, saying that was her *worst nightmare*, being betrayed by a man you've loved for a long time.' Which raises the question: Which man was Sara talking about? Who do you think she loved for a long time, only to be hurt and betrayed by?"

"I would say her dad," Rex ventured.

"Exactly," said Lathon. "Her father hurt her terribly. And that pain took in all three categories that we've talked about—separation and loss; shame and humiliation; even fear of bodily harm, from a man who could hurl a knife. That's a heavy thing to carry around all these years, and we'd really love to take some of it off you."

"But *how?*" Sara cried. "How can you take some of it off me when, for the fiftieth time, I don't *remember* it?"

Lathon waited a moment, letting the echo settle. "Group," he said, "in the wreckage of her childhood, Sara lost something important—the little black box that contains some of her story. Where would you now, as flight inspectors, suggest that she start looking for it?"

The five of them put their heads together, thinking it through out loud. Lina proposed that Sara talk to her sister, whose memory was probably better than hers. Dylan suggested a hypnotist, something he'd done himself when he first got sober. And Rex, ever the helpful one, advised a tab of acid. "You might not remember anything you didn't before, but at least you'll have a good time," he cracked.

"Yes, thank you," sniffed Lathon. "Another county heard from, as usual."

Reaching to his left, he held up the notepad. On it was blocked, in big letters, PHONE HOME.

"At the risk of repeating myself, it's time to talk to your dad, Sara. He can't hurt you anymore—he's six thousand miles away. And while it may not be joyous for you, we can't do without him. He's the missing witness in this case."

Sara shook her head in trepidation. "Those horrible little questions of his, prying into my business—'Who're you seeing these days?' 'Have you thought of adoption?' I mean, *gak*! Just the thought of *talking* to him about that stuff . . ."

"It's hard to blame him for being interested in his daughter."

"No, but you don't know what it does to me; I get physically ill from just a *courtesy call.*"

Lathon nodded, stroking his chin contemplatively. "You're right," he said. "We don't know what it's like—and there's not much we can do until you tell us. And so, we ask you respectfully to go find out. Just talk to him, as one adult to another, and report back on its effects in your body. You might be surprised and find he's not the same bully. That this man, who does, after all, speak five languages, and has traveled the world over on business and pleasure—you might just find that he's interesting, and inspires other feelings besides fear and loathing. But even if he doesn't—if it's just pain and more pain—that's what we're set up to listen to. Pain we can help with, whereas 'bored' we're stumped by. That's become an old story, Sara, and frankly, a *dull* one. And after three or so months of it, we're starting to get a sense of what drove those hundred men off."

eleven

It was the first warm afternoon of the year, and the city took to the streets, dazed and sun-drunk. On Park Avenue, bankers lolled on concrete plazas with their ties slung over their shoulders while temp workers grazed in Bryant Park. Walking the cross blocks, you could suddenly smell the vegetation, as dogwoods and plane trees showed out in splendor, shrugging off the insult of soot.

Though I'd walked much of the way, savoring the rare mood on Broadway, I was early for my meeting with Jack. I met him in his lobby, where he was fetching the mail, having just returned from a power walk. He lived near the park and took his exercise there, traversing the stretch to Ninety-sixth Street and back in a shade under forty minutes. A runner and power lifter into his fifties, he had been forced to gear down when a hip started to creak, but was otherwise in admirable shape. He was wearing tennis shorts and an Andover sweatshirt, and his thighs, though slightly varicose, were rippling.

"I work out around one," he said. "That's when the casting agents are at lunch. The rest of the time, I'm either by the phone, or racing around town doing callbacks."

"Yes, how's that going?" I asked, walking him to the elevator. His building was one of those prewar monoliths whose charms are impervious to developers. Its grand old lobby was paved in marble, and gave off that whiff so inveterate to West Siders, the odor of mold and trapped air. It had lately suffered a makeover and sported garish suede couches, as well as a series of large oils from the Draw-this-dog school of Impressionism. In all that gray space, though, the redo hadn't taken, and the property soldiered on, inexorable.

"I'm sorry, what did you say?" asked Jack, looking up from his mail. He'd paled as he flipped through the stack of bills, the muscles in his jawline hardening.

"I say, how's it going there? Any line on a good part?"

He grunted, giving back a sour smile. "Eh, well, I've been out a lot, and had a couple of callbacks—a sitcom, and a national commercial. Nothing fancy, but I could sure use the dough about now. It's starting to get tight around here."

He explained, as we walked through the door into his foyer, that he'd been waiting on a check for several months. It was for his share of the proceeds from a touring musical, the last of his former productions still on stage. At the time of his arrest, such checks arrived weekly. Now, he was happy to get two a year, and for a fraction of their former amount. He'd been calling all morning, in fact, trying to reach his ex-partner, and found it galling to have to stick out his hand. He had looked diligently for work and practiced every economy, abandoning all traces of his prior lifestyle. Where once he kept a limo and driver downstairs, now he stinted on riding the subway, walking to all his auditions. He rooted in his change drawer to buy the *Times* each morning, and hadn't seen a play or had a meal in a restaurant since—well, it had been a long time.

"I can't afford to get down, though; something'll pop for me soon. This run I'm in just can't go on forever."

He smiled as he said this, but there was a tenor of entreaty in his voice, as if he were addressing some unseen agency. These last six years had dealt a series of blows—the seizure of his co-op and beach house for taxes, and the auctioning off of all his assets; his subsequent migration from hotel to motel, in the very letter of downward mobility; and the loss of old friends to whom he'd turned for money and been unable to repay. And so here he was now, with his wife and

German shepherd, in a cramped two-bedroom on Seventieth Street. There was a fractional view of the Hudson River, and some pieces he'd held back from the IRS fire sale—an eighteenth-century oak escritoire; a tall, bombé chest that tapered like a wedding cake. But as you looked around the apartment, you had a sense of the wagons being circled—a line drawn, and a last stand declared. I wondered, but decided against asking just yet, how he managed to pay the rent.

On the wall above the sectional was a cluster of framed photos. Most were of Jack's family in its current configuration—his wife, Marcia, a pretty redhead some sixteen years his junior; and his four grown sons and their spouses and progeny, many of whom favored Jack with their cleft chins and color. By dint of its vintage, though, one picture stood out. It was a sepia shot of a man at a train station, his head cocked over the trestles. He was tall and quite handsome, with the sort of taciturn glamour that Hollywood once codified into a tintype of manhood. In his square-shouldered suit and snap-brim fedora, he could have been mistaken for any one of a dozen stars— the young Kirk Douglas or Robert Conrad, following his chin into action.

"Oh, he was a looker, all right," said Jack of his father. "I remember him coming up the street in the evening, and thinking, 'My dad is the handsomest guy in the whole world.' I'd go running down to meet him and grab on to his leg and hug it, and he'd kiss the top of my head and let me carry his briefcase. In terms of affection, though, that was about all I got from him. My father was *not* what you'd call a warm, affable guy—though everybody else seemed to think he was."

He recalled his boyhood visits to the *Daily Mirror*, where his father chronicled the exploits of the mob. Some kid or other would be roped out of copy to show Jack around the building, letting him get his hands dirty pulling first-run pages, or setting the slugs for a Yankees story. And on each and every visit, people would take him aside and tell him what a great man his father was.

"It wasn't just the usual, backslapping bullshit; they were genuinely in awe of him," he said. "He had that effect on people, including the kids on my block. When I was eight or nine, I remember joining the Cub Scouts, and my mother coerced him to be a troop leader. She did that a lot, you know, playing the go-between, trying to get us closer together. At any rate, all my squad-mates fell in love with my father. They'd come up to me on hikes and say, "What's it like to have a dad like that?' And I'd shrug and go along and say, 'Oh, it's great, and blah-blah-blah,' while all the while thinking, 'I'm the *last* to know.'"

"Sounds like a page out of Cheever," I said. "The suburban father who's too wrapped up in himself to pay attention to his son. And the son who, to get back at him, goes and cleans out the liquor cabinet, and knocks up the girl next door. . . ."

"Well, I don't know about the girl next door," he said, laughing, "but the rest of it's pretty close. We had a house in Harrison, and spent our summers on Long Beach, where my father'd drive out on weekends. But, to be fair about it, remember that this was the forties, when *most* men didn't relate to their kids."

"Really? I thought it was the *last* time they *did* relate. Driving them around on their paper route, teaching them how to drag-bunt, and so on. . . ."

"Yeah, well, I didn't get that, and I'm very sad about it," he said. "I really did love him a lot, you know, in spite of his coolness to me. And, of course, in his later years, he became much more loving with me. Actually took me aside and said, out of the clear blue, 'You know, Jackie, I made so many mistakes raising you. If I had it to do over again, I'd be a much better dad,' and I said, 'Stop it. You did the best you could.' "

Small tears appeared in the corners of Jack's eyes. In a man of such adamant spit and polish, sentiment was the last thing I expected. But on the subject of his father, we'd apparently hit a pocket of deep feeling.

"Did you ever ask why he was so cool to you as a kid?"

"Oh, God no, what good would that've done?" he winced. "The past is the past; he felt lousy enough as it was. What's the point of hashing out regrets?"

Over the course of the next hour, though, that was precisely what Jack did, kicking over regrets about his father. Like many a jilted son, he held himself to blame, bemoaning both his abject neediness as a kid and his remarkable bad timing. His father, he said, put in twelve-hour days, then came home and got a start on the next day's story. Whenever he spared an evening for his son, however, Jack took the occasion to fall all over himself, blowing his lines in the high-school play or finishing up the track in the hundred–yard dash.

"And, I mean, Christ, the look on him when he'd come down out of the stands," Jack said. "It wasn't anger so much as plain embarrassment. As if he was thinking, 'How could someone as great as me have *possibly* produced someone like you?' And then, when I did do well at something, he'd be off on assignment, or fishing in Canada with his buddies. I mean, not for nothing, but I graduated sixth in my class, and made Phi Beta Kappa at Chicago. You'd think that'd entitle me to *some* respect, or at least . . ."

He stopped, his eyes suddenly pinpoint hard. But, as quickly as it flared, the heat went out of him and he returned to his cautious regret.

"I guess by then, though, he was busy with his novel, and I didn't want to rub his nose in it."

"Well, what about later, when you were a big producer? Did you take him someplace expensive and order the magnum of Cristal? Say, 'Here, Dad; here's the kid you didn't have time for. How do you like me *now?*' "

Jack shrugged, his great, florid face gone slack. "I really wasn't aware of being angry at him then. Or if I was, I don't remember it."

Clearly now, we were deep in Cheever country—the rage and resentment so thick under ice that they came back as little pearls of melancholia. Jack was *sad* that his father skipped his shows; *sad* that they'd waited so long to make up to each other; *sad* that he'd never discussed this with his former therapists—

"What? You didn't *discuss* it with them? How could you've avoided it?"

He gave a little laugh, swirling the last of his Pepsi. "Oh, there were lots of things I avoided in therapy," he said. "My drinking; my addiction; the state of my marriages . . . I could go on, if you want."

"Well, but what *did* you talk about, if not your problems?"

Jack rubbed his hands, a merry light in his eyes. "Ah, well, let's see," he said. "With Marvin, I mostly talked about my celebrity pals, who he was very interested in. With Albert, who'd invested his money in a glue factory, I talked—or I should say, *he* talked—about the hassles of the glue business. And with Carole, who was top-dollar, I actually talked about things that mattered to me. Until she showed up, bombed, to session."

"Really?" I said. "You had a therapist who was drunk? What, did you smell it on her breath?"

"Oh no, no, nothing so crass," he said. "Carole was teddibly Park Avenue. But every third session or so, she'd greet me not with her usual 'Hello,' but with this drawn-out, high-pitched, 'Hill*ooo.*' And I said, 'Fine, I'll fix you, honey,' and started showing up drunk, myself. And after a while, it was like being front row at a farting contest—you couldn't tell which of us was more gassed."

By now, I was laughing in spite of myself, and Jack had ramped up into full raconteur mode, telling the story with delight. Far from ending treatment or reporting Carole to the board, Jack went away with her and a dozen of her clients to a farmhouse in Maine for a weekend. These "gang-bang group therapy trips" were all the rage in the eighties, he said, sort of like a cross between an Apache sweat lodge and co-ed sleepaway camp. After an intense first day of it, they'd all gathered downstairs for dinner, and Carole had a glass of wine with her meal. Then she had another, and another, and another.

Along about the fifth, she was warbling "La Vie en Rose," and opining that all rapists should be castrated in a public square.

"Well, needless to say, I took her aside the next morning. I said, 'Please don't be offended, Carole, but you *should* slow down around your patients. It sends out the wrong signal when they find you passed out in the bathtub.'"

I laughed and closed my notebook, abandoning all hope of continuing the interview. "Was she mortified when you said that?"

"Mortified?" he howled. "Hell, she socked me in the jaw! Nearly knocked me out flat with a right cross!"

"Stop it!" I cried, meaning more, more, more. "You're telling me your therapist *hit* you?"

"Word of honor," he said, tapping the side of his jaw. "And let me tell you, she didn't *punch* like no Freudian."

We laughed a while longer about the methods of Carole Troutman, and the various other harebrains he'd so happily subsidized. He made a delicacy of being seen by the halt and incompetent, on the premise that they were too impeded by their own dementia to intervene in his drinking and drugging. In the sweetheart logic of the alcoholic, this made perfect sense. It allowed him to pretend that he was getting help for his boozing, when what he was really getting was license to continue.

Unlike most of the other boulevardiers of the era, however, Jack was actually paying attention during the eighties, and could recite to you now every one of his adventures with great, self-lacerating charm. Part of it was the ingrained confessional of AA, mixed in with a portion of rue. But the better part, by far, was that he was a born performer who loved nothing more than playing to a room.

So it went for the balance of the afternoon, the sunlight dissolving into orange shadow, the last, sweet fireball of day. Jack kept telling stories, one more antic than the next, about his travels with the pleasure circus. There was the blond chorine that he fixed up with a rock star, who, in the throes of enthusiasm, knocked over a candle, setting fire to their room at the Plaza. There was his longtime coke dealer who began smoking his own inventory, and was last seen on the corner of Gansevoort and Washington, enbroiled in a knife fight with his own shadow. After several hours of this, I felt glutted and stoned, as if I'd been snacking on rum cake and triple sec. I also, truth to tell, felt like one of Jack's therapists—regaled and diverted, but decidedly not engaged.

With a light head and a heavy hand, then, I returned to the subject of his father. Jack shot me a look of dull exhaustion, as if acknowledging he'd wasted a grand evasion. His defenses low on power, though, a couple of memories eked through. The first was about his father, and an injury he suffered as a boy. Jack's grandfather, it seemed, was an Orthodox Jew who forebade all manner of childishness in his children. The playground was off-limits to them, the wearing of shorts out of the question, and gum-chewing grounds for a beating. Nonetheless, there was Jack's father, chomping on a wad in his room, when up the stairs rumbled his father. Terrified, he pasted the gum against his window and pulled the drapes shut to avoid detection. The next day, though, as he was prying it off, the penknife slipped and freakishly lodged in his eye. It took three operations to save the cornea, after which he was ordered to lie in a darkened room for a period of more than a year.

"My mom told me that," he said. "She thought it would explain my father to me. I'd gone to her and said, 'I want Mike Kragen's dad to be my father; he's much nicer to me than Dad is.' And my mom, who was usually a great ally of mine, said that was a hideous thing to say. That my father'd had a much harder life than me, and I ought to be grateful for what I got from him."

It was while talking about his mother that the second memory cropped up. Among her many virtues, she was a wit and prankster, her playfulness the tonic to her husband's gloom. One day, she and Jack played a joke on him. As usual, she drove him to the station in the morning, only this time concealing Jack under a blanket. En route, she mused aloud about what their boy might someday be.

"I'd bet my nickel on movie star," she said. "That is one handsome kid we're raising."

The gag was that as soon as he ventured a guess, Jack would pop up and say, "Nope, I'm gonna be a spy!" But his father was engrossed in the morning *Times*, and didn't take the bait.

"What's *your* thought about it?" she tried again lightly.

"Of what?"

"Of Jack."

He shrugged, not looking up from his paper. "He's all right, I guess. Nothing special, either way. Don't forget about the cake for the Riordans."

It was by now nearly dark in Jack's living room. The sky was a violet wall over his shoulder, and the shadows under his cheekbones were livid. He sat there with his legs crossed, one foot drumming the air. It may have been a minute before he spoke.

"I understand it was tough for him growing up," he grunted, "and that his dad didn't know fuck-all about being a father. But still, you know, my God—"

He broke off, his blue eyes radiating the gloom.

"But?"

A sigh, and the force of his anger escaped him, replaced by a dilution of sadness. "I mean, how can you even *think* that about your eight-year-old kid?"

twelve

april

The weather held fair through much of the week, and the members
showed up in a sprightly mood, chatting as if they were poolside. Rex
was just back from a weekend at Winged Foot, where he'd golfed, he
said, with a Pro Bowl quarterback. Dylan reported that he'd joined
the Y on Twenty-third Street, and was going there every morning.
"Any day now, I'm gonna shatter the twelve-minute mile," he
quipped. Even Lina seemed up, drawn out of herself. She'd been
digging in the yard at her house in Saltaire, and was sporting the first
blossom of a tan. "Divorce or no divorce," she said, "I've got veg-
etables to plant, and weeds that have to come up. Legally, it isn't settled, but that house is *mine* this summer. Tomatoes are nine-tenths
of the law."

About the only one not in high spirits was Peter, who kept crossing and uncrossing his legs. Owing to the heat, he'd removed his tie
and jacket, and unfastened the top button of his dress shirt. Still, he
seemed hemmed in somehow, unable to make the downshift from
work talk to banter. While the others chirped away, he sat with his
hands folded, waiting glumly to get started.

At six-thirty, Lathon called the session to order, and announced
that he was making some changes. "This is the ninth of our twenty
meetings," he said, "and as I expected, you're ahead of schedule.
You've learned how to recognize pain when you hear it, and to tell
it from its imitator, suffering. You're also getting the hang of distin-

guishing pain by kind, breaking it down into its three compounds. And so, kudos to you all: you've picked up the basics of serious listening in a little more than three months.

"Now, what that means, practically speaking, is that we can move to phase two, go from diagnosis to prescription. We all know what pain sounds like now; the question is what do we do about it? The answer, of course, is that we go ahead and treat it, using all our delicacy and courage. For the past three months, I've been talking *ad nauseam* about suffering conversations. Now, I'm going to harangue you about *effective* conversations, in which people tell each other the truth of what hurts them, and design action to heal the wound. It's a process with certain kinds of risks, to be sure, and I'm not going to understate them. But done right, it enriches the partnership, and sets the stage for phase three, which is serious fun. And that, dear friends, is where we all want to go—or, more accurately, where we want to go *back* to."

Sara put her hand up timorously. "At the risk of being an idiot, could I ask you to explain some of your terms?"

The others laughed at this, as much from relief as levity. Several, it seemed, felt shaky with his lingo, and were glad that someone else had copped to it.

"By all means," said Lathon. "Though you're hardly an idiot."

"Well, but that's what I feel like half the time. I mean, I practically get a migraine when I hear *true story* and *false story*, and yet everybody else seems totally fine with them. And what *is* a suffering conversation, and am I in one right now, and if so, could someone get me *out* of it?"

"Hey, I *would*," said Rex, "but I'm stuck in one myself, and it's got me real good around the ankle."

"Great, I hope you get gangrene," muttered Lina, grinning a death ray at him.

"Now, now, no fair picking on Rex," said Lathon. "This is my fault, rattling on as if I were speaking plain English. Okay, then: the short, abridged glossary of Dr. Lathon. A 'suffering conversation' is something we do or say to prevent a problem from getting solved. It may be arguing about the problem, or pretending it doesn't exist, or inventing a new problem to distract from the old one. In other words, it's good, old avoidant behavior, like Sara's obsession about being ten pounds heavy, when her real problem is that she's angry at her father. Or it's Dylan's drinking, or obsessing about his wife, when the real pain is that his marriage is over.

"Which brings us up to 'true story' and 'false story.' The false story is what we tell the world to try and get something we want. An example would be Jack's playing the big high roller in order to buy people's company. The true story, as we know, is that he felt crummy and worthless, but as long as he kept buying drinks for the house, he didn't have to deal with that. It takes guts to tell the true story, because it requires you to *do something*, to acknowledge the pain and yearning of being human. The false story, on the other hand, requires nothing at all of you. You can sit there all day, playing it over and over until you run out of friends or quarters. Ultimately, the false story doesn't draw people to you; instead, it drives them away."

Now it was Peter's turn to raise his hand. "So the false story, if I hear you right, leads to a suffering conversation, whereas the true story leads to an effective one."

"Pre*cis*ely," said Lathon, awarding praise with a nod. "The true story, declared with dignity and courage, is the first step to the end of suffering."

Peter made a face, deflecting the praise. "Well, I had a conversation with my girlfriend today, only I'm not sure if it was suffering or effective."

"Well, tell us about it," said Lathon. "We can use it as a teaching example."

Peter wiped his palms on the flaps of his pockets, physically oppressed, still, by the task of revealing himself. It seemed that he and Kara had been on the subway to work that morning when she began chatting about a friend of hers. The woman, who was pregnant in her early forties, had developed complications, requiring her to take to bed for several months. "As I don't have to tell you," said Kara, "I'll be forty myself soon, and I don't want that happening to me. When are we going to cut this messing around and actually get down to business?"

"Well, I looked over my shoulder," Peter said, "and there were at least five people listening to us, not even *pretending* to read their papers. I said, 'Isn't there a better time for us to discuss this?' and she said, 'Hey, no time like the present.' So I said, 'Well, wouldn't we have to get married first?' and she said, 'If that's your proposal, I accept.' I mean, it's a quarter to eight in the morning and my eyes are barely open, and suddenly I've got a wedding in September."

After a moment's uncertainty, the others checked in with congratulations. Lina, sitting next to Peter, reached over and squeezed his arm. Jack half stood, offering a wry ovation, exhorting the others to join him. And Rex, who'd once groused to me that it "fucks up the alignment of the planets when a stiff like Peter marries money," dipped into his pocket for an expensive cigar. Handing it over to Peter, he joked that they could get married on the A train, and catch the shuttle to Kennedy for their honeymoon.

"Yes, that's right," said Lathon, laughing along with the others. "This gives a whole new meaning to getting railroaded!"

There was more laughter and catcalls, and more shaking of hands. The mood in the room, already bright to begin with, turned downright festive now, as the members badgered Peter for details. They asked how it felt to be an instant millionaire, and if they could apply to be houseboys on his boat. About the only one not swept up in the merriment was the perspiring husband-to-be. Sunk in his seat, he looked qualmish and heat-struck, as if they were discussing the removal of his appendix. Curiously, though, no one noticed but Sara, who watched him with pensive eyes.

"You know, I'm starting to get the feeling," she said, "that Peter isn't a hundred percent with this."

"Oh no? What makes you think so?" asked Lathon.

She scanned Peter again, as if checking her data. "Well, he doesn't *look* very happy, for a guy who just got engaged. And for his girlfriend to have to corner him on the IRT, with all those people listening in . . . I don't know, it doesn't sound real spontaneous to *me*."

"Mmm, good listening," said Lathon. "It does sound like a shotgun proposal. Is that how it felt to you, Peter?"

Peter's head scrunched down beneath his shoulders. He peered out between them like a turtle. "Well, I—I thought we'd agreed that now wasn't the best time for me. I mean, here she is, making a million-plus a year, and I'm still a half-assed accountant. And on top of that, she wants to have a baby soon, and a great, big wedding at the Royalton—I mean, it'd wipe me out financially just paying the *coat check girl*. Meanwhile, if I try for a new job and come up empty, it's going to really bum me out. I am *not* the kind of person who can brush off rejection—I obsess about it for months on end. But on the other hand, if I *don't* do something soon, I'll get stuck where I am and—"

"Folks, didn't I say this would be a good teaching case?" said Lathon, laughing. "What would you call the speech we just heard?"

"A suffering conversation!" they chimed.

"And a first-class case of it, too," said Lathon. "Notice how the thinking goes around and around, picking up momentum as it goes. This is what all good panic attacks are made of: these miscellaneous fears pumping adrenaline into the bloodstream. Worry then starts to feed on itself, telling the heart to beat faster, and the lungs to work harder to move the extra oxygen, and before you know it, your stomach's churning acid, and your palms and the soles of your feet are wet, and that sense of foreboding is now palpable terror, only you can't figure what you're even terrified of, except that it's somewhere in the room behind you—"

He pulled up short and looked around, gauging the jitters he'd evoked. "See, even just talking about it gets the engine racing. Whereas talking about the *pain* takes the terror down. The truth has a way of restoring order."

Peter stared at him, sweat pebbling his forehead. "Well, but I'm not even sure what I'm actually *afraid* of, let alone what's hurting me."

"That's all right," said Lathon, "why don't you just sit back and listen, while the rest of us mull it over? Group, in that speech now, Peter said something instructive—'I'm not the kind of guy who can handle rejection; it stays with me for months.' Now, that strikes me as odd, given that this very morning, a woman proposed to him on the subway. So my question is, if it's not his girlfriend, then who's he afraid of being rejected by?"

The other members sputtered a moment, caught off guard. Lathon was fond of springing such questions, often stopping an interview to ask them. It was all part of the training, he said; a way of thinking with your ears, and hearing with your heart and viscera.

"Well, he's talked about wanting a new job and more money," said Rex. "So maybe he's worried what her rich family'll think. Look down on him as the deadbeat in-law."

"All right, the class angle," said Lathon. "That's one idea: Park Avenue turning its nose up on Buffalo. Anyone else with a thought?"

There was a second pause, the members skulking in their seats, as if they'd neglected to do their reading.

"Well, that whole job-search thing is pretty hairy," said Sara. "Going on interviews, being scrutinized by strangers—"

"No, no, come on, people, you're going backwards," chided

Lathon. "Peter just told you that he's afraid of rejection—what category of pain does that suggest?"

Again, a round of vacant stares. Lathon tapped his armrest crankily.

"What, have I slipped into an alternate universe?" he said. "Are you the same people I *complimented* a minute ago?"

The babble of a car alarm wafted up, sluicing the mild evening. Jack leaned over and shut the window.

"Of the three kinds of pain, I would say humiliation," said Lina.

"Ah, *thank* you," said Lathon, patting his forehead dry in a pantomime of relief. "And of all the rejections, which one hurts the most, and can shame and humiliate you for life?"

Sara nodded before he'd finished the question. "Being rejected by your parents."

"Ahhh," said Lathon, softening his voice for emphasis. "Did everyone hear that, because that is the baseline: the experience of early shame. As kids, every one of us had *two* sets of parents—the idealized parents who were loving and generous, and their all-bad counterparts who were mean to us. That's not psychosis, it's just the way kids' minds work. They truly believe that if their nice mommy screams at them, she's been taken over by an evil witch. Hence, all of the fairy tales about good queens and bad queens, and princes turning into toads. Kids aren't able to think abstractly, and so they split the world up into black and white.

"Now, the theory is that if we get good enough parenting, we'll eventually grow out of this splitting. We'll see that the 'good' and 'bad' moms are the same person, and learn to view life pragmatically. But in practice, it doesn't always work that way. Most people were sufficiently stung by the 'bad' parent that they court the 'good' one with a false story. Who among us doesn't go home for Christmas and tell our parents what they want to hear—that our lives are better than they really are, and that we bear them no lasting grudges?

We may say to ourselves, What's the point of hurting them now, but the truth is, we're afraid of them hurting *us*. They're still our parents, and they can still cut us dead, with a look or a bitchy remark."

Sara, who'd slid so far down in her chair that she looked like she'd been thrown against it, shook her head morosely. "So what you're saying, then, is there's no hope."

"On the contrary," he tutted. "There's *always* hope, if you can show up as yourself with them. But that's a subject for another day. For now, let's hear about Peter's parents, and see if we can't see what they did to shame him, and why he's still afraid of them."

In his loping cadences, Peter described his parents to the group. Both were physicians in private practice who had affiliations with a hospital in Buffalo. Of the two, though, his father had had much the harder going. He was a torturously shy man with no instinct for self-advancement, and his reticence had held him back. For many years, he'd toiled obscurely in research, unable to catch on with an established practice or attract the capital to start his own. One night, after hearing that he'd been passed over for a position, he came home and put his fist through an heirloom. Another night, upon learning that a colleague had been chosen over him, he picked up his briefcase and threw it clear across the lawn, screaming "Fuck" loud enough to alarm the neighbors.

"It was the first—and last—time I heard him curse in my life," said Peter. "For that matter, it was the first time I heard him raise his voice. He had a policy, he and my mom, of never discussing things in front of us. We'd sit down to dinner—me in my bow tie, my sister in her dress—eating a 'proper supper' by candlelight. And as far as I can remember, no problem ever came up there, even though there were lots of problems. My father was pissed off at being stifled professionally; I had some kind of low-grade depression that made it hard for me at school, and my sister, from early on, was showing signs of being gay. But to this day, none of that stuff has ever been talked about openly. In fact, they *still* don't know if Janet's gay or not. My mother once asked about it, but Janet was so devastated, it freaked them both out for months. Now, neither one of them has the nerve to raise it again, and it just sits there, hanging over us, when we're together."

"Whoa, hold on a second," said Jack, furrowing his brow. "As a kid, that's a hard thing to talk about, especially in a place like Buffalo. But even up *there* now, it's 1995, and we're all more adult about this, no?"

"Actually, the time and place are irrelevant," said Lathon. "All that matters is the story in that household. And the one I want to know more about is the mother, not the sister. Obviously, someone was running the ship in this family, and I'll lay you ten-to-one it wasn't the father."

He delegated Jack to follow that up, quizzing Peter about his mother. He depicted her as a brusquely efficient woman who made it her business to protect Peter's father, heading off problems before they got to him. When Peter, for instance, told her that the crazy O'Dwyer kids were chasing him home after school, she marched across the street and browbeat their mother, threatening to have her two boys deported. And eight years later, when she discovered a joint in Peter's shirt pocket, she quietly made his life hell for months, bringing it up whenever they were alone.

"I hadn't even meant to smoke it," he groaned. "I—I was just going to my first rock concert, and thought maybe you needed it to get in, or something. But she was just *relentless* about it, telling me how I had broken her heart, and brought a pestilence down on the family. And I tried to tell her that I was one of the few kids in school who *didn't* have a drug problem, but she didn't want to hear that. All she'd ever say was, 'There's no getting out of this. If your father found out, it would kill him.'"

"Wow, that's just a *little* bit over the top," Rex chortled. "And the best part is, she's not even Jewish. Where'd she get so good at slinging guilt?"

"Probably from my mom," said Lina, pursing her lips. "She could teach anyone in three short lessons."

"Now, now, there's no monopoly on guilt," said Lathon. "It's as abundant in Taipei as it is in Crown Heights. Only, in this case, it seems to have inspired more than just shame—it brought, in his mother's words, a *pestilence* on the family. That's a big load on a young kid's back, and she kept adding to it every day. Meanwhile, behind her hysterics was an implicit indictment: You're not *good enough to be in this family*. What a kick in the pants for a lousy joint—not just penance, but the threat of expulsion."

Staring at his wing tips, Peter allowed that this was so. As a kid, he'd spent a lot of time worrying that he wasn't loved. There were his undistinguished report cards, a source of deep concern at home, and his parents' seeming preference of his brilliant sister. But above all, there was the lack of warmth in the family, and the ban on all expression of feeling. No one ever hugged or kissed good-bye, beyond the occasional peck from his mom. And none of them ever cried or lost their temper, comporting themselves like strangers at an inn.

"I don't know where I got it—maybe from TV, which I watched a lot as a kid—but I always thought that families should be . . . closer, you know," he said. "I had friends who were really tight with their parents and siblings, and I was always jealous of that. Going to a Bills game with their father, or packing up the car and heading to the beach together—it might not sound like much to you, but I know that *we* didn't do it. And I'd always think to myself, why don't we do that? Why are we so different?"

"And there you have it," said Lathon. "In aspiring to be Mc-Keons; this family forgot to be *human;* to love and connect in some creaturely fashion. It met its moral burden, but there was no heat or light, none of the emotional sustenance to flourish. And so you had Peter coming down with childhood depression, and the father eating his humiliation in silence, and the sister becoming a sexual exile, and the mother who went native over a lousy joint—folks, *this* is not the way to raise happy children. In fact, they remind me of another Scottish clan. A warm and fuzzy bunch called the Macbeths."

Everyone laughed at this, including Peter, briefly released from his stew of worries. But then his face dimmed, and he resumed his position inside the fog bank. Though the room had cooled off since the onset of nightfall, he had sweat clear through his blue cotton dress shirt, darkening the broadcloth at the chest and collar.

"But how can I expect them to change," he asked, "when it's been like this for hundreds of years?"

Lathon grunted and let his head recline, rocking in his Italian desk chair. "To be honest, I don't know the answer to the McKeon problem. There's a rich tradition of inertia and silence that may just prove impenetrable. But what *you* can do—in fact, must do—is start your own tradition. You can decide that in *your* family, children will know that they're loved, as demonstrated by hugs and kisses. You can decide that in your family, it's okay to be human, to get angry and sad and even bruise each other occasionally. And you can decide that your family honors true stories—that it speaks its heart and mind to each other, and says to hell with the tradition of silence."

From his seat beneath the window, Jack smiled and shook his head, rolling his eyes at the skyline. "That's very elegant and sweet and all, but just a tiny bit glib there, don't you think? Number one, you're asking a guy who grew up in the deep-freeze to start acting like a New Age touchy-feely. Number two, you've got him married with kids already, but you didn't even ask him if he *loves* this girl, or if he wants to go through with the wedding."

Lathon drew the smallest sliver of a smile. "No, you're right, Jack; my mistake. Why don't we ask him, then? Peter, do you love Kara, and how do you feel about getting married now?"

Hunched over his knees, Peter's brown eyes widened, as if he'd spotted a Krugerrand on the floor. "Yeah, I . . . I mean, I do, you know. In fact, I'm crazy about her. It-it's just that . . ."

"Yes?"

Peter winced, blinking back the sweat on his eyelids. "I-I'm just worried that maybe I'm not good enough for her, and that I'm gonna screw this up somehow."

A hum of sympathy issued from the others. They eyed him with a solicitude that was almost tactile.

"Then go home and tell her that," said Lathon, softly. "Tell her that you love her and feel blessed to have her—and also, that you're scared to death. Explain how bad it hurt when your first marriage cratered, and how important it is that this one go the distance. The first step toward an effective conversation is to acknowledge that you're in pain. It may be that she, too, is scared and nervous, and for some of the same reasons that you are. So *talk* to her; let the *partnership* go to work now, and design action to treat the wound. Because that's the strength and beauty of the unit—it has the resources of two to solve problems."

Peter prized at the dirt beneath his nails. A smile inched across his face. "How about I bring her in here and let *you* tell her for me?"

Lathon laughed with his entire trunk, shimmying the chair beneath him. "Nope, sorry; nothing doing," he said. "I mean, I'll be glad to take your money, but you're going to do the talking. It might not come out as music at first, but you'll get the hang of it soon enough. Confidence, they say, is the product of competence, and competence comes from three things: practice, practice, practice."

thirteen

Lina's agency, a community mental health clinic in the Bronx, was situated in a particularly bleak stretch of Southern Boulevard. Walking the five blocks from the IRT was like walking Sniper's Alley in Sarajevo—the firebombed buildings, vacant for years, reduced to urinals for neighborhood strays; the beer cans and bus transfers blowing like phantoms through empty intersections. Finally, near the clinic, the odd bodega appeared, with three or four hardboys idling in front. Slouched against the plate glass in their G-funk attire, they eyed me with a look of bald derision, cackling as I came abreast of them.

Lina's clinic was a three-story bunker overlooking the Cross Bronx Expressway. Buzzed inside the door, I stepped into a waiting room under construction. Three walls of Sheetrock, as yet unpainted, supported a drop-ceiling lacking its tiles. I spotted them soon enough; they were in boxes on the floor, beside a cart containing chunks of the former ceiling. Lumpy and ringed with concentric whorls of mold, the remnants were encrusted with what I hoped wasn't asbestos. I presented myself to the receptionist, and sat as far as possible from the cart.

It was midafternoon, and the room was beginning to fill up with schoolkids of various ages. Slumped in hard, yellow plastic scoop chairs, a couple whiled away at pocket video games. Others put their heads down or stared out the window, as sullen as wildcats in a ramshackle zoo. Belatedly, it occurred to me that virtually all of them were Hispanic, and that the triptych on the wall was a shrine. It bore the names of the 187 immigrants, mostly Dominican, who had died in the torching of the Happy Lands disco down the block. I looked again at the faces in the room, and recalculated what it cost to be a kid from these streets.

At a quarter past the hour, I spotted Lina down the hall, her arm around a stout, elderly woman. She was talking to the woman, who nodded agreement, but who seemed barely to have the energy to continue walking. Behind them was a girl, perhaps nine or ten, trailing her fingers along the fake wood paneling. In her free hand was a paint box with a red ribbon around it.

"Remember now, we have a deal," said Lina to the girl. "You owe me one beautiful painting of you and your cat, Bernie."

The girl nodded shyly, grinning at the floor, then made an impressive fart noise with her mouth.

"Lakeesha, *tell* Mrs. Stavros thank you for the paint set," scowled the woman.

Swiveling at the hips, Lakeesha windmilled her free arm, as if there were a twister inside her trying to get out. "Thank you." She giggled down the front of her blouse, and ran off in the direction of the door.

"Girl—!" cried the woman, limping after her. Her wheeze could be heard from the foyer.

Walking back to her office, Lina told me Lakeesha's story. She was what the staff psychologist called a "scapegoat child," singled out for abuse by her crackhead mother. So enraged was she when brought in three years ago that she lay facedown on the linoleum floor and refused to answer questions. Lina pulled strings to get her placed with Alma, a foster mother who had literally loved her back to health.

"Every day, she'd take her into her lap and just hold her there, telling her stories," said Lina. "Lakeesha was like one of those kids from a Chinese orphanage—she had practically no experience of human touch. *Now*, look at her—she's a grade ahead in reading level, and is blossoming into a little Hieronymus Bosch."

She gestured at the pocked white walls of her office, which were crowded with watercolors. Most were of trees and cats and such, with the odd portrait of Michael Jordan tucked in. But on the wall above her desk, enjoying pride of place, was a slumscape of lunar detail. Witches on broomsticks flew over projects, their black hats trademarked by Nike. Big rats with devil ears traveled in packs, devouring a man with a halo. And sprawled in a corner trash can was a woman with snakes for hair. Above her, on a light pole overarching the street, was a placard I mistook for a parking sign. Bending in, I read, in careful red lettering: NO CRACK, TUESDAYS AND THURSDAYS

"Amazing," I said. "It's like a bird's-eye view of hell."

"Yeah, well, she's *been* there enough," said Lina. "But this is one that isn't going back."

And then, as if closing the case file on Lakeesha, she stood up and took me on a tour of the clinic. Two doors down, we looked in on the art room, where several kids were working in clay. Across the hall, in a room laid with gym mats, a gaggle of boys were engaged in smashmouth soccer, evincing only vague interest in putting the ball in the net. And at the back of the building, in what was formerly dead storage, lay the product of five years' planning—a theater. The front of the room was taken up with a stage, a plywood affair under strips of track lighting. Ten rows of seats, four abreast, were screwed into the concrete floor. On a riser behind them was the director's booth, consisting of dimmer switches, a microphone, and a video camera.

We went and sat down in the last row of seats, which had been salvaged from a cinema on Tremont. Onstage, working in clamorous subgroups, were a dozen kids painting scenery for a play. I saw an oak-tag backdrop of hulking tenements, and a cache of cardboard bats and guns. Evidently, *A Christmas Carol* this wasn't.

"Yo, Miz Stavros," one of the boys called, "you said we could have a deejay with this, right?"

"Absolutely, Hector," said Lina. "As long as you can fit it into your budget."

"But that's only like fi'ty dollars," he protested. "Why you can't get Mayor Giuliani to break you off some dough?"

"Um, I don't think he's taking my calls." She laughed. "Besides which, isn't your cousin Angel a deejay?"

"Yeah, but he won't bite for no fi'ty dollars," Hector groaned. "Especially since we're down to about twenty-two."

Lina laughed again, despite her best efforts not to. She hadn't stopped smiling since the moment we entered, and was clearly in her glory among these kids.

"Well, then, you better write a letter to Spike Lee," she said. "Because the bank of Ms. Stavros is closed."

Some first-rate bitching and moaning ensued, including the grumble from a boy who couldn't have been older than ten that this was another case of keeping the black man down. But then the work resumed, more or less unhindered, and I prevailed upon Lina with some questions.

Asked about her experience in group thus far, she said that it was painful and helpful in equal measure. Barely a session went by that she didn't burst into tears, so badly did it hurt to discuss her marriage. There were things she hadn't even brought up there yet, like Anton's treatment of her daughter, Jorie, and his lies about Lina to their mutual friends. There was so much to tell, and never enough time in which to do so, because the others had to be heard from, too. And even if she had the whole session to herself, she *still* might leave things out—but then, that was what the one-on-ones were for.

"How often are you seeing Lathon, outside of group?" I asked.

"Oh, once a week, at least, and sometimes twice," she said. "It's ridiculously expensive, but I can't do without it. I've got a crisis with my son, who I think is doing drugs, and an insane amount of pressure dealing with Anton. Did you know, his latest stunt is, he wants to kick us out of the apartment? Wants to evict his own kids from the place they were born in, because he says it belongs to his father."

She said that, sixteen years ago, when Anton's parents gave them the co-op, it was clearly understood that the title would be forthcoming. The "sale" price was to be nominal, along the lines of a thousand dollars, and that only to satisfy state tax laws. The deed never appeared, though, and Lina thought it bad form to complain. After all, they were living debt-free on Park Avenue, in an apartment that, in the early going, was far beyond their means. Nonetheless, as she grew to love the place, it worried her to have no stake in it. She pleaded with Anton to ask his parents, and always, he'd promise to and then forget, or blow up at her for being greedy. At the time, she ascribed it to his fear of his father. Now, in hindsight, she saw it for what it was—a plan to deprive her of legal standing in her own home.

"What does your lawyer say?" I asked. "Surely, you have rights, too, no?"

"Well, it is their house, even though I haven't seen the deed, still—like everything else, he's withheld that. And as far as my lawyer goes, she thinks it's a bluff. Anton's way of trying to intimidate me before our hearing. After two and a half years, she thinks he's running out of tricks, and this is just a last, desperate ploy."

She scowled, but her voice trailed off uncertainly. She gazed at the stage with vacant eyes.

"But what do you think?" I asked. "Are you worried he'll make good on it?"

She drew a long breath and released it slowly, weighing out her answer to the quarter ounce. Now, as in group, I was struck by how careful she was, and what a high degree of seriousness she brought to bear.

"Look, I'm not a greedy person, and I don't want what isn't mine," she said. "I never asked for half his money, nor would I take it if it were offered. But when it comes to that apartment—I mean, that's where my *kids* were born. It's where all of their friends live, either in the building or down the block, and where all their happy memories are from. So, if I'm greedy about that, it's on their account; I want them to come out of this without their lives ruined. I told him he can have it back when they're off to college, but I'm not going to let him trash what's left of their childhood."

She said this loudly enough to prick up ears onstage. Hector, the boy who'd petitioned for a deejay, broke into a lovely smile.

"Yo, I hope they gonna film this, Miz Stavros," he crowed. "Because this show is gonna be the *joint!*"

Lina waved at him and sent down a smile, momentarily roused from care. When she turned to look at me, though, her eyes had hardened.

"He can hassle me all she wants, file every motion under the sun," she snapped. "But when he screws with my kids, that's when I get nasty. No one screws with my kids if I can help it."

fourteen

may

It wasn't friendship, exactly, since they didn't connect between meetings. Nor could you really call it intimacy, since it stopped and started every fortnight. But as the spring wore on and the sessions mounted, a bond built up among the members. You could hear it in their tone now, a kind of genial rhythm, and a companionable pleasure at being together. They looked forward to these two hours, eager to hear the changes in one another's stories, and to tell the latest progress in their own. More, they prized the tenor of the conversation, relishing its candor and resonance. They'd begun to sense the privilege of being among peers—the luxury of speaking a feeling without having to explain it, and of being accounted for without raising a hand.

One night, between sessions, Lathon and I met for a drink, and I remarked on this change in the air. He surprised me by being skeptical about it, saying it felt fluky to him. It was predicated less, he thought, on parity or kinship than on an unusual run of good luck. All six members were moving forward, making slow but steady progress. Lina's divorce case was being heard by a new judge, who was evidently more scrupulous than the last one. Dylan was keeping to the straight and narrow, and inching toward a settlement with his wife. Jack had landed a couple of regional commercials, which, if nothing else, would see him through the summer. Peter had all but made his engagement official, taking lunch hours off to find a ring.

These and other developments had spawned an air of false confidence, the notion that the big leap was just ahead. But life was rarely so accommodating for long, and undoubtedly had some shocks in store. And that, he said, would tell the tale of this group—how it functioned when the wheels fell off.

I was puzzled by his take, and told him so. I reminded him that my group, which was less polished and well matched, had hung together through all sorts of strife. The recovered memory of a childhood rape; the emotional blackmail by an addicted daughter—if anything, those trials had knit us tighter, made us something like family to one another. Lathon granted the point, saying that was how it went in most groups, but this one felt different to him. There was something missing, some thread or necessity that he couldn't quite put his finger on. By way of trying to change that, he was going to add some sessions, offer a complimentary meeting on the off-weeks. Given people's schedules, these might not draw a full house, but he thought it was worth a try. If nothing else, the members would see more of one another, and familiarity might put down roots.

Not surprisingly, the members welcomed the free sessions. They, too, sensed that something was lacking—a "flow, a feeling of momentum," said Rex. Dylan said that the process felt "shallow" at twice a month—that everyone was being "awfully polite" to one another, and on their best behavior. A little more frequency might knock people off that, and bring some "reality" into the room.

It wasn't quite clear what he meant by "reality," but Dylan certainly disposed of any excess politeness when he showed up drunk for the eleventh session. He was the last one to arrive, walking unsteadily past the circle and plopping into a chair by the window. Wearing a cracked grin and a soiled safari shirt, he leered at the other members. Though he couldn't have been drinking long—he'd been sober the week before—his eyes were bulging, and venous as old cue balls. His skin hung off him; his cheeks looked seared in their own juices. Watching the group watch him, I saw its energy sag, re-placed by a sullen fatigue.

"I'm pissed that Jack didn't show tonight," he said, to no one in particular. "I was really looking forward to what he'd have to say. Him being the big AA rabbi."

Jack had called in sick, stricken with acute colitis. Judging from the faces of the other members, it was clear there were those who en-vied him.

"What happened?" Lathon snapped. "I thought you were going to call me if you were about to pick up again."

"Yeah, well, I didn't have your number on me when I stopped off at Flashdancers." Dylan snickered. "Too bad, too, 'cause there was this dancer from Czechoslovakia who had the most perfect, little a—"

He pulled up short with a rueful smirk. "Oops, sorry, ladies. Forget I even said that. I wouldn't want you to hate me like my wife does."

The group sat back in acid silence, rankled by his snide self-pity. Sara, in particular, seemed shrift of patience, biting down hard on the stem of her Persols, and blowing hot air out her nose.

"I don't hate you at all," said Lina. "In fact, I understand com-pletely what you're going through. I just wish there was some way we could help you."

"There is a way to do that, and we've offered it freely," said Lathon. "He comes here, clean and sober, and tells us where it hurts. Beyond that, there's nothing we can do."

Lina held back a moment, surprised by Lathon's vehemence.

"Is there anything you could tell us about why this keeps hap-pening?" she asked. "Or, at least, why it happened this time?"

Dylan conferred a smile, as if indulging a small child. "I could tell you that, 'cause you're nice to me. I can't tell *him*, though"—he pointed at Lathon—" 'cause he's not nice to me. And plus, I don't like his suit."

Lathon glowered at him, then looked away. You could hear the bones scraping in his jawline.

"Was it something with your wife again—is that what started this?" asked Lina. "Or was it all the other stuff with work, and money, and trying to overcome your partner's . . . absence?"

Dylan fed her his snarky smile, but Lina looked back at him, inflexible in sympathy. Losing the staredown, Dylan made a crude joke, mocking her euphemism for Greg's death. But with all eyes on him, he began to quail, and soon enough, the words poured out.

"Yeah, I mean—*yeah*, it's about Jeannie, who I'm sick enough to *love* still, even though she hates my *guts*. I keep asking myself, what'd I do that was so awful, besides buy her the big house she always wanted? Was that where I fucked up, being too nice a guy to her, after her father beat the crap outta her for fun? Well, I'm sorry, but I couldn't do it, babe; I couldn't be a bastard, even though you ruined my life. We had this perfect—thing there, this perfect little unit, with the girls and—and the lap pool, and your fucking English garden, which God help us if it didn't rain on schedule. And you *threw* it out the window because of what? What for? Because I'm a *man*, and I remind you of your father, who I'm *not?* I am not your goddamn father, and I didn't fight in Korea, and I didn't knock you around when I got toasted. I'm me, I'm Dylan, and I have *nothing* in common with him, so *fuck you* for not having eyes in your head. . . ."

He went on awhile longer like this, letting the grievance discharge. And then at some point, it stopped and fatigue set in, and he talked about the pressure behind his eyes. It would start, he said, with thoughts of Jeannie, and soon the other things would follow. He'd remember life with Greg, who made all things possible, charging up the room with his Irish charm. He'd remember being with Harold, their agent and best friend—the three of them laughing and drinking at Jets games, or hopping in a limo at two A.M. and cruising to Atlantic City to play the tables. And then, as night follows day, he'd start thinking about money, and the whole, sick mess would begin swirling in his head, until the only thing he could think of was to *blow it out:* throw a case of beer down his throat. He didn't even care that it made everything more awful. All he cared about was making the pain stop. Make it stand in the corner for a while.

Lathon nodded, working the buttons on his blazer, trying, it seemed, to settle on a tone. "Dylan, you know, we hear that you're in a lot of pain, and we're very sorry about it; life has been bitterly unfair this last year. But I'm always here to talk to and grieve this with, and the group is here to talk to and grieve this with, and there's an AA meeting within blocks in any direction. And *that's* the way to resolve this pain—to tell it till it doesn't hurt so bad."

Dylan gazed at a cut on his ring finger, which had formed an igneous scab. "Yeah, well, like a lot of what you say, that sounds great at seven o'clock. But at three A.M., when you're lying wide awake in your dogshit, little, fleabag apartment—I'm sorry, but that just doesn't get it. What I need is something *real*, something to stop my mind from going, and let me finally get some rest—"

He paused, his eyes bulging, perhaps envisioning more wee-hours panic. "It also wouldn't hurt to have someone to talk to," he murmured. "Someone I could call if things got bad."

This was Sara's opening, and she took it. "But that's what they do at AA," she put in. "You find someone there and make them your sponsor—you can call them at any hour of the day or night. I mean, if that's what you need, some kind of round-the-clock support, why wouldn't you go there *immediately?*"

"You mean, instead of coming here and bothering you?" he sneered. "You know, I bet if I leave now, I can still make a seven-thirty meeting."

"You know that's not what I mean," she shot back. "I'm just saying, you're in crisis now, and group alone isn't enough—you need more than we can give you. And if I were you, I'd be there morning, noon, and night, going to as many meetings as it takes. I mean, even if you don't talk there, if you just go and listen, and be with people in the same sort of pain as—"

Dylan mocked her with a braying laugh. "Yeah, a roomful of people whose wives kicked 'em out, and—and their best friend died on them, and their agent has cancer, and they live in a rat hole where people go to *die*—"

"Or worse," said Lathon, cutting him off sternly. "There are people at those meetings who've lost everything they have, and are only there because it's a warm, dry room. I don't want to get into wound size, but trust me, there are people who can beat you. So let's not play that game."

But Dylan shook his head, relapsing into a sulk. "No, no, no, no, no," he gnashed, "I'm not going back to AA. I don't need their little whispering, and—and their asshole sanctimony. What I need is someone who can listen and keep their mouth shut—*'Ooh, didya hear, Dylan's drinking again?' 'What—no! He fucked up again? Wait'll his family finds out!'* Well, his family already knows, and they're *shocked*, I tell you. Shocked and mortified!"

After another tirade met with bitter silence, Dylan told the story of his slip. He and his wife had gone back to the arbitrator, where they'd laid out revised proposals. Though Jeannie's was actually reasonable, dropping claim to his retirement fund, there was something so dismally final about the meeting that Dylan went home and took to bed. There he lay, replaying scenes of their former life together, when suddenly he envisioned her in bed with her lover. Helplessly, he ran the loop over and over, imagining the woman who'd been so cruelly unavailable to him engaged in grunting sex. Weeping and furious, he ran riot through the house, throwing over bookcases and punching the walls, putting a fist-sized hole in his stereo speaker. At some point, he stormed downstairs with his car keys, ready to drive to Montclair and "settle things." Luckily—at least for Jeannie—he stopped off at a bodega, and sat for hours in his car, pounding Heinekens.

A couple of days later, having "drunk himself sober," he picked up the girls and drove them to his brother's on the shore. The occasion was his mother's seventieth birthday, and the whole family had turned out for the occasion. A pitcher of margaritas awaited them on the deck, and both the upstairs and downstairs fridges were lined with Guinness, while cases of reinforcements filled the garage. Temperance was never the word with his family, and when together, he said, it tended to double its intake. By dinnertime, such was the abundance of cheer that Dylan had fled to the basement. His mother, well along on her fourth Manhattan, had really put the screws to him for "driving that nice woman off." And Jim, whose house it was and to whom he was closest in the family, had somehow let it slip that he'd asked Jeannie and the girls to spend the Fourth of July weekend with him there.

" 'You know Alison and I love you, and that hasn't changed,' " said Dylan, unctuously quoting his brother. " 'But we love her, too, and don't want to lose that connection, just because you guys are splitting up.' "

"My God," said Lathon, "this family's right out of O'Neill. All they do is kick you when you're down."

"That's right," Dylan muttered, "and I'm an asshole for letting 'em. For some unknown reason, I thought it'd be different this time. That they'd rally around their own for once, instead of twisting the knife. But hey, they're the 'sober' ones and I'm the alky, so put it on me again. As usual."

Most of the members sat by, tongue-tied and dismal, shaking their heads in futility. But Sara, with her leg draped over an armrest, cut him a look of appraisal.

"You think maybe some of their hostility had to do with you showing up drunk?" she asked.

The others turned to Lathon, expecting him to intercede. Instead, he put his feet up on the ottoman, designating himself a spectator.

"What, are you my *wife* now?" said Dylan, glaring back at Sara. "That's just the kind of angle *she* would take: 'What did *you* do to get your ass kicked?' "

Sara shrugged, folding her arms like a breastplate. "Maybe she's right; maybe you do look for trouble. Like driving a hundred miles with all that alcohol in your bloodstream, and your two little girls in the car."

Again, the others stirred, uttering grunts of agreement. Planted on the sidelines, they turned now to Dylan, who looked around the circle accusingly.

"Hey, what *is* this?" he squawked, glaring at Lathon. "I show up and tell my story, and this one nails me for drunk driving. Is *that* what I'm paying for, this fucking twelve-step double-talk? Where's that 'serious healing' that you sold me?"

"I didn't sell you anything," said Lathon, coolly. "I made you an invitation, and you accepted it. And that, beyond the listening, is all we can do here: make you invitations to respect yourself. There are plenty of invitations to *insult* yourself—have a beer; go to a strip joint; let 'em rub salt in your wounds. Those places are in *business* to fleece lonely men. In fact, if they were smart, they'd open up right next to Divorce Court. They'd make more money than Disney."

Dylan was slouched into the well of his chair, morosely studying his knuckles. "Yeah, well, you can say what you want, but at least they listen to me there. This Czechoslovakian girl, she might not've known much English, but she understood what I was talking about. She started stroking my neck. I'll tell you, man, it felt so good, I almost broke down and cried. To just be *touched* again like that, to have someone being *nice* to me—I can't even say how long it's been."

Lina shook her head in heartsick circles. Sara sent a glare in Lathon's direction, as if to blame him for this sad spectacle. Peter sat forward in an odd half crouch, poised, it seemed, to rise and render aid. Only Rex gave an air of being unimpassioned, modeling his stubble with two fingers.

"I'm kind of curious about something," he said. "Was this happening at the club, or did you take her back to your place?"

"Both," said Dylan, "but it started at the club. You know, they're not supposed to touch you there—in fact, they can get in big trouble for it. But she took me in the back, where they have these private rooms, and cuddled with me and talked for four hours."

"Right," said Rex, with his studied cool. "It's just that I've spent a lot of time in that particular club, especially in those places in the back. They're called Fantasy Rooms, you know, and they cost three hundred an hour, not counting tax and tip. So, figuring on four hours, plus whatever you tipped her, her 'niceness' probably ran you fifteen hundred."

"What!" cried Lina. "You spent fifteen hundred dollars! But how could you *do* that when you're not even working, and have a wife and kids to take care of?"

Dylan grinned forlornly, as if such things were beyond knowing. But Lina stared back at him, her mouth hanging open, badgering him for an answer.

"Actually, it's pretty easy," said Rex. "What happens is, the girl's all over you for three songs, then tells you how bad she wants to be with you. And you, meanwhile, have had massive quantities to drink, and are in the worst possible shape to make important business decisions. But she's breathing in your ear and having orgasms just thinking about it, and you're all, 'Damn, I think she *likes* me, I can't hurt her feelings.' And so, back you go with the 'free' bottle of champagne, which is actually six-dollar horse piss that even the homeless wouldn't drink. And it's dark in the room, and the couch is big enough to lie down on, and things start happening that maybe weren't happening outside, but the real deal, the main event, never comes off, and—"

"Uh, thanks, Rex, that'll do; I think we got the point," said Lathon. "What you're describing here is the mother of suffering invitations: the love and understanding of a gorgeous stranger. She rubs the back of your neck, finds you handsome and brilliant, and wants you to the exclusion of all others. She's the genie in the lamp, the check from Publishers Clearing House—she solves all your problems, and any others that might come up. That's the great lure of the suffering invitation: *the promise of a pain-free future.* 'If only I had X, then Y would go away.' Only, instead of going away, Y comes back with a vengeance—in this case, the credit card bill from hell."

Dylan looked down as if perusing said bill. There were tears in his eyes and a dead exhaustion, as if he were a man lost at sea and letting the wind steer.

"I've spent twelve thousand bucks in the last ten days," he murmured. "That's money I had put away for my retirement."

This last roused the group into a storm of umbrage. Lina demanded he call his accountant and block the charges. Sara, who found the whole business deplorable, insisted that he go home and cut up all his credit cards, including those from Sears and Texaco.

"Well, wait a second, let's hold off on the card-cutting," said Lathon. "These are wartime conditions, and we treat the chest wounds first, and send the toothaches and trenchfoot down the line."

Dylan stared out the window, as if watching his Keogh fund float by. "Well, but what the hell do I *do* now?"

"What do you do?" said Lathon. "Well, you stop living like a fugitive, and accept the honest pain of being human. Which means that, instead of going to strip clubs, you come here twice a week, and we thrash this whole thing out until it's tolerable. And instead of numbing out with a case of beer, you take a course of Paxil or Effexor. But, above all, it means that you cut the denial and get yourself to AA. You're an active alcoholic, and they treat that there. We're not set up to do that."

Dylan pondered this prescription gloomily. "And if I don't do that? If I ride this out with just the occasional beer, to medicate myself till the divorce?"

Lathon flipped his notepad shut. "Then you'll probably die. Or lose custody of your kids, or hit someone else's in a crosswalk. That would make us very sad, but, hey, it's your story. All we can do is invite you not to."

Dylan hung his head, morosely weighing the options. With his eyes cast down and jaw clamped shut, he looked like someone choosing between the noose and lethal injection.

"Ah, fuck it, what the hell, I'll try a meeting," he said, sighing. "I wouldn't *dream* of disappointing my fans here."

fifteen
june/july

No one was was very surprised, though, when Dylan missed the twelfth session, and declined to phone in with his whereabouts. Weeks went by without word from him, and attempts to reach him at home raised only his shrill recording ("Oh, *hi*, everybody! No one home but us *machines!*") Concerned at first, the others soon grew resentful, and after a month or so began to write him off. They no longer asked Lathon if he'd heard from Dylan, or if he would be welcomed back whenever he got sober. The whole thing was just so nauseating, said Lina; sad, and such a waste. How could he turn his back on his daughters?

Dylan's absence might have caused more turmoil had there not been a greater diversion: summer. The week after Memorial Day, the group's attention flagged, as several members pursued their private agendas. Jack landed a plum role in summer stock, and took off for the Berkshires clear through Labor Day. Rex launched a boutique trading firm with three partners, and began to trot the globe in search of clients. And Sara went on a series of tense vacations, burning up the wires from Bordeaux and Lisbon to her beleaguered assistants at work.

But while the others breezed in and out during the summer, Lina and Peter were faithfully on hand, and got a handsome return on their labor. Of the various ways of measuring that progress, none was more dramatic than their change in aspect. Lina seemed to get

195

younger by the week as the grimace of fixed oppression peeled away. She put on ten pounds, shed her mortuary colors, and began showing up in pastel skirt suits, looking like Jackie Onassis on Ari's elbow. What you saw more and more as the summer wore on was a quality of maidenly freshness, as if she'd somehow channeled herself at nineteen, the girl as yet unspoiled by Anton's insults. In fact, one of the assorted men who suddenly came calling remarked that she looked like a "virgin." But I'm getting ahead of myself.

As for Peter, the man in the gray flannel suit box, the changes were subtler than tailoring. To be sure, he surprised everyone with his crisp new dress shirts, and had the group in a near-swoon once with a taupe double-breasted. But what held their attention and enlisted respect was a shift in his bearing and energy. Where once he was all but invisible in session, now he emerged as a voice of rigor. He told Rex off for his no-show frivolity, and pressed Lathon to fish or cut bait on Dylan. He stopped sweating profusely and let his hair down in group, exhibiting a certain street sense and a sly, *menschkeit* wit.

But the thing you were most struck by, as the summer progressed, was the force of his emerging ambition. Like a green second lieutenant who had just won his first firefight, he seemed to grow into his own authority suddenly; to take charge of the atoms around him. It was stirring to watch, as theatrical in its way as a birth, or a revolution—Peter's life taking wing on the strength of the idea that he, too, was entitled to be happy.

For months, the group had been urging him to stop worrying about what other people thought. Jack, in particular, had pressed the point, calling him a fool for staying on at his current job out of concern for his bosses' feelings. "You really think they care about you there?" he harrumphed. "You think they're losing sleep over *your* morale? Go out and get a job that you really want, then tell 'em all to shove it with a pitchfork!" So, too, with Peter's fears about proposing to his girlfriend without first consulting his mother. "Oh man, screw *her*," said Rex with his usual tact. "If she doesn't want you marrying the girl of your dreams, go buy yourself a new mom with Kara's money."

And then, one stifling night in June, Peter came in with a brimming smile and announced that he'd gotten officially engaged. "All these months of thinking, why *me;* what could Kara possibly see in me? But it finally dawned on me—why *not* me, goddamnit? Why *shouldn't* I be entitled to someone nice? And plus, I got tired of her constantly bugging me about it. We'd be sitting on the sofa, eating take-out or watching *Seinfeld,* and she'd look at me with this smile and say, 'How'm I doing, Peter? You like living here all right? The cuisine up to your high standards?' And I thought, damn, you know, I better get a move on here. This offer may not last much longer."

The group poured out its congratulations, though the news by now was a foregone conclusion. Even Sara, for whom every wedding was a rebuke, showered him with smiles and questions. Where were they getting married? Had they picked out a dress yet? Oh, this was all just *so* romantic!

Peter laughed it off in his embarrassed way, saying it was the first time that his name had come up in connection with the word *romantic.* Shyly, he suffered the group's thirst for details, explaining that he'd popped the question at Ellen's Stardust Diner. He and Kara were having cheeseburgers and chocolate malteds when a doo-wop group came over, serenading them with "The Chapel of Love." Peter produced a jewel box containing a deep-fried onion ring, and slipped it on Kara's finger. "I love you a lot," he said, "but this was all I could afford now. Will you take me for richer or poorer?"

"Oh!" cried Sara, "that is such a great proposal. I would *kill* to have a man go to that much trouble for me. I wouldn't even care if he was gay."

Lathon laughed, saying it could be arranged. "For starters, you can run your own ad in *New York* magazine. In fact, we'll help you draft it."

Sara shuddered, raking a hand through her hair. It wasn't the first time that the idea had been pitched to her, nor the only such suggestion from Lathon. He'd been urging her for months now to call her father, or, failing that, to sit down and write him a letter, spelling out the terms of her resentment. It needn't be mailed, merely brought in and shown, as a means of sawing through her thick inertia. But Sara would nod yes and then promptly forget, or come in and say she'd tried to but couldn't go through with it; the very effort made her violently ill.

"I was talking it over with my girlfriends," she said now, regarding the singles ad, "and we all agreed that the personals aren't my style. A couple of them did it, you know, as a goof last year, and the letters they got back were pretty appalling. One guy wrote that he was a Knights of the Round Table buff, and sent a picture of himself in full mail armor. Another one was crazy about shoveling snow; said there was nothing quite as satisfying as digging out your driveway. I mean, I'm sure most of these guys are sweet and well meaning, but I'm probably a little too jaded for them."

"You mean, for men like me," said Peter.

"Um, well, no," said Sara, brought up short. "It—it's just that I'm very critical, you know, and hard to please, whereas—"

"Whereas Kara would obviously take all comers," he snapped.

"N-no, that's *not* what I meant," she said, the panic edging in. "Look, this isn't about you, Peter, it's about *me* and *my* problems; my fear of making a fool out of myself, and—and—"

"Actually, you're wrong," said Lathon. "It's about both of you, and two people at the same impasse. In a lot of ways, you know, you had mirror childhoods—Peter, with the dominant, critical mother and the emotionally crippled father, and you with the dominant, critical father and the emotionally crippled mother. Both of you grew up so stung by the opposite parent that you withdrew from the company of their sex—Peter into an empty, joyless marriage, and Sara into long stretches of manlessness. And as you've both discovered, it gets lonely on your little island, and depressing taking yourself out to dinner on Saturday night. And so, after years of isolation, Peter said the hell with it, already; I'm willing to risk a little humiliation for the chance to get off this rock. Whereas you sit by, Sara, reapplying your lipstick, waiting for a handsome sailor to come find you."

Mangling a coffee stirrer between her fingers, Sara bristled in frustration. "But I *am* trying to meet people, I go to parties all the time. And whether you believe me or not, at least ninety percent of the men are either married or gay. Or both."

Lathon looked at her, not quite stifling a smile. "I repeat, Sara: there *are* no romantic rescues at sea, except in really bad Kevin Costner movies. All there are are people like us, poking around in the dark with our lousy flashlights, trying to find a person to make some history with. Peter did it, but it took guts on his part: the courage to defy his mother's rules. *Oh, we're McKeons, we don't go in for that sort of thing.* Well, Peter did, and we urge you to do the same, by throwing the family's rules out the window."

The talk came back to Peter's engagement. Kara's parents were thrilled by the news, and sent a huge bouquet the next morning. Peter's father was also delighted, suggesting a prompt meeting of the families. As expected, though, his mother was a different story. When told of the engagement, she muttered something perfunctory, then handed over the phone to her husband. For Peter, this created a scrim of dead air on which to screen his ready self-doubts. Immediately, he wondered if there was some flaw in Kara that his mother saw and he didn't. After all, she'd seen through his first wife, Amanda, after an acquaintance of twenty minutes. Now, her silence had Peter in a lather. He'd been waking up soaked from dreams each night, even with the air conditioner going. In one dream, he was fleeing an ax fiend and tried stashing himself in a mailbox. His hips, however, wouldn't fit through the slot and he was trapped like Pooh Bear, with his rump out. In another, his assailant was a dwarf with a crossbow, raining arrows at his ankles as he jogged the FDR Drive.

"And then, last night, Kara and I went ring shopping," he said, "and something really . . . weird came over me. We were at this place in the diamond district, looking at rings from the twenties—Art Deco stuff that Kara loves, and which, by the way, was very afford- able—and suddenly I went into this, like, mini tailspin, sweating and feeling faint, and having all these bad memories."

"What of?" asked Lathon, squinting in attention.

"Well, of my first wedding, mostly—it was like I was back at the hall again, with all eighty of Amanda's guests, and all six or seven of mine. I—I mean, it was just so . . . vivid to me, how nauseous I was, and what a fiasco the whole day was. There was the fight that broke out between her and my uncle Hubert, who's seventy-something years old and tried to stick his tongue down her throat; and this big mix-up with the cake, which was supposed to have been hazelnut, but which was loaded down with rum and had all her little nieces throwing up.

"And, meanwhile, as I'm standing there, remembering all this stuff, suddenly it was like she was *there*, in the store, with us. Maybe it was the air-conditioning, but I suddenly started to shiver, think- ing, Christ, what a putz I am. I mean, I hit this million-to-one shot— find a wonderful, sexy woman—and I'm dragging her to a discount jeweler, for Christ's sake. And I could hear Amanda over my shoul- der, saying, 'Boy, this gal must be *desperate;* look what she's cutting herself in for!'"

Rex, doing the interview, followed up on this point, and learned that Peter was anguished about money. As Kara had large holdings, her lawyers drafted a prenuptial agreement, which set out the terms of their finances. Peter was stunned, if a little uneasy, about the large sum Kara offered to fund their account. What galled him was seeing, in triplicate form, how little *he* was expected to contribute. It was a mere fraction of their overhead, just enough to cover the food bill, and it left him feeling queasy with shame.

The others picked up there, inquiring about this feeling, when

Lathon headed them off. What *he* had been hearing was a different kind of shame, one that had nothing to do with money. Peter had alluded to it earlier, describing the debacle of his first wedding. What humiliated him was less the comedy of errors than that *it occurred in front of his family.* There were "six or seven" McKeons there, not to mention all the ghosts—that mighty pageant of the undead and undivorced who dropped in for a laugh. They played grab-ass with the bride and spiked the wedding cake, too, having a high old time at Peter's expense. *That* was the wound here, the basis of his "romance PTSD"—the experience of being humiliated before his clan.

"Now, the question I see forming on Peter's lips," he went on, "is, How can I prevent *future* outbreaks of romance trauma? The answer is, you do two things, the first of which you just did. You tell us how painful it was to be embarrassed like that, and let us draw the sting out with our listening. The second is to take possession of a new idea, which is that now that you're engaged to Kara, your family's opinion is worth zero. Not less than before, or approximately the same, but zip, zero, nada. Only two views count now, yours and Kara's, and any dissenters are to be ignored. You can't stop your mother from running her beauty contests. What you can do is tell her to keep the results to herself, and to respect your feelings for your wife. Because, whether she likes it or not, you're launched on your own story now, and your only duty is to the principals of that story. Parents not included."

Peter said nothing but his eyes grew wide, as if to encompass this larger understanding. He withdrew a bit at the next session, speaking briefly about his job search, and about an upcoming dinner for the two families. The following week, though, he showed up in a new suit and declared that he'd put his foot down with his mother. She had been keeping her own counsel about the bride-to-be, but had a lot to say about the wedding plans, particularly "her" half of the guest list. This time she wanted to invite the whole clan, including relations from Wales and Scotland. Peter seethed; he and Kara had their hearts set on a small affair on Block Island. Instead of submitting, though, he read her the riot act, telling her that this was *their* day and they'd do as they damn well pleased.

"The line went dead for, like, fifteen seconds—I was afraid she'd passed out, or dropped the phone," he said. "Then I think, 'Great, now I've done it, here comes the counterpunch'!—But instead, she backed off and was actually nice about it, saying that she understood and that she respected our wishes. At which point, it was *me* who almost dropped the phone. I mean, all my life, I've been afraid to get angry at people, like there was this—unspoken threat that the sky would crack open and strike me dead if I did. And I think of my father, who was afraid of it, too, and who just sat there and said nothing while the world screwed him over. I mean, what's so terrible about speaking your mind, about saying, 'Hey, look at me—I've got ambitions, too.' And she, of course, protected him. Said, 'Oh, we mustn't upset your father; it would *kill* him if he knew about the joint in your pocket.'"

Suddenly, Peter was spitting the words, aloft on a jetstream of rage. The others stared as if he were inhabited by spirits, so unused were they to this tone from him. Even Lathon did a double take, jerking his head back, like a horse that had spotted a rattler. "Wow," he said. "Where did that-all come from?"

Peter balled his fists, glaring like a hockey goon. "I'm just tired, that's all," he spat. "Tired of all the bootlickers who take credit for work they didn't do. And I'm tired of being treated like a faithful dog, waiting for the big men to throw me a bone. Like last week, the firm announced a golf trip to Maui, and guess who they picked to stay behind? 'Oh, but, Peter, you're indispensable, we need you to run the desk.' Yeah, *balls*, I'm indispensable. The reason I'm not going is because I don't sing karaoke, or—or whore around after work with the bosses—show 'em I'm a real man by stuffing fives in a stripper's garter!"

The room went silent for an awkward stretch. In the apartment above, you could feel, rather than hear, the restless thump of children running. Elsewhere, a door banged open and shut; life, and its quotidian vibrations.

"Actually," said Rex, in for one of his rare guest appearances, "a real man tips *twenties*, but who's counting?"

"That's right," sniffed Sara. "After all, you wrote the book on it: *The Real Man's Guide to Stripper Etiquette.*"

"Actually, you know, that's a good idea," said Rex. "I mean, I've already done the grueling legwork."

But Peter was unamused. "I've bent over backwards to make people happy—let Amanda have the bedroom while I slept on the couch; went in to the office on Saturdays to handle some of the overflow. And the upshot of that is that people played me, and laughed behind my back. 'Oh, *Peter'll* do it, he doesn't mind staying behind. He's the lonely Maytag repairman.' "

Another silence greeted this speech. In perfect stillness, the others watched Peter, reappraising him in light of his vehemence.

"Folks, what did you hear there, besides Peter's anger at his bosses?" asked Lathon.

"Well, I heard anger at himself, for letting people use him, which I can certainly relate to," said Lina. "And there was some anger at his father for being a doormat, but I had a thought on that. I think what he's more angry at him for is not showing him how to be a *man*. To stand up and tell people, 'Hey, enough, already; I want what's coming to me.' That is one of the things a father does, teach his son how to fight for himself."

"Yes, well, that's part of it," said Lathon. "Boys identify with their dads, and it hurts them to think their old man is a wimp. But that's shame, for the most part, and what we saw now was *bitterness*, which is anger turned to stone over a period of years. From what we know of his family, what offense do you think they did him that's being triggered by his frustration at work?"

"Um, well, we know that his folks favored his sister," said Rex.

"They always bragged on her, whereas with him, they didn't say much, which, obviously now, pissed him off. And I guess he feels like they're doing that at work. Playing favorites with other people."

"You're getting close," said Lathon. "What thing was denied him by both his bosses and parents, and which he's getting now in spades from Kara?"

The others glanced at each other, thoroughly baffled.

"In a word, it's *respect*," said Lathon, softly. "Peter's finally getting the respect he's been craving since boyhood, and which the world has so unjustly held out on. He wanted it from his mother, not for being a star like his sister, but for being a good, clean, hardworking kid. But sorry, that wasn't enough; Mom demanded a McKeon, someone they named a hospital for. He wanted it at work, where he wasn't asking for a corner office—just some acknowledgment for a job well done. But it seems that they only promote sycophants there; all candidates with dignity apply elsewhere. More than infuriating, it's corrosive; it eats at who you are. You start to think, well, being myself isn't working—I have to do something else. Get a nose job or dye my hair, go try on identities, until I find one that plays to the room."

Peter, who'd colored at the word *respect*, gave a puzzled look. "But I thought we agreed that I didn't do that; that part of what's held me back is I can't play politics."

"No, but nor do you act on your wishes," said Lathon. "Instead of making your own story, you become a character in theirs, killing yourself to make people happy. To please your mom, you stayed married to a woman you loathed, and hung around in a job to suit your bosses. If there's a running theme here, it's that you defer to others, give their needs precedence over yours. Which is fine if that's your temperament; if you're born to be a butler. But as we heard tonight, that's not who you are. Who you are is someone with the need and will to make your mark in the world."

"But could we just cut the Lathon-speak for half a second and talk about the mechanics?" said Sara. "What I want to know, in plain, simple English, is how he gets from here to there."

Lathon smiled at her, closing his notepad.

"The same way you will, when you get tired of being alone," he said. "You go out into the world and you ask for it."

But Peter wasn't the only one troubled by dreams. At the start of the twelfth session, Lina put her hand up exhaustedly and said she was sleepless from a recurring nightmare. In it, she was driving across the Queensboro Bridge when she stopped, got out, and climbed a girder. Standing on the cable, she looked down and felt the piers shake. The wind picked up, shimmying the bridge in sections. Clinging to her perch, she saw the waves yawn beneath her, and woke up, moaning, with the sheets tangled.

"It's miserable," she groaned, "I can't function like this—I'm out on my feet all day. Four in the morning I'm wide awake, and I just lie there, shaking, till seven."

Lathon condoled with her about the lack of sleep, saying it was the last thing she needed these days. But before offering his thoughts, he wanted to hear a little of what was going on at home—specifically with regard to her children.

"Eh, well, that's been a nightmare, too," Lina sighed. "There was a period of a couple of months where I thought things were better. My son, Todd, who was great until his dad walked out . . . well, I hoped we had turned a corner there. He was buckling down to work after a rough semester, when he was cutting class to be with kids who drank beer and sold drugs. He'd started being more responsible around the house, and was getting along better with his sister, Jorie, who he'd been tormenting since before the separation. But then, last month, when Anton threatened to evict us, the bad stuff started all over again. Todd stayed out one night till five in the morning, going to some 'rave,' I guess they call it. He got into a fight with

Jorie in which he was literally throwing *punches*—I had to jump in and pull him off her. And then, last Thursday, when I went in to wake him for school, I saw this bag of pills on his dresser. I asked him what they were and he got real nervous, saying they were herbal supplements to build muscle. Well, it's true he's into bodybuilding and has started to get bigger, and so the first thing I thought of was steroids. And I snatched them up and said I was going to get them analyzed, at which point he leapt out of bed and started screaming in my face, saying I'd never make it as far as the door. But instead of backing down to him—he's six-foot-one suddenly, if you can believe it—I stood there and yelled back at him, saying I wasn't having this in my house. I said, if you want to take steroids, you can go live with your father, or his parents in Westport, Connecticut. And after a while, he broke down and told me what they were—said they were Ecstasy and some other drug that he was holding for his friend Darren. And I know the kid he's talking about, and boy, do I dislike him. He's one of these little rich boys who thinks he's a gangster and acts like he's fresh out of Sing Sing. I told Todd, 'I want those given back to him and the friendship ended, or you'll find your things in the hall.' And, of course, he just laughed at me, and said, 'Ooh, I'm so afraid, Ma.' But he wasn't laughing the next day, when he came home after school and found his stuff by the door. I had taken the day off and was waiting for him in the living room. I told him, Look, I know you're unhappy about the divorce, but this is not the way to show me."

"Hey, good for you," said Sara, pumping her fist for emphasis. "That's exactly the way I would've done it."

"Yeah, I'm totally behind you," said Peter. "When it comes to things like drugs, you can't be too tough."

"And how'd he respond when he saw you meant business?" asked Rex.

Lina sighed, looking utterly spent, her eyes sunk deep in their sockets. "Well, we fought again,—a real knock-down-drag-out, with him hulking over me shaking his fist. But I managed to stand my ground, though I admit I was scared; he's got a temper like his father, and then some. After more screaming and name-calling, though, he finally broke down—said that everything was going wrong for him since his dad left. And I cried, too, and told him I loved him with all my heart, and that I was trying to be strong for the three of us. I said, I know this has been horrible, but we *will* get through it. We just need to stick together, and support each other."

In the week since the fight, there had been some hopeful signs. Todd had returned the pills to his friend, and—so far as Lina could tell—broken it off with him. He had also agreed to come in and see Lathon about his feelings around the divorce. Toward his sister, however, he remained a tease and a bully. He ragged her about her height, a current sore spot of Jorie's after a growth spurt left her towering over her classmates. He cranked up his stereo when she was trying to study, pointing his speakers at the wall between their rooms. And he never missed a chance to slip her an elbow, or hip-check her as they passed in the hallway. In so doing, he was largely aping his father, whose treatment of Jorie was flippant and cruel. When she was a toddler, he called her names like "Flagpole," because of her stringy frame. Years later, as she filled out, becoming lean and graceful, he shifted his line of attack. Now, she was a "dummy," "the blonde in the woodpile," "Little Miss Malaprop." Todd adopted his jeering tone, and the two of them often had her in tears.

"I take the blame for that," said Lina. "I should've put a stop to it years ago. I mean, yes, I stuck up for her, but then he'd do it behind my back, and when I confronted him, he'd tell me she was exaggerating. Now I'm seeing the results of not taking a stand: I've got a son who talks to women like his father does."

This pained Lina greatly, and she was trying to correct it. She chewed Todd out every time he baited his sister, telling him that real men never stoop to boorish insults. And she went to great lengths to boost Jorie's confidence, attending all her soccer and basketball games, and taking every chance to say how proud she was. Evidently, it was paying off, because Jorie was beginning to bloom. After years of shyness, she was asserting herself in class, such that one teacher remarked that she was like a "grad student in braces." She'd branched out socially, making friends with some of her teammates, and was spending less time roaming chat rooms on the Net. Where Todd had been thrown for a loop by his father's absence, Jorie seemed to be thriving. No longer did she have to skulk in her room, ducking Anton's sarcasm.

Peter broke in with praise for Lina, but she promptly cut him off. She still hadn't gotten to the biggest problem, which was that, at long last, she was broke. Anton was two months late with the child support, saying that he wouldn't send it until she vacated the apartment. Nor had he paid the past due maintenance, and a notice had appeared in her mailbox Friday, threatening action by the co-op board. She was down to practically nothing in her checking account, and had maxed out all her credit cards. In fact, when she tried to pay for her groceries this week, the cashier informed her that her account had been canceled.

"My God, what a bastard he is, to take food out of his kids' mouths," Peter fumed. "But I don't understand something—why didn't you tell us this before? I mean, I knew things were tight, what with the legal bills and all. But I had no idea it'd gotten this bad."

Lina looked dismally at her hands in her lap. "To tell you the truth, I . . . I didn't either. I mean, I assumed he was bluffing, and that, at some point, he'd pay me; after all, you know, they're his kids, too. But I see now what a fool I am, how naïve and trusting still. It's like there's a part of me that can't admit how vile he is; I keep thinking, 'But wait a minute, this is a man that I used to *love* very deeply, and who I looked up to, and respected, and—and raised two kids with—"

"And who—truth be told—you're still afraid of," said Lathon.

Lina's gaze returned to her lap. "Yeah, I am," she said. "In fact, terrified; he's capable of just about anything."

"Like what?" asked Sara. "What are you afraid he'll do?"

Lina exhaled, blowing her bangs out of her eyes. "Well, nothing physical; he's too much of a mama's boy for that. But believe me, this is someone who'd stoop to any level to beat me down in court. Last night, he called at eleven o'clock and just screamed abuse over the phone. 'You're a thief, you're a liar, you have no character—' "

"Wait a minute, hold on," said Peter, beetling his brow. "You're locked in this bitter fight, where he's trying to starve you into submission, and yet you're still taking his calls at all hours of the night? Why're you even talking to him, let alone fielding abuse—isn't that what you're paying a lawyer for?"

Lina blinked at him, as if the idea of resistance was foreign to her. "Well, but what do I do? He's got kids in that house. I can't just block him out with caller ID."

"No, but you can hand him over when he calls for them, and hang up the rest of the time. It's like you're trying to appease him, to 'yes' him into a deal, in hopes that he'll see reason and call a truce. But I *know* these kinds of guys, I deal with 'em in business, and I can tell you that they don't quit until they've cut your head off."

Lathon nodded, bestowing approval; among the group, it was well settled that Peter and Lina were his pets. They faithfully did their homework, used the buzzwords with confidence, and were demonstrably getting better every session. This reflected well on Lathon, but less so on the other members, and a few of them, like Rex, resented their progress. Over beers with me one night, he had said, apropos of Peter, "Why doesn't he just change his name to Poindexter already, and get it over with?"

"Sara," said Lathon, "you look like you wanted to weigh in."

"Yeah, well, I wanted to say that I know those guys, too—one of them, in fact, is my father," she said. "And it just seems to me that you're being awfully nice to this creep, when what you really want is to cut *his* head off. If it's war he wants, then give him war; don't even let him speak to his kids until he sends you a check. And if he calls again at night, hang up and change your number. Let him know, like you let your son know, that the rules have changed, and that you aren't going to sit around and take his crap."

"Oh God, if only it were that simple," said Lina, rolling her eyes. "What I wouldn't give for some of your toughness."

"Yeah, well, you can have it," said Sara. "I'm letting it go for cheap. In fact, I'm having a garage sale on toughness this Sunday."

The others laughed at this, as did Lathon, who said that a lot of men would be glad to hear it. As for Lina, it didn't take a degree from Princeton to decipher her dream, he said. Her house was caving in, under pressure from Anton, with all his wind and bluster. Even the escape route was blocked—the bridge to her new life knocked down—by the gale-force strength of his tantrums.

"And understand, Lina: tantrums is exactly the word for it," he said. "Anton isn't Godzilla; he's just a loud, tiresome brat who always got his way as a kid. Only in *your* mind has he ever had any stature—first, as the dashing prince in college, then later, as the bully over dinner. But those are just projections, an old fairy-tale fantasy in which he's either come to save you or kill you. We all do these projections—they're a holdover from childhood—but in your case, you take them literally. You think of Anton as a force of nature, when what he really is is a putz. How many forces of nature, after all, hire their mothers to clean their toilets?"

Lina laughed her desolate laugh. "It's funny you should say that, because I just saw her last week, and she looked like one of those horses who'd been worked too hard."

Turning to the others, she said, "I don't know if I said this, but Anton's mother cleans his office. At sixty-eight years old, she's down on her hands and knees, scrubbing his stupid bathroom. And mind you, her husband's worth twenty, thirty million, but she goes around like a bag lady."

"But of course she does," said Lathon. "In that family, the women all are slaves and the men are little sun kings. Just look at the way Anton treats his kids: Todd, the boy, gets whatever he wants, while Jorie gets called *stupid* and *Dumbo*. It's an old, old story—or I should say, an Old World story—but whatever you want to call it, it's their story. Your story, on the other hand, is about dignity and independence, and it's time you unhitched these two stories. So stop taking his phone calls, be it ten at night or ten in the morning. Stop letting him push you around about money—your lawyer can get you a hearing next week, on an emergency basis. And *start* being the tough broad you are with other people. I mean, you run a crisis center in the *South Bronx*, for God's sake. If Anton ever ventured above Ninetieth and Park, they'd have to send a SWAT team to save him."

Lina received this counsel with a wan smile, and went home looking done in. It was much the same the following week, when she recounted a meeting with Anton and the lawyers that dissolved into a shouting match. But for the fourteenth session, she showed up tan and elegant in a lilac power suit. Her hair was done smartly in a chin-length bob, taking away from the length of her face. She had on pearl earrings and a modest gold necklace, and, for the first time, was wearing full makeup.

The others, consisting only of Sara and Peter, showered her with compliments. Sara made much of her "swinging new 'do," which took ten years off her, she said. And Peter asked Lina if she'd been working out, saying that she looked "stronger, somehow, almost chiseled."

Lina laughed, a little fazed by the attention. Yes, she had been working out, although no one had noticed until she gained back some of the weight she'd lost. As for her new look, well, it was mostly the lawyer's idea. She had finally gotten a hearing in front of the new judge, and was polishing up her image for court.

"Well, I like it," said Sara. "It's totally you. You look like a strong, sexy woman—which you are."

Lina laughed again, blushing to her breastbone. "Well, I don't know if I would go *that* far."

"No, it's true," said Peter. "I started noticing it last week. It's like you're more—vital suddenly, more confident in your actions. You can see it in how you're sitting; you're not clenched as much. Not tied up like a pretzel."

"Really?" said Lina, checking herself out. "Well, it's good that at least my posture's improving!"

She laughed for the fifth time in as many minutes. "Actually, I *am* in a better mood, since we got this new judge. He's totally no-nonsense, and doesn't put up with any stalling. Anton tried for a postponement already, but the judge said no way. He said this has dragged on long enough as it is."

"Ah, well, finally—a judge with some common sense," said Sara. "When is the hearing scheduled?"

"Next Monday," said Lina. "It should be pretty cut-and-dry. Anton's clearly in default on his payments. At any rate, that's the good news, or the potentially good news. The bad news is, I just found out over the weekend that Anton raided a joint account that we had frozen. It was money we'd made from the sale of some property, and since we couldn't agree on how to split it up, we were going to let the court decide."

"How much did he take?" Peter asked.

"A lot," said Lina. "About eighty thousand. I—I thought it was sealed, and that neither of us could touch it, but obviously there was a way around it. And, of course, I called my lawyer, and she filed a complaint, and said this would kill his chances when we go to court. But meanwhile, who knows if I'll ever see that money again—it's probably buried in some account offshore. And the moral of the story is, I feel like a jerk. Like a passive, trusting dope who never learns."

Peter and Sara shook their heads, as if to retract their earlier praise. No one spoke for several moments, a tacit censure of Lina's naïveté. Finally, Lathon sat up and cleared his throat.

"You know, on any other night, Lina, I'd have jumped right in and corrected what you said. I mean, obviously, you're not a dope who doesn't learn from experience; you've come as far as anyone in here. But tonight, I wanted you to stay with the shame, the pain of being suckered again by Anton. Because while it takes guts to fight a bully, sometimes it also takes being embarrassed—the pain and rage at being violated. I want you to savor that feeling, Lina, really steep yourself in it, so that it's fresh and clear in your mind. When you walk into court, this feeling will make you stronger. Trust me, there's nothing like a little righteous indignation when you're marching into battle."

Lina's day in court was actually a pretrial hearing, called to settle the arrears in child support. She showed up bright and early in a dove-gray suit, minus the pearls and mascara of the previous session. Anton and his lawyer, however, were a full hour late, causing the case to be bumped to the end of the line. Anton was a tall, florid man who walked bent forward, as if he were entering turbulent airspace. He had a high, burnished forehead and commanding eyebrows, and seemed to glow the way some men of substantial means do. What he lacked, however, was a certain quality of judgment, as he was dressed, essentially, for a day at Hialeah. He wore a white linen suit over a beige silk sport shirt that was unbuttoned to expose his pumped-up chest. On his feet were a pair of two-tone Ballys that were the envy of all the fourth-floor security guards. And in the event that you still hadn't noticed him somehow, he had topped things off with an actual boutonniere. All told, it was a getup that would have raised eyebrows in *Vice Court*, to say nothing of the stares it drew here.

Seated across the hall from him, Lina gaped over her newspaper. "What the hell—is he on drugs?" she whispered. "He looks like he's here to teach the Hustle."

"Amazing," her lawyer murmured. "Wait'll the judge gets a load of this. He'll be lucky to walk out with a dime."

The wait grew to hours, and Lina and I walked downstairs to stretch our legs. At a newsstand, looking for something nutritive among the chips and year-old "health" snacks, Lina remarked, apropos of nothing, "God, you know, it's just so disappointing."

Mistaking her meaning, I said, "Yeah, it really shoots the day, having to wait around like this."

"I'm talking about Anton, and how ridiculous he is," she snapped. "I mean, all these years of living under his shadow, and he turns out to be some guy in a—a pimp suit."

"I imagine, though, that must make this easier for you."

Starting away from the counter, Lina received this without comment. "Could he have always been this ludicrous, and I not seen it?" she brooded. "Was I that deaf and blind that I missed that he was a clown, or did this just come over him recently? Oh, I'm just so furious at myself, to have wasted years on such a—a twit."

By midafternoon, our wait had become a vigil. Anton riffled the pages of *Esquire*, avoiding eye contact with his wife. His lawyer, however, to whom he bore a resemblance, stalked the halls angrily, working his cell phone. He had on a black double-breasted with chalk-dust pinstripes, and a tan that seemed to have been applied with paintstrokes. Even his bald spot was perfect, somewhere between burnt rose and bronze, a color rarely seen since Veronese. Barking into his portable, and jumping up and down out of his bench seat, he looked like one of those millionaires who coach basketball in Kentucky, making the conference finals on fear and Ritalin.

Finally, at three o'clock, our suffering ended. We were let into a room that smelled of trapped air, and whose heat was undisturbed by creaking fans. Sun poured in through the tall, dull windows, imparting a Southern tedium to the proceedings. The judge, a large man who seemed miserable under his robe, sorted through a sheaf of papers.

"I've been going through this file," he said, weighing its heft. "I see two and a half years of motions and countermotions, and changes of attorney, and so on. What I *don't* see is why this isn't settled."

"Your Honor, if I may," said Anton's lawyer, leaping up. "My client has tried repeatedly to negotiate with the plaintiff, but she keeps moving the goal line. We've made a number of fair offers, granting child- and spousal-support, but now she wants the deed to his parents' apartment. And even were it his to give—which, assuredly, it is *not*—they have no right to simply *expropriate* it without title. And then, to drag him down here on a false and fallacious complaint, when it is *she* who's in violation—that is a disgrace, and I won't—"

Lina's lawyer cut in, offering her version of the story. The judge, however, stopped her in midsentence.

"I agree, Mr. DaVola," said the judge to Anton's lawyer. "It's a disgrace for *any* of us to be here today, what with the air-conditioning not working. But help me understand something, if you can—what does the issue of the co-op apartment have to do with child support?"

Anton's lawyer, who'd just sat down, jumped to his feet again. "Your Honor, my client has made every reasonable attempt to secure that apartment for his parents. And when, after *months* of appeals, there was still no compliance, my client had no choice but to withhold payment. Moreover, the other side failed to return an important—"

Once more, the judge held his hand up for silence. "But doesn't Mr. Rizikh feel obliged to feed his children? To see that their tuition bills are paid?"

"Well, of course, he does, Your Honor. And he's perfectly willing to pay them, provided Ms. Stavros vacates the—"

The judge cut him off, saying that the apartment was not at issue. The purpose of today's hearing was to determine why the support money hadn't been paid—and thus far, no reason had been advanced. This sent Anton's lawyer into a fit of speechifying, enumerating a list of complaints. There was the matter of the summer house, which Ms. Stavros had "ruined and ravaged" by leaving the windows open during a rainstorm. There were a number of paintings, "important new works," that had not been turned over in due course. There was a "documented" effort on the part of the plaintiff to turn her daughter against his client, whose "parental overtures" had been rebuffed. Here and there, Lina's lawyer objected, endeavoring to set the facts straight. Each time she tried, though, Anton's lawyer cut her off, lecturing her in the sort of singsong cadence with which one addresses the mildly retarded.

Finally, having exhausted his list of grievances, Anton's lawyer sat down. Admonishing him to keep his seat, the judge called on Lina's lawyer. She reviewed the case tersely, establishing a pattern of "evasion." Anton's lawyer jumped up, decrying "this scurrilous slander," and demanded that she be slapped with sanctions. The judge, eyeing him balefully, ordered him down again. Lina's lawyer resumed, documenting her client's hardship. She produced a set of bank statements showing how Lina had been "bled," all but bankrupted by ruinous legal bills. She furnished copies of canceled checks, indicating the sums Lina had borrowed to keep her children in private school. Anton's lawyer objected, but the judge lost his temper, telling him to sit down and be quiet. It was at this point that Lina's lawyer played her hole card—a letter from an officer at the Republic National bank, certifying the raid on the joint account.

Adjusting his glasses, the judge studied the note, reading it twice for clarity. When he looked up, his eyes had narrowed to slits, hooded beneath fleshy lids.

"Oh, this is bad, Mr. Rizikh; very, very bad. I don't look kindly on midnight bank raids. I also don't look kindly on spouses who withhold payment, and then come in with some cock-and-bull story about an apartment. As of five o'clock tomorrow, I want a check in your wife's hands for the amount you owe in back child support. In addition, you're going to bring—not send, but *bring*—a check to the co-op's lawyer for arrears. Oh, and one more thing. If those funds from the marital account aren't restored by Friday, I will fine you in the amount of a thousand dollars a day. Please see my clerk before you leave."

Anton's lawyer leapt up, marshaling a complaint about fairness, but the judge, baring his teeth, threatened expulsion. Anton, meanwhile, sat stunned at his table, his head propped up on a fist. Out of the corner of his eye, he was staring at Lina with what I at first mistook for outrage. But on further inspection, I saw that it was something quite different, a look of bewildered appraisal. It was as if some old, ruminant interest had kindled in him, predating the wedge of acrimony. Or perhaps he was noting the changes in her, and betraying his approval. Whatever the case, his gaze went unreturned, and he bent down, glumly, to gather his papers.

Outside, in the hall, Lina waited for her lawyer, who had stayed behind to sign some forms. Not far away, Anton paced in a circle, jingling the change in his pants pockets.

"How does it feel to be the slam-dunk winner?" I whispered, mindful that he was within hearing range.

"Ask me a year from now, when my stomach calms down," she muttered. "Right now, I just want to get out of here."

Though her back was to Anton, apparently her antennae were up, because he pivoted and stalked over to us.

"Can I talk to you a minute?" he asked, peering at Lina with an expression that was both supplicant and cool.

She looked at her watch and actually shook it a little, as if it contained some microtransmitter to beam her elsewhere.

"Well, but *just* a minute," she said. "I've got to make a call to my office."

They walked off several paces in the direction of the stairs, and I obliged them by walking the other way. Once out of earshot, though, I stopped and looked back, anxious to know what they were talking about. Lina was standing with her head turned from Anton, presenting her left ear for petition. He, for his part, was bent in close, pouring words into the ear made available to him. In this theater of formalized sexual contention, they made for a curious sight— a husband and wife talking at intimate range, enacting the last stanza of courtship.

And then, abruptly, it was over. Whirling on her heel, Lina stomped away, shaking her head incredulously. Anton stared after her, his mouth hanging open, both arms out in entreaty.

"I'm leaving," she said, shaking her head as she blew by me. "If you see my lawyer, tell her I'll call her in the morning."

Pocketing the notepad on which I'd been scribbling, I scrambled to catch up to her. "What happened?" I asked, as we rounded the corner. "What did he say to you?"

She glared straight ahead, not even pausing to downshift. "I'll tell you what he said," she snorted, jabbing the down button. "After two and a half years of torture and humiliation, he asked me to *feel sorry for him.*"

On the last Tuesday in July, a damp, torpid evening, the group met for the final time before summer break. A month or so earlier, Lathon had made an announcement that his practice had outgrown this space, and that he would be moving to larger quarters in the Flatiron district. As work on the new place was going to be extensive and required his oversight, he was extending the break until mid-September, when he would be delighted to receive the group in his new offices.

"I apologize for the interruption," he'd said then, "but I simply need more room, and figured this would be the least bad time to do this. Also, I won't miss the patter of the little monsters above us, and the clanking of that damn radiator all winter."

Tonight, the group arrived to find the office in boxes. Along the wall that met the window, cartons were stacked five high, ribbed like turrets in a child's game of fort. The omnifarious art had been taken down and packed carefully, bulky in cardboard carriers. And in the middle of the room, on a console of Bekins boxes, was a spread of hors d'oeuvres and soft drinks.

"It would've been nice to have wine," said Lathon, "but I hadn't heard from Dylan in a while, and if he was coming, I didn't want to lay temptation before the weak."

Dylan, of course, hadn't come, to no one's chagrin; it was assumed by one and all that they'd seen the last of him. Jack, meanwhile, had sent a card from summer stock, saying, "I'm as happy as a kid who ran away with the circus." Enclosed was a favorable review from a local paper. Everyone else was on hand and punctual, one of the larger such assemblies of the summer. Even Rex had shown up, passing around the latest batch of snapshots of his much-photographed year-old daughter.

It turned out to be a convivial gathering, as cheers and glad tidings made the rounds. Peter had just interviewed with an investment bank, and thought he "might've hit a homer the first time up." He'd researched the company thoroughly, analyzing its position in foreign markets, and pitched them several ideas that knocked their socks off. An offer was forthcoming, he thought, that would be a full step up the ladder, but he wasn't going to get excited until they'd had the "money talk."

"I know what I'm worth," he declared, "and I'm not taking one dollar less from them. My days of bending over backwards for people are *through.*"

Sara also had news to report. She'd met a wonderful boy—"Excuse me, a man; I've gotta stop saying that," she groaned—although he was awfully young-acting for thirty-two. It seemed he was quite the beauty, a slightly more streetwise Ethan Hawke, with a touch of the hip-hop white boy in effect. He directed videos for a living, and was doing well enough at it to spend half his time doing volunteer work in Bushwick. And for all his rough edges (he hadn't bothered to finish high school, nor to clean his kitchen since the year Bush left office), he was affectionate to the point of reverence with Sara.

"I'm a little worried about that, frankly—the whole puppy-dog thing," she said. "His friends all say he lights up around me, but I'm going real slow with this. We haven't even had sex yet, which, at two weeks and counting, is a new world record for me. I'm just going to try and enjoy myself and see where this goes, and not sweat the small stuff, like his personal hygiene."

Lina, meanwhile, balanced a plate in her lap, looking as relaxed as we had seen her. She'd taken the day off to spend with her daughter, Jorie, who was lonesome with most of her friends gone for the summer. They'd gone shopping in the morning, then to a matinee of *Miss Saigon*, in honor of Jorie's interest in Vietnam. She'd written a terrific paper on the Tet Offensive, and between acts, dazzled Lina with her erudition.

"She's such an amazing kid," Lina marveled. "She just has this mind that thinks in paragraphs. I asked her why she thought we were over there, and she starts giving me Cold War theory and the missile crisis. And on top of being smart, she's also very funny. Last night, for instance, the phone rings during dinner, and she beats me to it, like always. Turns out it's one of the guys I've been dating lately, and she says, 'Which are you, the lawyer or the French guy?' Well, needless to say, it was *neither* of them, but he was so charmed by her that all he could do was laugh. And for the next ten minutes, she grilled him about his intentions, and said, 'You'd better be *nice* to my mom; she's had a bad year.' "

"Yeah, well never mind that," said Rex. "What's with you and all of these guys suddenly?"

"Yeah, that's right," said Sara. "You're stealing my headlines. I come in here, finally, with a guy to talk about, and you're sitting over there with *three* of them."

Lina tossed her head back, laughing without her usual plangency. "Well, I finally decided I'd had it with all this mourning, especially since no one had died. And so I joined a new church, where I'm meeting tons of people, and signed up at this tennis club in Saltaire. And suddenly, men're coming from everywhere. I can't keep up with it, it's happening so fast!"

"Damn," said Sara, "now I really *am* jealous. I want to hear everything that's happened, and don't leave a word out."

Lina laughed again, and took a breath to slow down; suddenly, the prospect of airing her love life seemed to daunt this circumspect woman. She described the first man as a fiftyish architect who was the very model of seasoned charm. He was learned on many subjects, loved baseball and opera, and listened with blue-eyed sympathy to whatever she said to him—

"Oh God, I hate him already," said Sara.

The problem, Linda continued, was that he was a little *too, too* sympathetic, and not shy about laying his cards on the table. He'd called a number of times since, and sent her a box of blue tulips, and on their second date asked her up to his place in Rhinebeck. But that was too fast, she said, and downright pushy when you stopped to think about it, and so she told him that she'd call *him* when she felt ready. Number two was also a nice guy, a lawyer involved in animal rights issues, but he turned out to be a wet blanket about the dating scene. He'd been seeing a bunch of sharpies who either lied about what they wanted or who were looking for the antidote to their exes. This turned Lina off, as she was the unspoiled optimist, determined to have a memorable new experience. It felt great, she said, just being out again, in the company of attractive men who found her likewise. It didn't matter that they weren't perfect, merely that they were pleasant; affirmative proof that the world didn't consist of Antons.

And then, lately, there was Jeffrey, easily the pick of the litter. He
was a tall, dapper man of disarming sweetness and a wry, easy calm
in conversation. An engineer by training, he'd traveled the world for
ITT, and later founded a company that installed fiber optics. He
was affluent, Jewish, and dotty about his three daughters, trotting
out a wallet that was fat with their pictures. The hitch, however,
was that he was suffering from lupus, a disease that sapped his
strength for weeks at a stretch. This nagged at Lina, who was bursting with new energy for all the life she hadn't lived yet. Nonetheless,
she liked Jeffrey and felt completely at ease with him, as if they were
two old friends who, now single, said why not?

The group was elated for Lina. Rex and Sara lobbed jokes her
way about being a "heartbreaker" and "the Greek Julia Roberts."
Peter effused about how great she'd been looking, particularly since
her "one-punch knockout" in court. And Lathon took the occasion
to indulge in some chest-beating, saying that this was what happened to clients of his who had the courage to write their own story.

"Ever since you opted out of *Anton's* story, it's been one victory
after another," he noted. "You have peace in your own house now,
you've got a judge on your side, and admirers hand over fist. If you
recall our little paradigm, there were three steps out of suffering.
Step one was to declare and feel the wound, to pay attention to your
body in pain. Step two was to take measures to heal the wound,
practicing the art of self-respecting action. And step three was the
stage called 'serious fun,' where you get involved in something mean-
ingful and joyous. For Jack, that meant going off to do a play, although I'm not so sure he'd mastered the first two steps. For Rex, it
meant having a daughter to spoil, although, again, I have my doubts
about steps one and two. And for Lina, who did do the work that's
called for, it means experiencing herself as a *woman* again, being
fussed over and found desirable by lots of men. That isn't just plea-
surable, it's downright restorative, a correction for those twenty years
of being insulted."

"Yes, that's right," she nodded, "it's been a revelation, frankly, getting all these compliments and phone calls. You have to understand that Anton was my first romance, and so when he rejected me, I had nothing to fall back on. I couldn't tell myself, well, at least other men found me pretty—I was pretty much a virgin in every sense."

"And that's why we applaud you for doing what you're doing, and urge you to keep on doing it," said Lathon. "Don't fall into the trap of thinking that this guy's wrong for you, or that that guy would be perfect if he were younger. This isn't the adult version of musical chairs, where you're out if the music stops and you're still single. It's a chance for you to have fun again and develop a relationship with *yourself*, to put your heart through a new range of motion. The worst thing you could do now is to rush the process, and settle for the guy who's least like Anton."

Lina poked the goat cheese around on her plate, musing on this counsel. "I don't know," she said. "I don't think I can bear to drag this out. I'm already feeling guilty for spending evenings away from my kids."

"Listen," said Lathon, "your kids can spare you for a while. They've *had* the lonely saint-mother who stayed home and cried her eyes out, and they're telling you that they like this version better. You've been a wonderful mom, Lina, the best thing that ever happened to them. But for everyone's sake here—and I do mean theirs as much as yours—you're going to have to make your way now as both mother *and* woman."

sixteen

september

In his life away from the office, Charles Lathon is a sculptor, crafting large works of high intensity. Many of his pieces depict a human figure either in flight from, or in pursuit of, another. Some are beautifully and elliptically rendered—a series of tall bronzes, their limbs attenuated like flame tongues, in a frieze of retreat and advance. Others, like the wall-mounted terra-cottas, are unsettling and phantasmagoric. In one, a frightened child reaches out for a woman, who transforms into a bird with huge talons. In another, a man is picnicking with a lover, kneeling to fondle her cheek. Out of his back steps a second man, whose cleft face leers at us. Though far from decorative, the work is highly accomplished, and has attracted the notice of dealers. Twice in the eighties Lathon was given his own show at galleries on lower Broadway. Some pieces fetched prices in the mid–five figures. One woman from Texas bought four of them, and created a grotto of lunging arms and legs.

Alas, for Lathon, demand cooled in the nineties, as it had for many artists of minor note. Nonetheless, he continued to spend the bulk of his afternoons at his studio on Avenue A. As a result, he now had some twenty finished pieces sitting, unseen, under tarp and cheesecloth. It made logical sense, then, that in his search for a new workspace, Lathon had opted for a loft. The move, he said, would bring his careers together, and spare him the transit from studio to office. It would also reduce the strain between his "two stories"—the sense that each was produced at the expense of the other.

That, at any rate, was what he told me in August, when I stopped by to see his new quarters. He had rented half a floor of a former bookbinding factory on Park Avenue in the lower Twenties. It was an enormous rectangle, roughly three thousand square feet, and in its raw state resembled a school gym. It boasted twelve-foot windows that faced onto the avenue, and a ceiling high enough to accommodate jump shots. But almost a month into the renovation, the job seemed to have barely begun. Workmen were still prying off chunks of the old Sheetrock, exposing long swaths of dank brick. Others were hauling up bundles of oak planks, to replace the rotting floorboards. It would be a week, at the soonest, before construction began, to say nothing of when it would be done. Moreover, new problems were arising daily, the latest being a pipe that had cracked during removal, spewing gallons of water. Though Lathon was paying overtime and keeping a stiff upper lip, it seemed unimaginable that he would reopen as scheduled.

I went back the Friday before Labor Day to check his progress. The bare brick was gone, now hidden behind walls of acoustic tile wrapped in white linen. And though not yet varnished, the new oak floor dazzled, basking in the late-day sun. At the north end of the space, a pair of rooms had been built: two tall, square boxes, glassed in on top, to take advantage of the ample light. One was fitted out like a mini-library, with floor-to-ceiling bookshelves, a plush gold carpet, and three of Lathon's sumptuous club chairs. This, he explained, was the office he would use for couples and one-on-one sessions. The other, packed high with unopened cartons, was for group work and seminars. Directly across the loft, following a convex curve, was Lathon's studio, where an inch-thick rubber mat was laid to absorb the sounds of his craft. Between the studio at one end and the offices at the other was a vast, open gallery for Lathon's art. It was a stunning space, airy and bounded by light, a sort of floating cloud-scape, with neighbors.

That, at any rate, was the good news. The bad news was that the rehab looked, at best, half done, with barely a week before group re-sumed. Wires snaked down from the unfinished ceiling, looming overhead like fish hooks. Spackling cans and lumber scraps com-peted for floorspace, a menace to the unobservant. The bathroom was uninstalled, the offices needed painting, and the waiting room existed only in blueprint. Meanwhile, the wall that separated Lathon from a Lamaze instructor was flimsy and untreated for sound, to the extent that the silence so essential to his trade was now breached by squalls of heavy breathing.

"A disaster," moaned Lathon. "The worst move of my life. I spent myself right into oblivion."

He was slumped on a chair at the head of the gallery, dispirited and exhausted. He had on work boots, a T-shirt, and spattered blue chinos. His hair had grown long, spilling over his ears, and was pulled back in a little pigtail with a rubberband. As he spoke, he dabbed at the corner of one eye, which was red and bleary from paint dust.

"I'd figured on a hundred thousand and I'm at one-sixty-five, with no end anywhere in sight. They still have to do the ductwork, and put up walls in the waiting room, then lay carpet and do the soundproofing so I don't have to listen to *that*—"

He glared in the direction of the class next door, where a room-ful of women respired to the music of whales. From the other side of the loft, though, came a more troubling noise: the piercing strains of Park Avenue South, circa five o'clock.

"Um, that may be a problem," I ventured, nodding at the open window.

He walked over and slammed it shut. The noise was only partly abated. "I saw this place on a weekend, when there were no trucks or rush hour traffic. Now, even when it's *not* there, I'm hearing car horns and brakes squeak. I mean, it's just been a certified New York nightmare—complete with night sweats and panic attacks."

He explained that there had been hassles from day one with the contractor: subpar materials and two-hour lunch breaks, and an aversion to working on Saturdays. Then, they'd run afoul of the building codes, installing fixtures not approved for this space. Finally, after a fight over cost projections, Lathon fired the first crew and brought in another one. It was at about this point that money became an issue.

Nor, as it turned out, was that the end of Lathon's woes. In the six years I'd known him as a client and collaborator, I'd learned only the most negligible facts about his private life—that he had a wife, a son, and a co-op in Tribeca. Recently, though, at one of our post-session recaps, he'd made reference to tensions at home. I timidly followed up, asking if it was something he wanted to talk about. He backed off, though, saying that it was just your domestic ups and downs, and nothing that a week in the islands wouldn't fix.

But now, as he sat caked in grime and paint splotches, he began suddenly to speak about his failing marriage. He and his wife had decided to separate in May, although, for reasons that involved their teenage son, they remained under one roof temporarily. The apartment was a large duplex, affording both parties some privacy, but the misery was so pervasive that he spent most nights on the couch in his office. His son was in a tailspin and barely speaking to Lathon, conveying his rage by gaining thirty pounds. All in all, it was a full-on disaster, and one of his own making, said Lathon. When confronted with suffering, he couldn't take the advice he handed out.

"I tell it to my patients every day: stop avoiding, and face the pain," he said. "If I'd just bitten the bullet and moved out in May, we'd all be a lot better off now. But I thought I could finesse this, do the leaving in stages, like I was LBJ in Vietnam. And what I was really trying to do was spare *myself*, not my son. I couldn't deal with not being around him."

I was stunned into silence, and embarrassed for us both. There are therapists whose sympathy draws you in, inspiring fondness and familial curiosity. They are the parent you never had, the friend you've always lacked, and in imagining their lives, you never fail to insert yourself. By contrast, Lathon's power was purely exclusive; he was effective insofar as he was inscrutable. You respected him because he was so confidently *other*, as polished and unitized as steel. You couldn't imagine his life because it was beyond all knowing, and it certainly didn't include you in it. Instead, you conceived him as the sum of his knowledge, and were content and grateful to receive it.

Lathon changed the subject, talking about his burnout workload. On a table, by the phone, was his leather organizer. He passed it over to me, and said to open it anywhere. Fixing randomly on a page, I read as follows:

Wednesday, April 12

9 A.M.: Gretchen	12 P.M.: Marvin
10 A.M.: Bob B.	1 P.M.: Zack and Daniel
11 A.M.: Lauren	2 P.M.: Craig W.

The next three hours were left unfilled, presumably set aside for sculpting. The schedule picked up, though, at six P.M., and ran through nine o'clock. I turned the page and saw the same thing for Thursday, the only change being a group from eight to ten. And so on, in lockstep, wherever I flipped, an endless run of twelve-hour days, with a pause on Saturday or Sunday.

I sat by, nodding and murmuring empathy, as he expounded on why he worked to exhaustion. It had something to do with his bilious father, whose response to Lathon's career was, "You get *paid* for that?" As I listened, though, or half listened, to Lathon's monody, I found myself distracted by a thought. Actually, it was less a thought than a constriction of the airways, and a sharp, torquing pressure between my ears. It was brought on by a split-second flicker of an image: the prospect of forty patients, lined up back-to-back, waiting with bated panic to see Lathon. I'd met some of those people, having sat in on several of his groups, and was acquainted with the tenor of their hysteria. By design or luck, Lathon was a specialist in crisis, in lives requiring acute and constant tending. Even now, as we sat in his half-built office, the phone rang every ten minutes. There were calls to return, and dosages to adjust, and a suicidal client at Saint Vincent's—and all this while he was still *on vacation*. It was a grueling life, and the responsibilities were endless. I began wondering why he hadn't cracked utterly.

"Have you thought about cutting back your caseload?" I asked. "Making it not so—oppressive?"

He smiled, and gave an exhausted grunt. "You know how many times I've closed my practice to new clients? And then a friend of a patient calls up, depressed and on the verge of breakdown, and I'm right back in it again."

"I understand," I said. "But you won't be much help to anyone if you go in for a breakdown yourself."

"Oh, don't worry about that," he said, struggling to his feet. "I'm paying a divorce lawyer, two mortgages, my son's tuition, and five thousand dollars a month rent here. I can't *afford* to go in for a breakdown."

In a perfect world, Lathon would have held off for three weeks, and finished the renovation in due course. But, strapped for cash, he couldn't finance that option, and so he reopened for business as scheduled. The electricians had finished their work, or at least contrived some hasty arrangement whereby wires weren't circling overhead. The debris was picked up and the dividing wall had been padded, so that the majority of the maternal spirit next door was silenced.

But for all that, the place was still a genteel shambles. The office reserved for groups was cluttered with cartons, and functioning as an ad hoc storeroom. In the studio, there was a miscellany of tools and paint cans, and more cartons lining the walls. And in the middle of the gallery, like a dais onstage, was the old configuration of armchairs. Lathon sat at one end with a phone on his shoulder, fetching his messages from his service. He waved to me, and went on jotting notes in his organizer. Waving back at him, I took my seat behind the circle.

It was several minutes before I could get my bearings, so disjunctive was it to sit in all this space. Somehow, I felt both puny and conspicuous, like the first one on the dance floor or into the pool. There are many things that flourish in big rooms, but therapy isn't among them. It needs the proximity of walls, the safety of enclosure, something to keep the words from spilling out. It also needs a minimum of distractions, and here there were distractions aplenty. Wherever you turned, you saw Lathon's sculptures, hulking and explicit. They roosted in the corners, casting baleful shadows, or hung upon the walls in stark relief. In the half-dark, they looked like flailing pod people, or like mummified patients from groups past. No matter where you sat, you could not fail to see them—and once you did, it was hard to look away.

The second thing that struck me, as I took in the scene, was the change in Lathon's appearance. In lieu of the tailored suit and Fratelli dress shoes, he sat before me garbed like a downtown salonista. He had on black jeans, biker boots, a work shirt and vest, and a Navajo bracelet fretted with turquoise. Wisely, he'd cut his hair, but had grown a goatee, and seemed only to be missing an earring to complete the look. He looked up, caught me staring, and laughed.

"No, I haven't lost my mind, if that's what you're thinking," he said. "I'll explain it as soon as I'm done here."

He dashed off some notes to himself, then greeted me in high spirits, and apologized for our last meeting. I'd caught him at low ebb after a truly horrible month, he said, but still, he shouldn't have burdened me. He was much more himself now that the worst was over, and hoped that I'd forget it ever happened.

Before I could answer, he leapt ahead, bringing up the state of his office. What remained to be done was mostly painting and un-packing, although there was a problem with the ductwork, and oc-casionally, the lights blinked on and off. But the group room would be finished soon, as would his studio, at which point he could resume his former life. He had done a crazy thing, moving to such grandiose quarters in the middle of a divorce. And it certainly wasn't lost on him that he'd done it in August, when the alternative was a grim va-cation without his family. But he'd survived his "personal hell month" and was up and running again, and had never been so happy to be back at work.

As for his new attire, he'd been considering the change for some time, saying that it was part of his evolution as a therapist. Where once he'd been the strict apostle of Freud, presenting a blank screen for his patients' projections, over the years, he'd come to see the utility of his own story. He'd stepped out from behind the couch, consulting personal experience in helping others practice the art of being human. It had made him a better doctor, more empathic and available, and much less impressed with received doctrine.

And now, in the spirit of that progression, he wanted to take down the wall that separated "physician" from "person" in his story. Particularly after this summer, when he'd screwed up time and again, it seemed preposterous to go on acting like the omniscient magus. He was a man like any other, with the usual mix of fears and wishes, and he felt increasingly false in his power suits, talking down from on high. Better that clients view him as he really was: a person who, though fallable, had built a thriving practice, and managed to produce the artwork on display here.

"At the session before the break, we talked about 'serious fun,' and the joy and calm you get from constructive making. Well, here's living proof that the paradigm works, because, at the moment, my sculpting is all that's keeping me going. My marriage is over, I'm up to my eyeballs in debt, and my son hasn't talked to me in a month. But every day, I know that I've got that block of three hours where I can head to my studio and get lost in something deep. It's funny, you know, I was in a cab last week, and I got to talking with the cabbie. I said, How do you do it, deal with the hassles and bad drivers, and the cops who've got a quota to make? He was a Puerto Rican guy, in his mid- to late fifties, and he was sitting there, cool as a cucumber. He says, 'You wanna know my secret, how I'm doin' this for thirty years?' He says, 'I put in my time here, work my sixty-hour week, and lose a day of work to fight tickets I don't deserve—I do that because I know that, at the end of the week, I got two days of fishing comin' up. Me and a friend of mine got a boat in Sheepshead, and we go out at six in the morning, fishing for blues. And when I'm on that boat, drinking beer and letting my line out, I am the happiest little *pinga* in the whole five boroughs, because I'm doin' the most best thing that you can do.' I thought, my God, this is the poster boy of serious fun. He's doing something joyous, he's loved it since childhood, and it makes all the other crap in his life endurable."

So impressed was I with this story that I forgot to ask the questions I'd been filing. Wasn't Lathon worried that springing these changes would disrupt the group's concentration? And what about the wisdom of displaying his art to patients, who could scarcely fail to be struck by it? It seemed such an odd and intimate thing, to put the product of your unconscious in front of your clients. It might even be said to co-opt the process, displacing their inner life with your own. I intended, as I say, to ask these things, but then we got off on this rhetorical siding, and before I knew it, his intercom was buzzing. I made a mental note, though, to gauge the members' reactions, and to follow up with them in weeks to come.

Jack and Lina arrived together, having met downstairs buying coffee. They were sharing a laugh as they came through the door, but stopped in their tracks once inside. Looking up, Jack squinted as though viewing an eclipse, his mouth hanging open in surprise. He tried to crack a joke, but trailed off and gaped. Lina said nothing, taking in the scene with wide eyes. She seemed dazzled at first, admiring the dimensions of the room, and the brilliant floor and cloth walls. By degrees, though, her expression turned to bafflement, as she studied Lathon's terra-cottas. She walked slowly toward us, a jacket over her arm, eyes locked on a piece near the window.

"Welcome," said Lathon, grinning at her. "What do you think of my new digs?"

Lina stood by a chair, holding her bag and coat close to her, as if afraid of touching something. "I, uh . . ."

She looked around again, perhaps searching for something to praise. "Well, it's certainly . . . big enough. I mean, you've really got some room here. Though the other place was fine for that."

Lathon explained to her that this was the gallery, and that their permanent quarters, the group room, would be ready soon. As he said this, though, Lina was eyeing his attire, checking out his boots and bracelet. She continued doing so over the next several minutes, her perplexity giving way to alarm.

There were similar takes from the other members as they filed through the door one by one. (Peter was out of the country on honeymoon, having married Kara the weekend of Labor Day). Each of them responded to the new environs with some mixture of praise and dismay. Sara pronounced it a great place for a party, though moments later, I saw her slip Rex a look, confiding her snarky contempt. Rex, for his part, complimented the sculpture, but tweaked Lathon about his outfit, asking if he was a bouncer at the strip joint around the corner. Lathon laughed and said he wasn't, but that if he ever applied there, he'd be sure to mention Rex's name. This loosened things up a bit, reducing the ambient weirdness, the sense that nothing was as it had been, or should be. Lathon told the story of the renovation, reciting the black comedy of botched plumbing and no-show workmen. He was regaling us with tales of a "dyslexic electrician" when Dylan came softly through the door.

Of all the surprises in store for the members, this one was, by far, the most jarring. They gaped at Dylan, or glared accusingly at Lathon as he welcomed him back to group. Among them, it was well settled that the worst had come of Dylan—that he was dead in some basement, or lost in the streets, one of those bundled figures in a doorway. They'd long since stopped asking about him, because the answer never varied; no, he hadn't been heard from. And though they wished him no harm, they were glad to be rid of him, and the intractable grief he brought in.

Dylan took a seat, and said hi circumspectly, sensible of the cool reception. He glanced at Lathon, exchanging a nod; it was clear they'd met earlier to prepare for this. He was dressed in a tweed blazer and tasseled brown loafers, and looked improbably, even preposterously, well. He had a deep tan, the kind accrued over weeks, and a bright-eyed clarity that belied the months of squalor. There is a subset of addicts—and they are in the tiny minority—who can abuse themselves savagely, then clean up like a pearl. Dylan was such an addict, and it had probably worked against him, deluding him about the damage done. He could look in the mirror, see that he was handsome when sober, and conclude that he'd been given a free pass.

Glancing at his watch, Lathon cleared his throat, and thanked the group for showing up early. There was a lot to do besides catch up on one another's stories, and he was grateful for the extra time. First, he wanted to apologize for the state of his office. As he'd explained on the phone over the last couple of days, this hadn't gone the way he'd planned. He'd been naïve about how long such a project took, and failed to make allowances for the standard glitches. And yes, some of those glitches were the stuff of science fiction, but at the end of the day, this was *his* fault. He asked them to bear with him, and promised that it would be over by the next session, when they would be meeting in the cozier confines of the group room.

Second, since Rex had been thoughtful enough to ask, he wanted to explain his new attire. No, he hadn't gotten a fashion makeover from Sara, or bought a motorcycle for his fiftieth birthday. This was what he wore when he wasn't doing therapy, when he was out there being himself and making his story. And since so much of what he did now was to coach that in patients, he felt uncomfortable dressing the part of someone he wasn't—someone he hadn't been, in fact, for five or six years.

"Well, I don't have a problem with the outfit," said Jack. "After all, it's your show; you can wear what you want here. But I am a little curious about the Fu Manchu. It kind of makes you look like one of the Village People."

There was some startled laughter from the other members, and then the group returned to its business. Lathon took up the third, and most delicate, point of order: Dylan's stunning return. He said that he'd thought long and hard on how to handle this, and that the decision was one of the toughest he'd had to make. Should he hold Dylan out, and put his reinstatement to a vote? Or should he invite him back in, but warn the others beforehand, so that they'd have a couple of days to sort their feelings? In the end, though, he thought this was the fairest solution—to bring Dylan in and let him be heard. Allow him to make his own case to the group.

No one said anything for several seconds. The members looked down, examining their nails or jewelry. Finally, Lina glanced at Dylan.

"Well, I can't speak for anyone else," she said, "but I'm glad to see you're healthy—and not just for your sake, but for your daughters'. And I'll also say that I'm . . . okay with you're being back here. My question is how long are you back for?"

"Yeah, that's my concern," said Sara. "I mean, you're in and out of here, and in and out, and there's no real rhyme or reason either way. I guess what I'm saying is, I don't sense a commitment. A burning need to get sober, and stay that way."

"And, of course, you *know* my criteria—are you going to meetings?" asked Jack. "Because if you are, that's one thing; I'll give anyone a second chance, as long as they're working The Program. But if you're not, then why bother? You're just wasting our time here, and we haven't got time to spare."

Another pause followed, arid and volatile. "Can I say what I was going to say now, or should I save it for later?" Dylan asked Lathon.

Lathon thought for a moment, plying his new mustache. "Actually, I would like to hold off for a bit, and hear from the others first. This is a complex issue, and I don't want it to dominate the session. But don't worry, I'll give you plenty of time at the end."

And with that, he moved that they get under way, and produced a jazzy card that Peter had sent him. It was addressed from an inn in the Italian Alps, where the newlyweds were spending the last of their honeymoon. Peter wrote that they had rented a convertible, and were flying around the hairpins like crazy people. They'd been diving in Corfu, gone topless in Ibiza, and bought matching leather jackets in Milan. "Oh, and by the way," he closed, "Kara's seven and half weeks pregnant—but don't tell my mom, or she'll *have a baby!*"

"God *damn,*" Rex said, "that boy is out of control. Driving a convertible going to topless beaches—I mean, who's he think he is now, *me?*"

"That's right," Lina chortled. "Except, in Peter's case, he's with his wife."

"See, there you go again," Rex aped his hero, Ronald Reagan. "If you only *knew* what a model husband I've become. I'm home so much of the time now, my wife is *begging* me to go out. She's like, 'Don't you have any old *girlfriends* you can call?' "

"Still, it's amazing how much Peter's changed," said Sara. "I remember when we first started, he was so shy and nervous, I sort of felt sorry for him. Now, he's got his life together and we're still sitting here—I guess he's the one who got the last laugh."

The others piped up, begging to differ with Sara. Jack declared that he'd had a great summer, and felt happier and more at peace than he had in years. Lina put in that she, too, wasn't just "sitting around here," that, with some help from the group, she'd met a lovely, wonderful man, and was enjoying her life just fine, thank you kindly. Even Dylan demurred, saying that, in some way he didn't understand yet, these sessions had probably saved his life.

Lathon cut in, to Sara's relief. He had read Peter's card, he said, merely to make the point that time and opportunity were fleeting. There were seven sessions left of the twenty contracted for, and for those who hadn't yet "used" the group, now was the time to get cracking. Nor was he keen on adding sessions unless all six members agreed to it—and judging from the fun Lina and Peter were having, he doubted they'd sign on for another minute.

"As I told you at the outset, life is to be lived *out there*, and not in therapy. Now, I'm not pie-eyed enough to think that a lifelong resistance can be eliminated in twenty sessions. Trust me, I know how obstinate it can be; that's why they call it resistance. But I'm determined that if you don't walk out of here with a new story, that you at least be clear about the terms of that resistance. What, specifically, is holding you back, and what action can we design to chip away at it?"

He went around the room, soliciting status reports. Lina went first, saying, that in her new "spirit of rebellion" she'd disobeyed Dr. Lathon and fallen in love. She'd really meant to hold off and have fun playing the field, but Jeffrey was just too good to keep waiting around. He was the wealthy engineer whose chronic lupus first spooked her, but whose calm and unshakable sweetness carried the day. He loved to cook dinner for her and hang out with her and the kids, showing off his "two-hand, Coney Island set shot" and his collection of Beatles memorabilia. They had been spending weekends with their respective children at his roomy house in Watermill, where he took the kids up in his twin-engine Piper, and howled with them through back-to-back showings of *Dumb and Dumber*.

"I'm telling you, he's everything that Anton isn't, and never was," she said. "I mean, Anton's idea of taking the kids for the day was handing them a fifty and dumping them off at the movies. Whereas Jeffrey genuinely likes kids and can relate to them on their level instead of saying, 'all right, that's enough of that. Let's talk about adult things now.'"

"Well, how wonderful," said Lathon. "And how perfectly apt— a man who loves kids as much as you do. That, of all his qualities, tells the tale for me; that he has the confidence not to be threatened by them. You can always spot a fake by how they react to kids. If they're bored or impatient with them, watch out."

"And how do your kids get along with *him*?" asked Sara.

"Ah, well, that's the best part—they utterly adore him," she said. "My daughter, who's a real techie, talks for hours with him about computers. If I'm lucky, I understand maybe two words of what they're saying. It seemed like, right from that first day, she sensed she could trust him, that he was a whole other breed from her father. Not many kids would do that, open up to their mom's boyfriend, especially after being burned by their father. But Jorie just has this ability to let stuff roll off her, to disregard the crap that comes along."

"Yeah, that is pretty rare, seeing how early it started with her," said Rex. "I remember you saying how Anton had dogged her since she was, like, five years old."

"And I remember it, too, because I could definitely relate," said Sara. "Although, as we know, I'm not exactly what you call re-silient."

Everyone laughed at this, none louder than Lina. It was as though her brain, having been regulated for gloom all these years, was having difficulty adjusting to joy. She looked terrific in a beige pantsuit, which set off her tan, and jingled a gold bracelet given her by Jeffrey for her birthday.

Jack, who'd been away all summer, marveled at the change in her. He was seconded by Dylan, who said it gave him hope, seeing someone rebuild her life like that from scratch. Sara, for her part, praised Lina's courage, falling in love so soon after such a long, bad marriage.

"I mean it," she said, "that really takes guts. Me, I break up after a *week* with someone, I'm no good to anyone for months."

Therewith, the praise turned to congratulations, bestowed most emphatically by Jack. "You're a terrific person, Lina, and this guy of yours is lucky to have you. And also, I'm just struck by how fitting it is, going from one of the meanest pricks in town to one of the nicest. Other women might have said, 'Ah, he's got lupus; who cares if he's nice?' But you were too smart to be fooled by that, and to that, I say, more power."

"Hear, hear!" said Lathon, raising his coffee cup. "Here's to two nice people finding each other."

The others joined in, toasting with whatever was at hand—an Evian, a Coke bottle, a half-eaten bagel.

"Well, thank you," she said. "That's very kind of you to say, though I sort of feel like you're being nice to me because I was such a wreck when I first came in."

Jack disputed this, reminding her that she had been a wreck for good reason—a husband who'd bled her dry for years, and a feeling of helplessness in court. Sara noted that her own problems were mild by comparison, and yet eight months later, she was still stuck in a relationship that barely had a pulse. And Rex, who was exceptionally tight with a compliment, applauded Lina's choice of "such a mature and together guy."

"As you know, us *immature* guys are pretty much a lousy bet," he said. "And by the way, if you ever need any investment help, I'd be more than glad to provide it."

"Well, good," said Lina, put at ease by his crassness. "I'm glad to hear you say that, because we're already talking about getting married next fall."

"Is—is that true?" blurted Sara. "Boy, you sure don't mess around, once you get going. I mean, zero to engaged in—what?—six weeks now? But are you sure this isn't a little . . . quick on the draw?"

"Well, actually, it's been three months since we started dating," said Lina. "And don't forget, we *are* talking about a year's engagement here; we're not even going to let our kids know until the spring. But aside from that, it just feels—*right*, do you know what I'm saying? I mean, I've never been so at ease with someone, and just *fit* together like we do. It's like everything he tells me about him, I already know, and vice versa about me."

"And that fit you're talking about," said Lathon, "is only something that happens when two people truly respect each other. It goes deeper than attraction, to a kind of neural recognition: I am safe with this person; I am valued. You know, we talk about family values in this country, but there *is* no family if it doesn't value its members; if it doesn't make clear to them that they're loved and respected. We saw that with Lina's last family, the one with Anton in it. He was incapable of valuing others, except as they were useful to him. That was particularly true of his children, who *have* no value to him, and, even worse, stole his spotlight sometimes. As a rule, you know, narcissists can't stand their children; they view them not as loved ones, but as competition. Whereas Jeffrey, from the sound of it, can nourish himself. He doesn't have to steal from the mouths of babes."

"That's right," said Lina. "That's one of the things that's so great about him—he doesn't *need* anything from me. He's already made his mark at two different companies, and established his name in the world. Now, all he wants is to just be happy, and to make me happy with him."

She talked a bit about their plans for the future—a house in Irvington or Hastings-on-Hudson, once Todd and Jorie were off to college; and a series of long and leisurely treks through back-roads Europe and the Far East. In the near range, the hope was to have Jeffrey move in with her, and visit the least amount of chaos upon her kids. Besides child support and a modest settlement, the use of the apartment was all she wanted from Anton—five more years in her children's lifelong home. But Anton refused to budge; it was his only card now, and he was playing it. The case was going against him and he would soon have to settle or risk half his assets at trial. But denying her this one thing meant more to him than money, and he seemed prepared to gut it out or go down bluffing.

"But that's insane," said Jack. "Does he really hate you that much, that he'd risk losing millions of dollars?"

"I guess." Lina shrugged. "Either that, or he loves that place. Although his last two years there, he was barely home, other than to sleep and change his clothes."

"Actually, from what I know of him, it's neither," said Lathon. "Just as there are people who're fixed on victimhood, there are others obsessed with domination. It's the old Hegelian master-slave trope, in which the master is the one who writes the history books, and the victim dies nameless and faceless. But as you've seen with Anton, it's a cartoon role—Bluto to Olive Oyl in *Popeye*. There's no story there, no movement or progress; everyone stays locked in their slots. And in the end, that's his punishment—to be trapped in a caricature, living an empty, cardboard lie."

. . .

Rex was next, and not to be outdone, said that he, too, had "changed his life around during the summer." There had been a "major growth spurt," and "a big development," which was sure to earn him points here with the others. He needed a couple of weeks, though, before he felt good and solid with it, and so was going to hold off on an announcement until the next session. He assured them, though, that he felt fine and dandy, and apologized for being a "withholding twit."

Naturally, this pricked the group's curiosity.

"My God, what could it possibly be?" teased Sara. "A 'big development,' and a 'major lifestyle change'—wait a minute, you're not thinking of becoming *monogamous*, are you?"

"Maybe he's gay," offered Lina. "That would explain all the strip clubs—he was just confused about his sexuality."

"Actually, I *have* thought about turning gay," Rex said, enjoying the speculation. "I mean, imagine if I hooked up with a guy like me—I could have sex and watch football at the same time!"

"Ah, now, that's thinking," said Lathon, shaking his head. "Just don't invite me to your Super Bowl party. Next!"

Sara took the floor then, though with her usual trepidation. She *hadn't* had such a great summer, she reported, having spent two weeks with, first her mother, then her father, and not enough time with her beloved niece, Amanda. ("My God, that little girl is just so delicious, and there is such a bond between us," she mooned. "She looks at me with just this love in her eyes—I swear, I have dreams where I run off with her to some desert island.") Then, there was the state of her affair with Christian, the beautiful, if bedraggled, video director. He was as passionate as before, e-mailing her mash notes at work, and talking in dead earnest about "having a kid with her someday." What made this problematic was that he wouldn't *sleep* with Sara, despite two months of heavy petting. Nor would he tell her why he was holding out, other than he wanted it to be "perfect" when it did happen.

"I'm just so damn frustrated—it's almost worse than when I was with *no one*," she said. "I mean, he's very sweet to me, and wants to spend every minute together. But then, when I see him, it's just more of the same—talking and kissing till three in the morning, and rolling around the couch with our clothes on. And instead of being happy, I feel fat and ugly, like he's messing with my head on purpose. And, *of course*, I've tried talking about it, but he's so vague and murky—although, the other night, he did hint that something happened to him as a kid. And right away, I told him that I'm completely fine with it, and that I could deal with whatever it was he had to tell me. But then he clammed up and wouldn't discuss it any further, and now I'm so angry, I feel like dumping him flat. Telling him to fuck off and die."

"Well, of course you do, and who can blame you," said Lathon. "I mean, here it's two months and you've been completely up front with him, and yet, for some reason, he won't turn his cards over. Obviously, he's attracted to you—you say he can't keep his hands off— but there's some deep, dark backstory that he won't share with you. And I suspect that that's what's driving you nuts. That you could handle having to wait if he just told you what it's about."

"Um, I *guess*," she said. "Though not for much longer. I'm so frustrated, I'm ready to go down and greet the sailors."

There was a peal of laughter from the men in the room, as well as some stealthy double takes. Rex, in particular, eyed her with something other than friendly solicitude.

"I don't know," he said. "This sounds like a bad deal all over. *My* rule of thumb is, never trust *anyone* who won't have sex with you."

Lina passed over this remark without comment. "Sara, how much do you know about this guy's sexual history?"

"Well, see, that's the thing—I know that he's definitely had a *lot* of it," said Sara. "Not from him but from friends in common, I'm told he had quite the reputation on the club scene. But then, according to those same people, he calmed down a couple of years ago, and got totally involved in his work. So, to make a long story short, I don't know what to think."

"Well, but what needs to be asked," said Jack, "is, what do you *want?* Do you want to hang around for more head games with him, or do you want to get off the ride? Because I'm remembering back to that guy last spring, the one who strung you along for a while, then wrote that bullshit form letter. And the thing *I'd* like to know is, why do you stand for it? You're way too good for this treatment."

"Yeah, really," said Lina. "As you said yourself, this is worse, almost, than being alone. At least if you were alone, you could spend your free time looking. Whereas now, it's totally monopolized by him, and you've got no chance to find someone real."

"Well, but it-it's not that he's not real," said Sara. "You know, I'm sure he does care for me, and he's got all these good qualities, which, if I could just figure out what the problem is, then maybe we could start to make some—"

"But see, there you are, trying to *potchki* around, instead of *demanding to be treated respectfully,*" said Jack. "For some unknown reason, you're willing to let these guys jerk you, instead of saying, 'I will not accept being done like this.' "

There was a thrum of agreement from the other members. It was as though the truth of the remark had struck in them some key of harmonic resonance. Sara, for her part, said nothing for several moments, fumbling with the lapel of her jacket.

"I—I see what you're saying, and, you know, I do put my foot down. If anything, my history is I'm *too* quick to do that, that I cut people off after the first sign of trouble, and—"

"Well, but what Jack is saying is something different," said Lathon. "What he's saying is that, at some base level, you don't respect your wishes. You don't stand up and say, 'Look, this is what I need, and I won't settle for less.' At thirty-eight years old, time is very much of the essence for you, and you need to know where things stand with Christian. And you also need to decide, if he can be trusted, whether it's worth the long-term investment. And that, too, requires respecting your wishes, i.e., thinking very carefully about whether to take on his problems or look for someone less damaged."

Sara's face dropped. "Oh *God*, the idea of starting from scratch again. . . . I get sick just thinking about it. . . ."

There was a gathering pause, perhaps five or ten seconds' length. In the silence, you could hear the whisper of trees, their crowns mussed by the soft, fall wind.

"It stinks being alone, Sara; I can hear it in your voice," said Jack. "But at some point, you've gotta decide what matters to you. Is it more important to have a body in bed with you, or a guy who really gets it that you're special?"

We heard next from Jack about his "joyride" in summer stock, and what a shot in the arm it had given him. He'd played the lead in *Volpone*, farcing it up as the old grifter, and said it was like being the guest of honor at a great party each night. His wife had come up for several weekends, and gotten a big kick out of seeing him command the stage. There had also been an agent on hand from New York, and talks were afoot about an Off-Broadway play, for which Jack had already done two callbacks. And more good news, at least potentially: a meeting had been scheduled by the D.A.'s office to review Jack's suspension as a producer. His ban didn't expire until next April, and a hearing this soon was very possibly a sign of their willingness to reinstate him.

"Now, I don't wanna get too worked up," he said. "For all I know, they're gonna *add on* to the damn thing, and if that should happen . . . well, I can't even afford to think that. But if, God willing, they do let me back, I've gotten a couple of calls from friends in the business. Just a line to let me know that there's a spot still waiting for me, if God in His heaven, et cetera."

He concluded with some bad news, which was that, though employed all summer, he'd never been so broke in his life. The job in summer stock had only paid scale, and then the Feds took theirs for back taxes. What with two rents to carry, plus his transportation, it had worked out to a big net loss. Over the course of these last sessions, then, he really needed to look at what the money signified. Why did he keep cutting his own throat financially, and what steps could he take to gain control?

Finally, it was Dylan's turn, almost three hours into session. As he took the floor, you could feel the climate shift. Suddenly, the other members looked sour and drowsy, the shadows deepening beneath their eyes. Dylan, too, seemed out of gas, slinging himself up in his seat. He glanced over at Lathon, as if awaiting instruction, before gathering his thoughts together.

"I—I had talked with Dr. Lathon—saw him twice this week, in fact—about what I should tell you guys. I figured, you know, what could I say that you'd even believe, since I'd broken my word twice before? Anyhow, he suggested that I tell you what happened this time; tell about the thing that finally pulled me back in. It happened three weeks ago, driving to my friend's house in Hartford. I was supposed to have started early, gotten out before rush hour—and before I had a case of beer in my system. But I had a late lunch at this bar downstairs, and then this woman came in that I—ah well, never mind.

"Anyway, by the time I looked up, it was ten at night, and I wasn't on the road till eleven-thirty. Well, somewhere around Norwalk, I got white-line fever, but instead of doing the smart thing and finding a room to sleep it off in, I decided to keep on going. And then, the next thing I knew, I woke up behind the wheel, and there were these big, blinding lights in my mirror. It took me a couple of seconds to realize it was a truck, and that it was bearing down on me, doing seventy. Apparently, I'd pulled over to the side of the road, except there's not really a shoulder on the Merritt Parkway and my back end was sticking out in traffic. And I started fiddling with the ignition, trying to get the car going, but I was too freaked out to realize that I was still in 'drive,' and meanwhile, the truck is practically on top of me. I didn't have time to scream, even, or cover my eyes—I just braced, and waited for the hit. But somehow—and I have no idea how—the guy swung wide, and just barely clipped my tail end with his hitch. It threw me into the steering wheel, and gave me a knot on the forehead, and basically shoved my back bumper up into the trunk.

"But *still*, you know, I was alive, and in pretty good shape, actually, besides a massive headache. And I was able to start the car and pull onto the grass and call AAA on my cell phone. It took 'em a while to reach me, 'cause I didn't know where I was, and couldn't even remember what road I was on. But I'll tell you what I do remember, and what I'll never forget: those high beams in my mirror. I—I truly believe that something happened that night; that there was some—some power or, you know, force that intervened to save me, to keep me alive for my daughters. And you can say what you want, but I know what I saw—there is *no way* that truck could've missed me. And so ever since that night, I've not only not had a drink, I've been going to a meeting near my house. It isn't the most—uplifting; in fact, I find it pretty depressing, and dominated by the same three blowhards most of the time. But I'll definitely keep going there, at least till I find another meeting. Because after eight or whatever months here, I finally got what Jack was saying—there's no chance I can do this by myself."

Rex and Sara shifted in their seats, crankily resetting themselves. Lina huffed a sigh, and studied the terra-cottas. No one said anything for a quarter of a minute. Out the open window, a breeze rustled past, casting its ease like a net.

"See, this is what I didn't want to happen," he said. "To come back here and make everybody uncomfortable to have me. I mean, if anyone should be uncomfortable, it's me."

Again, arid silence. Dylan glanced at Lathon, who was cleaning his nails with a Post-it.

"It's just . . . I don't know," said Sara, flicking her hair. "There's something the doctor said that I thought was really true: 'Trust equals promises kept over time.' I mean, we've been here for eight months and you haven't kept your promises. So why, at this stage, should we trust you?"

Dylan nodded, fielding the question gravely. Meanwhile, one of his eyelids began to flutter, twitching like a shade that had flown up.

"I—I, you know, I understand your feelings," he said. "I haven't really contributed here, been a part of the team—"

"Yeah, you could say that," Rex snickered. "We thought you were dead, or sleeping on a bench at Grand Central."

Dylan swallowed in parched anxiety. His eyelid was batting furiously. "I—I agree that I should've called, let you know I was okay. Even though I was blitzed, I could've done that, at least. It's just . . . I didn't want another lecture on how I was stuck in suffering. I *know* I was suffering—believe me, no one knows it better than me—and I'm trying to dig my way out of it. But it's like they tell you at every meeting: all you can do is one day at a time."

He apologized again, while conceding that "sorry" didn't cut it, since they'd heard it all before and seen how much it stood for. But he said that he really did mean it this time, and had taken some steps to improve his life. He'd finally sold his house, absorbing a sizable loss to get out from under his mortgage. He'd found a condo in Nutley for Jeannie and the girls, at a fraction of what the house had cost him. And he'd begun to look around for an agent to replace Harold, hoping to catch on with one of the "young tigers" in the business. For the first time since Greg died, he was ready to roll up his sleeves and pour himself into a project. After being idle for most of a year, he saw now what a blessing it was to work, to do something you were good at and admired for. Most people didn't have that, and just thrashed away at whatever they fell into. If you were lucky enough to do better, you owed it to yourself to bust your tail.

The others conferred with darting glances, weighing Dylan's penance. For all its sharp edges, there was a quality of mercy in this group, a tendency to err toward optimism. Even a cynic like Sara held a place in her heart for the possibility of change, of human betterment. If she believed in it for herself, she couldn't deny it to Dylan, no matter how fuzzy his prospects. His stumbles notwithstanding, he was one of them still, a member of the tribe of self-improvers.

"Well, I like that you're taking action, and doing stuff to turn it around," said Jack. "And, most of all, I'm glad that you're going to meetings, and urge you to make as many as you can—say, ninety meetings in the first ninety days. What worries me is you saying that you find them depressing, as if you were expecting to make friends or be entertained. I mean, even in a bad meeting—and not all of 'em are great—there should be a couple of things that help you out. It might be a chunk of someone's story, or just an expression that you hear—a phrase that, for that moment, gives you strength. And if you aren't getting that, then absolutely change meetings—maybe find one in the Village, where there's more musicians. Because if you're bored, it's a cinch you'll stop going sooner or later—and then you're right back in the shit."

"Yeah, actually, you know, that's an idea," said Dylan. "There *must* be a meeting of artists and musicians. I'm going to ask my counselor if he knows of one."

"And what about your daughters—you haven't mentioned *them*," said Sara. "How'd you explain your wandering off to them?"

Dylan's face hung, welling up with color. "I, um . . . well, you know, we told them that I was sick. That I had a problem with my prostate, which was true, you know. From the alcohol . . . I had to go to the hospital for a couple of . . ."

He looked down, ruddy with shame. Even his ears had turned scarlet. "You know, they're really good kids—I don't know how we did it. Their mother's a mess, bringing home one guy after another— Olivia, the funny one, calls them 'mommy's dummies.' And as for their dad—well, I'm fine, you know, when I'm sober. I love them to death, and always tell 'em how great they are, and go out of my way to try to make things fun for them. Like this weekend, I took 'em to Great Adventure, and then we came home and had pizza and sat down at the piano, and made up silly lyrics to old Beatles songs. And they had a great time and wanted to stay the whole week, now that I've got the place fixed up a little. I bought bunk beds for the back room, and a big TV with Sega Genesis, and this melamine toy chest so that they can bring some of their stuff over. And I have to say, it was the happiest I've seen 'em since the breakup, and the most we've felt like a real family again, laughing and playing roughhouse, and talking about getting a dog. And then, Sunday night, when I drove them home, Rebecca just suddenly started crying. I took her in my arms, thinking maybe she was overtired, but then she said . . . she, uh, said that . . ."

He brought the heel of his hands to his eyes, holding them like a compress. When he took them away, his eyes were wet with tears. He bent forward, studying his palms.

"She said, 'I don't want you to leave, Daddy. You're going to get sick again. Every time you leave, you go get sick. . . .' "

He put his head in his hands, weeping in short, tight bursts. He held himself taut, elbows tucked to his ribs, rocking in short, tight movements. Watching, Lina pressed her fists to her chin, as if to scourge herself for chiding him. Jack pursed his lips and stared out the window, blinking back tears of his own. Even Rex seemed ashamed, cinching his broad face up into a mask of self-chastisement.

At length, Dylan stopped and rose from his crouch, looking around for a tissue. Lathon passed a box over from which Dylan took freely, satirizing his grief with loud honking. The other members laughed at this, grateful for the gesture. Dylan wrung the wad out and used it to pat himself dry. This drew more laughter, and an infusion of goodwill, a tacit camaraderie that included him. Without a word having been said, it was clear where he stood, and his relief was all but tangible.

"You've lost a great deal, Dylan, and much of what you lost is irreplaceable," said Lathon. "You had more than just a friend and partner in Greg. What you had, in the most basic sense, was a brother. The same goes for Harold, your former agent; in some ways, they were your real family, and certainly more loving to you than your birth family. The sad fact is, that's how it is for many people. They get shortchanged the first time around with their families, and so, when they're older and smarter, they make themselves a new one. It starts with a spouse and, at some point, children, and includes friends and pets and maybe even some in-laws, as well as the one or two siblings who mean them well. And if they're lucky and they've learned something, that family grows as they get older, and now includes grandchildren and daughters-in-law and parents they've made peace with, closing the loop on the old and new families.

"Now, through no fault of your own, Dylan, that family you made has been taken away from you. And while it's only right that you should honor that loss, it's time to note an overlooked truth, which is that, having made a new family, you can do it again—and with a much better partner than Jeannie. You've got two beautiful kids, your health, and your faculties, as well as a marketable skill. You've also got some hard-earned wisdom now about the way your story works. You know that you're vulnerable to the seductive ice queens, to the Jeannies of the world who promise heat and light, but make off with what little you've got. And you know, or at least you told us, what you really want—someone who's warm and unshakably herself; an adult, in other words; a *partner.* You're a young man still—fifty is just the beginning of the prime years—but not so young that you can afford the same mistakes. You see, for me, intelligence isn't a cluster of facts, or the ability to hold two ideas at the same time. No, intelligence is the capacity to learn from error. To be taught, at great pain, who you really are, and embody it with courage and humility."

seventeen

october

In New York, there is a trick of the light in autumn that makes the tawdry seem epic. Refracted through the ozone and carbon monoxide are filaments of gold and bronze. They dress up the streets in a coat of false majesty, and an iridescence the color of memory. People look crisper, more compactly themselves, sensible of the stark changes to come. Old cars hulk at the curb, like reliquaries, their windshields ablaze in the sun. Even the bricks of dank row houses throb with pigments, waiting for their Hopper to come paint them.

It was in just such an ambience of soot and elegy that Peter and I met before a session. We were sitting on the balcony of a restaurant called Metropolis, feeling the planet turn under our feet. It was a little after five, and the sidewalk was filling up with the foot traffic peculiar to the Flatiron district: beautiful young women in various shades of black, and the balding young businessmen who seek them. Wiping his new glasses on the sleeve of his shirt, Peter sat back and surveyed the scene, watching with the calm of a man who has nothing at stake.

"Man, I can't tell you how good it feels to be married." He grinned. "Especially when I come to a place like this."

On the table was a stack of wedding pictures, funny color snaps taken with disposable cameras that Peter and his bride had provided for their guests. In many of the shots, husband and wife were

sublimely silly: poised over the cake in matching pink poodle sun-
glasses, pretending to try and slice it with a Swiss Army knife; or
hamming up the dance floor like Groucho Marx and Margaret Du-
mont, gazing toward the heavens cheek-to-cheek. Flipping through
the pile, I saw why Peter was so relaxed now, sitting there, tan and
cheerful, above the fray. He'd had the good fortune to marry a
woman of spirit, someone who got the joke that life was less dire than
elsewhere reported. In her smart, brown eyes and encompassing
smile was the conviction that not all knowledge was tragic; that there
was truth and measure in the comic view, too. Such, in fact, was the
charmed confidence in those pictures that you could easily envision
future pictures: Peter and Kara dandling their two-year-old boy,
and, years from now, the brood playing golf in Scarsdale, his sons
making mock of Peter's backswing.

"It sure looks like your second wedding went better than the
first," I remarked.

"What first wedding?" he cracked. "You trying to tell me I was
married before? Funny, I don't remember it."

He waved for another round, and told a story about his pre-
wedding dinner. The meal itself was a small affair, just the immediate families and their significant others at a fancy inn on Block
Island. Though a tad overformal, things were going along smoothly
until Peter's father and Kara's got into an argument. Both were avi-
ation buffs and held strong opinions about which plane had ruled the
skies in World War I: the British Spitfire or the German Messer-
schmitt. Voices were raised, and a tense silence set in. And then,
Kara, in her light way, tweaked the two of them, saying that everyone knew that the real hero was Snoopy, who shot down the Red
Baron over Hamburg.

"As ridiculous as that sounds," Peter said, "it stopped the argument cold, by getting them to laugh at how childish they were
being. And it showed me again how tough Kara is, that she wasn't
going to let any nonsense ruin our day. You should see her with my

mom, she's got her eating out of her hand. When my mom found out
that Kara was changing her name to mine, she almost collapsed with
joy. She said, 'Peter, if you don't hurry up and marry this woman, I'll
find someone who will.'"

"Well, hey, congratulations on making your mom happy," I said.
"God knows, that's no small matter."

"Ah, it's only temporary," he said. "She'll find something to piss
her off. But she better be careful how she crosses that line. My wife'll
show her who's the boss here."

He laughed as he said this, savoring the words *my wife*. He was
so tickled to be a part of this brave, new launch, and proud of the
ease with which it sluiced the waters. Before the wedding, Kara had
adroitly settled the money issue, funding their joint account to the
tune of six figures. In kind, Peter had unloaded his pride and joy, an
old Porsche, and settled on a prudent Volvo. And though they could
well afford a larger place uptown, they decided to sit tight in Kara's
Chelsea two-bedroom, agreeing that ostentation was a needless way
to tempt fate.

"So then, those fears you had when we started out eight months
ago?" I asked. "About making the wrong move again, and looking
like a fool in your mom's eyes?"

"Gone," he said, breezily. "Or, I should say, almost gone; I'll
probably always worry a little what my mom thinks."

"And do you still look around at the great apartment and the
pretty wife and say to yourself, 'Man, I don't deserve this?'"

Peter laughed his nasal laugh. In the dusk, his gold rims
sparkled. "Listen, let me tell you," he said, leaning forward. "Anybody who's taken as much crap as I have deserves all the happiness
they can get."

At the session later that evening, the room was teeming with new developments. Jack had just come from his meeting at the D.A.'s office,

where things had gone even better than he'd hoped. In the weeks leading up to it, he'd collected forty affidavits, most from prominent figures in the community. In addition, there was praise from his probation officer, who bore witness to Jack's good offices at AA. The assistant D.A. had been duly impressed. While making no promises, he hinted that approval of Jack's return was a formality. On his way out, in fact, Jack was approached by one of the investigators, who thought it a travesty that Jack had gotten seven years.

"He said, 'Personally, I think that *two* years would've covered it,' but I thought, nah, it wouldn't've been enough," said Jack. "See, two years out, I was still drinking and drugging, and if they'd've let me back in then, I'd be dead now. I really needed that time to get solid in my sobriety, and to see how my actions had hurt people. Of course, after *five* years, I'd pretty well gotten the point, but I didn't think the D.A. would want to hear that."

Next up was Dylan, looking donnish in a tweed jacket, with news of his own to relay. He'd been steered by his addictions counselor to a meeting downtown consisting mostly of musicians and artists. There, the emphasis was on story, not platitudes, and the "preachiness" was kept to a minimum. As an added bonus, they were tough on windbags, such that those who ran their mouth for no reason got shot down fast by the regulars. He had been going for a couple of weeks and hadn't said much yet, preferring to sit in back and listen. Nonetheless, he liked what he was hearing so far, and had gotten some good reinforcement. And it couldn't have come at a better time, because an old pal from his drug days had moved into the building across the street. Nicky was a bouncer who had always had the best coke, and would deliver it, like a pizza, to your door. Now, he was living fifty feet from Dylan, and calling twice a day to hawk his wares.

"It's amazing, I finally climb out of hell, and the devil himself moves next to me. I'm letting the machine screen my calls now, but

I still see him in front of the building, like he's got nothing better to do than sell me an eightball. And you could understand why—I used to be a *real* good customer of his—but come on, already; no means no. Meanwhile, I'm like a prisoner in my own apartment, wondering how to get away from him. Do I give up the apartment? Get, like, a restraining order against him? *Your honor, that man keeps trying to sell me cocaine. Please make him go do it on Eleventh Avenue, where I can't see him.*"

Though this was just the first phase of session, where the members announced their concerns for the evening, the group fell to work on Dylan's problem. In lieu of past hostilities, they seemed bent on protecting him, handling him with tact and care. Jack took the lead, pressing Dylan to leave Hell's Kitchen. "Why would you want to stay there, in that awful apartment—or, as *El Jefe* would say, what are you afraid would happen if you moved someplace nicer? You think your wife'll come after you, trying to get a better divorce deal? Do you worry that this pusher'll follow you there, maybe bribe the movers for your address? All I'm saying is, it's nuts to live like a hostage—and the worst thing imaginable for your recovery."

"I agree," said Peter. "Even if you have to leave town for a while; rent a place in Connecticut and commute. I'm not just worried about your sobriety but your actual safety. I mean, what if this guy tries stronger tactics, like banging on your door at three in the morning?"

Dylan nodded solemnly, stroking the tip of his fine beard. "You know, I hear what you're saying, and I agree, to a point. But with what I'm paying Jeannie, and not having worked in almost a year, I—I'm barely scraping by in *this* place. There are still checks, thank God, from the stuff in syndication, but my income's probably a sixth of what it was. And as I'm sure you all know, it's three grand a *month* now for a small two-bedroom, not to mention the five grand up front to pay the realtor. And with no work coming in, and my

Keogh fund running down, I'm worried about just keeping a roof over my head."

The group took this under advisement, thinking the problem through out loud. Lina asked if he'd considered a neighborhood in Brooklyn, like Carroll Gardens, where his rent dollar might go farther. Jack suggested he talk about a buyout with his landlord, who could paint and sand the floors and charge triple what he was getting now. And wasn't there some cash from the sale of his house, which Dylan could use to carry him till he was back on his feet?

Dylan was moved by their concern, but raised difficulties about each suggestion. The sale of his house was not yet final, and what money he stood to clear was going to Jeannie and her lawyers. As for a place like Carroll Gardens, he knew people who'd looked there, and found it nearly as pricey as Manhattan. And about the buyout idea, it was certainly worth a shot, although he doubted he could get more than a couple of thousand.

The group flagged somewhat, dismayed by the stubbornness of his problems, when Lathon stepped in to prod them. In their haste to rescue Dylan from the big, bad drug dealer, they had neglected to get an answer to Jack's question, namely, what was so scary about leaving Hell's Kitchen? There were plenty of decent towns on the other side of the Lincoln Tunnel, where he could live in modest comfort and not fear for his life. To be sure, it wasn't Manhattan, but nor, on the other hand, was it permanent. When his finances allowed, he could move back and have his pick here. So what was keeping him from doing so?

Though it was long since cool enough to require closing the window, Dylan had begun to perspire. He rummaged his pockets for a handkerchief and sopped up the glare on his forehead.

"I wouldn't call it scared so much as—oh, I don't know," he said. "I guess it's just something that didn't occur to me."

"Really?" said Lathon. "It seems odd that it wouldn't. The rents are sky-high here, and you're low on cash, to the extent that you've had to borrow from your Keogh fund. I'd think it'd be the *first* thing that occurred to you."

Dylan looked away, screwing down farther into his chair. "I mean, I've already done it, moved out to New Jersey, so it's not like I'm afraid of that. In fact, I really liked it, living in Montclair; I had everything I ever wanted there, except the right woman. So no, I don't think that that's the problem. It's just that—"

"Is it because your wife's there, and you want to be as far from her as possible?" Jack offered.

"Um, no, not really; New Jersey's a pretty big state. I doubt we'd run into each other jogging."

The group kept probing, trying to decode his resistance, but got no further than a kind of generalized aversion. Then Rex put his hand up, as he did when he knew the answer, making less-than-subtle mock of his class-clown rep.

"You know, as I was sitting here listening to you talk about New Jersey, I was thinking about Dylan's *last* place—the house in Montclair. I was picturing the pool in back, and the landscaped yard, and the porch that wrapped around half the house—and then I pictured the kind of place that you're all talking about. Basically, it'd be some pillbox in East Rutherford, the kind with popcorn ceilings and that stank shag carpet, and those fake-wood cabinets with the veneer peeling off. And, like, forget about the fact that it's built on swampland, and you've got mice running around the size of coyotes, from scarfing up all that radon. What would scare me to death is going home to an empty house there. I mean, who the hell're you gonna call in *East Rutherford* at two in the morning?"

The grunts from the others were like murmured amens. Even Lathon was startled by the force of the remark, eyeing Rex with a half-smile. Rex stretched out his legs, fingering the cigar in his shirt pocket.

"Pretty good, huh, what I come up with when I stop playing," he said. "It's just a shame I don't use my superpowers for good."

But while the others commended Rex, Dylan's response went unnoted. His eyes lost their luster and stared ahead, dissolving in soft abstraction. For ten or twelve seconds, he seemed lodged in a trance state, frozen in perfect stillness.

"What about it, Dylan?" asked Lathon, finally. "Did Rex put his finger on the problem?"

Dylan blinked, climbing out of himself. "I'm sorry. What'd you say?"

"I asked if Rex was right about your reluctance to move—the fear of being alone and invisible?"

Dylan stared off, still half in his null state. "Yeah," he murmured, after several moments went by. "Yeah, I'd say he hit it."

The group got a report from Lina about life with Jeffrey (ever better), and from Sara about her affair with Christian (on life support). And then, Rex took the floor to announce his news from the last session, which turned out to be the evening's main event. After reflecting on it all summer, and having been cornered by his wife and parents, he had come to the conclusion that he was a "raging alcoholic," and would be dead by thirty-five if he didn't stop now. It had been fourteen years of mass consumption, and the effects were starting to add up all around. He'd begun to suffer migraines and bouts of prolonged depression. Looking into the matter, he'd learned there was a high rate of alcoholism in his family, particularly on his mother's side. One of her sisters was a regular at Hazelden, where she checked in twice a year to dry out. And her father's brother plowed his Harley into a light pole, after knocking off a quart of Jack Daniel's.

"I don't know why she never told me that before," he said. "Though I guess we're pretty much known for not talking. Anyway, it scared the hell out of me when she did tell me, because I do a lot of that over-the-top stuff when I drink. Like, for example, I'll be out partying till two in the morning, then we'll all pile into a couple of Jeeps and do these Death Race 2000 deals in Central Park. We'll be blasting around the turns, going, like, seventy miles an hour, just blowing through the stoplights like they don't apply to us. And whoever's behind the wheel—usually me or my friend Blake—has had a couple of pitchers of beer, as well as an assortment of mixed cocktails. And it's, like, one bad turn and you've bought yourself a tree, which almost happened last time, when I spun out on the grass—scared the fuck out of these four little Latin *esais* who were sparking up a blunt in Sheep Meadow."

Rex paused for effect here, shaking his head in self-rebuke. He was still as tan as a surfer and comparably dressed, in overalls and an old work shirt from which he'd chopped off the sleeves, exposing his massive arms. His blond hair was platinum, after months of heavy sun-time, and cropped flat and close to the head, Caesar-style. Taken top to bottom, he didn't look much like the stricken penitent.

"Anyway, my point," he continued, "is I realized I was a wreck in progress, and decided it was time to squash that. So, three and a half weeks ago, I went to my first AA meeting and haven't missed a single day since, whether I'm here in town or in Amagansett on the weekends. And it's exactly one month today since I had my last drink, and I'm pleased to report that I haven't felt this good since high school, when I was basically your home-by-dinner, no-friends-having, sex-starved little tool."

There was an eyeblink pause, in which the group seemed to teeter, unsure how to respond. And then, one by one, they fell into line, praising Rex's decision. Peter commended him for getting sober while his buddies were partying on. "In *that* kind of crowd," he said, "it takes guts to order a seltzer. I just hope they don't get to you with that macho pressure, because this is really a good thing you're doing." Lina agreed, saying she was happiest for Rex's daughter, who might finally spend some time with him now on weeknights. And what Dylan found admirable was that Rex had acted before the worst happened—before a kidney failed, or he'd hit an oncoming car, or driven his wife out of the house.

"Trust me, I know," he said. "It's harder to quit while you're ahead. But a whole lot cheaper, in the long run."

"As a matter of fact, you were kind of my inspiration—you and Jack both, and what happened to you," Rex said. "It might not've looked it at times, but I was paying *dead* attention to you, and thinking, Damn, I could really do this; I could lose everything I have. And the more I thought about it, the more *ass* it seemed to me—to have access to your story and not learn from it. And I'm sure that must sound like the typical capitalist—getting something of value, while giving up next to nothing—but I really am grateful to you guys, and I'll try to repay you somehow. Like, maybe, come on time here, for a start."

"Well, I'm sure we'd all appreciate that, but no, you don't have to pay us back," said Lathon. "Some people contribute here by telling their stories, and others by listening to them. And as we saw again tonight, you're a first-rate listener; you hear right down to the pain. So don't concern yourself with paying us back—although, if you've got any stock tips, we're all ears."

The others laughed at this, then moved on to a related matter, probing Rex's taste for chills and spills. Even when sober, he liked to go rock-climbing without a rope, and gun his Italian racing bike in the rain. He could work out all day, he said, and kill himself on the StairMaster, but it just didn't get it unless there was some element of risk—the juice, as he put it, "of maybe being dragged out on a gurney." That was what he missed about college hockey, or doing coke deals on the West Side of Philly: not the payoff so much as the thrill of action, that "speed-burn when your balls are in your throat." And without booze to damp him down now, he had all this loose energy, and was afraid he'd find some other jones to sink it in.

"Actually," he said, in a long, loping self-interview, "I've already got a little problem with gambling. I only used to bet on weekends, you know, and only then on college football; small-time action, like maybe a hundred bucks a game. Then, it kinda leached into Monday Night Football—not to get even, you know; just to spark up a dead night. Now, suddenly, I'm waking up on Sunday morning and checking out the weather in *Oakland;* trying to find what the forecast is before I bet the over/under. And even though it's still in the 'expensive-hobby' range, I could easily see me going up the ladder with this. Becoming one of those tools who bet the mortgage on a teaser."

Lathon cut him off there, saying that the group pretty well had the picture. What Rex was describing, he said, was something common among addicts—a cross-addiction to high-risk behavior. The two things seemed to be linked biochemically and were often predictors for the other, so that people who were chronic speeders, say, or who had multiple sex partners, had a high incidence of alcoholism, and vice versa. It was also well settled that these risky stunts were how addicts dealt with their feelings—or, more accurately, *didn't* deal. And so, while he joined the others in praise of Rex's temperance, he wanted to take a look now at the pain his drinking masked—a subject that Rex had avoided thus far.

Rex stroked his stubble and let slip a grin, winking that they'd finally got him. It wasn't, he said, that he was averse to confession, just that he wasn't much good at it. Both his parents, while Italian, didn't fit the mold, and were more like Midwesterners than anything: stout and cheerful, never a bad word to say about anybody—

"Ahh, *balls,*" Jack sneered, flicking his wrist disgustedly. "I don't believe a word out of your mouth."

A bright, blinking silence fell over the group. Rex looked at Jack and arched an eyebrow, eyeing him like a comic does a heckler. Tilting his head, he smiled in good humor, as if to say, Surely, I misheard you, old friend.

"You go on and on," said Jack, "about your macho stunts, and your wake-up call about drinking, but do you know what I hear? I hear *bragging*. I hear the exact same thing as when you told us about your girlfriend. No sorrow in your voice, no 'Christ, what was I thinking?' Instead, it's, 'Hey, dude, aren't I cool for doing these things, and aren't I twice as cool now for not doing 'em?' "

Rex went on staring at Jack and stroking his chin, but the drollery had gone out of his eyes. "Except I think I *have* changed," he said with forced calm. "I'm much more considerate now, especially to my wife, who, if she were here, would tell you how I've grown. How I book home after work to be with Marisa, and how I'm the only who can give her a bath at night and get her to stop crying when she's teething. And now that I've stopped drinking, Claudia raves how nice I am, whether it's bringing her little presents when I come down off a road trip, or telling her that I love her and that I'm lucky to have her—"

"Yeah, yeah, but it's all bogus," Jack sniped. "It's just a big fucking act with you. Before, you were playing at being the bad guy, and now you're doing the good guy. Same difference, really; it'll last a couple of months, and then you'll be on to the next thing. There's no *there* there."

Now Rex bristled, sitting up at attention. "Excuse me, but who are you to tell me that? What, are you just back from some mountain in Tibet, that suddenly you know all and see all? I admit that I did dirt, I told Claudia I was sorry for it, and we both got on with our lives. Was that not enough? Was I supposed to ask *you* for forgiveness? I mean, what's the fucking drill, that you've got this hard-on for me? What, do I remind you of one of your sons?"

"No, you sure don't, pal," Jack snorted. "My sons know to treat a woman with respect."

"Oh, and I guess they got that from you, with your twelve bad marriages," Rex said.

"All right, that'll do," said Lathon. "Both of you go to your respective corners, and let the group react to what they heard."

In lieu of the usual shilly-shallying, several hands went up at once. "Well, from what I heard, there was something missing in Rex's story," said Peter. "It felt . . . light, somehow, like he was talking about his golf game—'Oh, I finally figured what was making my tee shots hook.' I mean, it's great that he's done this and I hope he sticks with it, but you don't really sense that it's *cost* him much."

"Yeah, I don't trust it, either," said Lina. "I mean, for nine months, we've heard nothing but great news from Rex. One minute, you're raving about your baby, the 'supermodel,' and the next, you're flying around the world, making millions. Then, tonight, out of nowhere, we hear that you were depressed and having blackouts, but where was all that when it was happening? You know, I thought we had a deal that we would tell the truth to each other, and for me, at least, that wasn't easy. I am *not* the kind of person who tells her problems to strangers, but it was important and I understood that, and we were all making the effort. But with you, I really feel like you didn't keep your end up, and, to be honest about it, I think that that stinks."

Another lengthy pause, this one stock-still and ringing, a silence of affirmation.

"I . . . see," said Rex, drawing out the first word derisively. "And what is it you want me to share here?"

"That you're *human*, like the rest of us, and not some jerk who's getting off on this," cried Lina. "It's almost like we're a *joke* to you!"

Rex turned away, his cheek coloring as if slapped. He opened his mouth, but for the first time, irony failed him, and he sat there, flushed under scrutiny. In the ensuing silence, he seemed to regress before our eyes, slouching like a child who'd been scolded.

"You see, Rex, that's the problem with the false story," said

Lathon. "It keeps us at a distance, so that we don't know what to think. The truth is, you have begun to change for the better; becoming a dad was the best thing to happen to you. You're calmer and less boastful, more responsive to others—in short, you're more of an adult. Unfortunately, though, your story's still lagging behind, making you sound like a guy at a keg party. Just listen to your diction: 'I drive, like, seventy miles an hour, dude, and my Jeep is, like, totally bitchin' . . .' "

Everyone laughed at Lathon's Ridgemont High–speak, reducing tensions by a notch. Even Rex joined in, covering his eyes in mock shame, and glancing at the others to read their mood.

"Ah, it isn't *that* bad," he groaned. "Just 'cause I look like Sean Penn . . ."

"Well, I'd say it's pretty close," said Sara. "In fact, I'd say it's dead-on."

"Oh yeah, like you're one to talk," Rex said. " 'Hey, you guys, I just met the cutest *boy.* I can't wait till he calls me up so we can go to the *mall!*' "

This also met with laughter, further lessening hostilities. Lathon tapped his armrest, revving up for a solo.

"Rex," he said, "do pay attention to this, because language ultimately matters. Words are neurotransmitters, and can lock you in place, unable to convey your true story to the world.

"Which brings us to the larger question, and one that's been lurking around the edges here: What, exactly, is your true story? What *matters* to you, what do you dream of making? Clearly, it isn't money, because you've made lots of that already, and you're so bored you've got to go rock-climbing without a rope. As you've begun to find out, there's no narrative in money. You can't hang it on a wall and say, I painted that, or walk it down a runway and say, I designed that. That's why there are so many vampires hanging around the art world, people with tons of money but no story of their own, and so they have to buy someone else's to feel reified. And it's why I see so many kids in my son's private school dressed up like Snoop Doggy Dogg. It's not that they're bad kids, but rather that they have no story, and'll try on any false one that scares their parents. Now, fair enough, they're fifteen, and by next month, they'll be hippies, but you, Rex, you're thirty-two. It's time to stop playing pirate and accept the task of adulthood, which is to figure out what you were sent here to make."

Rex made a face, blinking dismissively. "Well, but when I'm *not* playing pirate, as you so kindly put it, I'm making a great living for my family. What's more adult than that?"

"Except that—to repeat—it leaves you hollow, having to bet on ball games to get a buzz," said Lathon. "And it also ignores the point of all that manic energy—the need to *make* something, to express what's in you. That's what I mean by 'serious fun': a craft that engages both body and story, and that utilizes all your passion. Every last one of us has that need, and it's our job to find out what fills it."

One eye shut in mockery, Rex looked around the circle, trying to recruit derision. None of the others took the bait, though. "And how are you supposed to do *that?*"

Lathon smiled, passing over the insult. "Serious fun usually derives from childhood, from an activity that engrossed us as kids. For Jack, it was acting, and being in plays at a young age. For Lina, it was science, and looking at stuff under microscopes, checking out life in all its forms. And you, if I remember right, loved to cook as a boy, and actually worked in a restaurant."

"Uh . . . yeah, I did," said Rex, his sarcasm wilting. "I worked at my grandpa's place, starting from age nine. And, actually, it *was* cool, hanging out with him prepping sauces, and going with him in the morning to buy fish. He knew about two hundred words in English, but he was like a thesaurus on fish—he could tell you every kind of fish that came in there. Thanks to him, I still get up at five A.M. some days and go down to Fulton Street to buy it fresh. He might've been old-school on some other things, but he was light-years ahead on fresh."

"Do you still cook?" asked Sara. "I mean, when you're not jumping out of airplanes?"

"Yeah, I do," he said, "though I don't take the time for it like I should. One of my favoritest things is to have a bunch of people over, and knock out a five-course *orgy.*"

"Well, then, instead of betting a thousand on the Giants," said Lathon, "how about spending it on a course with Jacques Pepin? They have classes now that put you side-by-side with the masters. You can learn bread making with David Bouley, or, I don't know, charcuterie with Pierre Franey. And these aren't just vanity deals— they really teach you, hand-to-hand. I mean, for someone who loves cooking, what bigger rush could there be?"

"Yeah, that's right," said Jack. "Put your money where your mouth is. Show the world what a great, big talent you are."

"I agree," said Lina. "Unless you're afraid you're not good enough, and they'll all see what a—"

"No, I don't *think* so," Rex sneered. "You should see what comes out of my oven. I have *definitely* got the skills to pay the bills."

"Well, but no one's suggesting you quit your day job," said Lathon. "Serious fun begins as an avocation; a sideline that can grow into a life. So take a couple of courses; put your passion into play, and see where the adrenaline leads you. Who knows, down the road, maybe you'll invest in a restaurant, or open up one of your own. Or maybe you'll be happy just honing your craft, and cooking for friends and family. But whatever the case, you'll be respecting yourself, and taking seriously this thing that gives you pleasure."

Rex squinted in thought, idly picking an ear. All trace of his usual irony was gone. "You know, I was actually thinking of something like that, but I kept putting it off because of work. And then I figured that I'd wait and do it right. Go at it full blast when I retire in three years."

"Except that if you wait three years, you won't be retired— you'll be divorced, and in hock to some bookie," said Lathon. "For other people, maybe, serious fun is an option, but for you, it's required medicine. It's like cortisone to an asthmatic: you either take it or stop breathing. So, factor that in when you do your cost-benefit. Yes, it's six hours that you could be spending making money—but on the other hand, what time do you want to stop breathing?"

eighteen
november

October barreled through, with its sharp stride and silver heels, as if it had a plane to catch. Everywhere, life seemed to have doubled its pace, racing against foregone conclusions. On Sixth Avenue, pedestrians sped home past the superstores, ignoring their blinking come-hithers. Fire trucks swarmed down Broadway in convoy, rushing to some millennial blaze. The air itself felt charged and animate, whooshing across Houston Street and circling the Battery in a shivaree of self-importance.

It was in something of the spirit of this backstretch drive that the group met for the last five times. Each of the sessions was fully attended, and crackled with pin-drop seriousness. Even Lina and Peter, in the bloom of their new happiness, came in with their game faces on, mindful of the upgrade in urgency. So, too, with Rex, who cut out the clowning, after a last sharp rebuke from the others. It was dreamtime therapy, all content and no filler, the six of them pulling together as they hadn't quite before, a *team*, finally, in the shadow of the goalposts.

Dylan, in particular, worked at top speed. Like a man who had badly overslept an exam, he seemed bent on filling in as many of the blanks as possible in the scant few minutes remaining. He began to remember how painful it was to attend his drunken mother as a boy. At the dinner table, polishing off her third Manhattan, she had mercilessly driven the stake into his hamstrung father, remarking what a poor provider he was and how life with him was one long insult. Nor were the children exempt from her barbs, least of all Dylan, the oldest. As the deputy parent, the one who held things together— getting his siblings to bed at a decent hour, and dressed and fed on mornings his mother slept in—he was the object of both her vitriol and favor. On her bad days, she was shockingly cruel, mocking his long hair and rock-and-roll dreams, calling him a "homo-in-training." On her good days, he was the light of her life, a son to make any mother happy. So seductive was her charm then that he racked his brain trying to promote it. He wrote songs to her in his head, thought up lies to amuse her, and brought home quarts of her beloved Dutch chocolate from his after-school grocery job.

"In so many ways, she was like Jeannie, my wife—funny and full of beans when she was in an up mood, and hell on wheels when she wasn't," he said. "And I thought, if I can just figure out where that 'on' button is, I'll have the coolest mom in Red Bank. In fact, now that I think about it, it seems like I've *always* been trying to make some woman happy. Whether it was the good-looking ones with the chip on their shoulder, or—or the nice-girl types who were sort of lonely and desperate—I'd think, hey, all they need is some affection and cheering up. I can make them happy! But instead of me making them happy, they would make me miserable, and I'd go off with my head in my hands."

At another session, relating his progress to the group (he had a line on a cheap two-bedroom near Columbia, and was up for a lucrative job scoring a show on Nickelodeon), he talked about the advent of hope in his life. He came, he said, from a family that believed in fate, or in its Catholic version, doom. Wherever you went and whatever you did, you were stuck with who you were and what God gave you. This genetic fatalism served a variety of ends, being advanced to explain everything from the family drinking problems to its rotten luck with used cars. It also accounted for his father's silence in the face of withering abuse. Instead of standing up to Dylan's mother, or packing a bag and leaving her, he merely sat there on his Herculon plaid recliner, "memorizing the box scores in four newspapers." Later, with the kids grown and out of the nest, he remained with Dylan's mother in the stated conviction that it was too much trouble to split up their possessions.

"Now, I'll grant you, he was at the factory day and night, taking every minute of overtime they would feed him, but still, how sad is *that?*" he said. "Instead of shoving off and finding a woman to love him, he basically said, 'Why bother? This is all I'm good for.' And God forbid he should have stuck up for *us*; told her, 'They're *my* kids, too, don't you talk to them like that.' I mean, I know that he loved us—or at least I think he did—but it was like, every man for himself in that house."

These memories, as well as other recent developments, were fueling his resolve to stay sober. He said that his little girls really needed their dad now, what with their mom coming apart at the seams. Sometime over the summer, Jeannie had taken it into her head that she had to make up for lost time. She broke up with the man she was dating and began running out to parties with her new gal pals from the health spa. Frequently, there were men staying over at the house, a new one every couple of weeks. They were nice enough on the phone with Dylan, and minded their manners around his daughters, but he'd had about as much as he could take. He'd talked to his lawyer about seeking custody, and launched into screaming fights with Jeannie. Yes, he was hurt and jealous like she said, but no, this wasn't about that. Plain and simple, it was about protecting his children. And whatever else his faults as a husband or father, he would never have it said that he didn't protect his children.

We got glowing accounts from Peter about the culture at his new company, as well as amused reflections about life with a pregnant woman. ("Out of nowhere, *I'm* the calm one in the family," he said, laughing. "Kara feels one small kick from the baby and right away, she's timing the contractions—and our due date isn't for four more months yet.") He had made a couple of friends playing tennis at Chelsea Piers, and was beginning to feel more "solid" about himself, like he was "laying down a base." On the weekends, he and Kara had been out looking at summer houses—nothing crazy, just a cottage on a couple of acres upstate—and that, too, felt like a big step forward. Ever since he could remember, he'd felt like a "party of one," a loner even among his family. More than anything, he had yearned to belong to something, to be admitted into a circle and made welcome. And now, finally, he had been—was at the center of his *own* circle—and it was bigger and more substantial by the day.

There were advances on the home front for Lina, as well, though the news there was somewhat more mixed. Having apparently seen the writing on the courthouse wall, her husband was now pressing to settle. He'd made her a cash offer that, while in no sense equitable, was far more than she had expected. On a number of other issues, the sides were well apart, though much of this was posturing by the lawyers. What remained off the table, however, was the thing that mattered most to her: the right to go on living in the co-op.

"I'm not even sure why I care so much, beyond how my kids feel about it," she said. "I mean, it's just an apartment, and I can probably buy one not far from it, if I use what he gives me in the lump-sum. But for some reason, I feel like I *should* fight him for it, like it's the morally right thing to do. We really do love that place, it's where we've lived all our lives together, whereas for him, it's just a—a chip in a card game. He doesn't want the apartment, he just wants to win, to prove that he's the tough guy and I'm the weakling. But I'm not such a weakling—at least, not anymore, I'm not. I'm growing muscles, though you can't really see them. And I just think it's so important that I stand my ground here, that for once with him I don't keel over."

. . .

That brought it to Jack, from whom little had been heard since his return from summer stock in Williamstown. He was a key contributor still, often driving the conversation, and bringing a tough, lawyerly edge to the questioning. But when it came to talking about his own agenda, he grew vague and oddly elusive. There was no news concerning his reinstatement, he said, and nothing much of interest doing elsewhere. He hadn't gotten the part he was up for Off Broadway, though there'd been a couple of regional ads to tide him over. Otherwise, he was lying low, waiting for the D.A.'s decision. Everything hinged on that phone call, he said, and until then, he was basically stacked up in limbo.

And then, one night, near the end of a session, he began suddenly to expound on how blessed he felt. Nothing had really happened, there'd been no change in his status—in fact, he was going stir-crazy, watching the phone. But last night, at dinner, he'd glanced over at his wife and seen how worn and tired she was. Marcia had returned to work after he'd been arrested, taking a job at a public relations firm. It was a touching gesture, though it didn't amount to much, practically speaking—what she earned barely paid the interest on his tax bill. But now, six years later, she was a senior publicist, and essentially supported him on what she brought home. She loathed every second of it, being on the phone all day with media hacks and their doltish assistants, but she did it without complaint. After the pain he had caused her, all the chaos and betrayal—the years she came home expecting to find him dead or in lockup with the other skells from Tompkins Park; and the day-by-day loss of all they had built up, watching friends and possessions melt away— even after that, she was right there with him, though she was only forty-four and pretty, still, and could start over with someone else. And he wasn't really sure how he had earned that loyalty, but he knew that it had saved his life.

"It's been eighteen years that we're together," he said, "and for twelve of 'em, I was out of my mind. And yet, somehow—she knew that there was a *person* under there, and—and that one day, he'd come out. I don't know *how* she knew that, because she didn't see me all that much, what with me coming home at three in the morning most of the time. But she just had this sense that, underneath the addiction, there was a guy worth sticking with. And I—I'm just really, really grateful for—"

He broke off, and put a hand on his chest, quelling the tears that sprang up. Surprised by his feelings, he tried making light of them, fanning himself like a hausfrau. Playfully, Rex leaned over to pat his back, and Peter went and got a cup of water from the bathroom. Jack drank it down with considerable embarrassment, and cleared his throat noisily to continue.

"Jesus," he croaked, "I don't know where *that* all came from; maybe I'm going through male menopause."

"Oh God, don't even say that word around me," said Sara. "I'm so suggestible, I just might get it."

The others laughed at this, teasing her about her age. Jack used the time to compose himself, sitting up at attention.

"Anyway, the other thing is that I saw my son, Michael, for lunch yesterday. He's getting married next month to a girl we're all crazy about, and I went over to his office to pick him up. He's a reporter, you know, like my dad was, and a very promising one at that. They've already given him a desk on the Metro side, and he was in on the team coverage of that awful subway crash, the one where the motorman was drunk. So, you know, he takes me around to meet the people in his department, and while he's off on some detail, his editor comes over to me. He says, 'I don't know if you know this, Mr. Perlman, but your son, Michael, never stops talking about you. He always tells everyone what a great producer you were, and how you inspired him to do what he loved for a living.' And he goes on to say how terrific Michael is, and that he fully expects him to become a major player, and I tell you now, the feeling that I had right then—"

He stopped again and laid his hand over his heart, this time in exaltation. "I mean, my God, to hear how much they think of him there, and that he's proud of his old man, despite my fuckups. . . . You know, it started me back remembering all those years ago, when I visited my *own* dad at the *Daily Mirror,* and the guys went out of their way to sing his praises to me. And last night, lying awake, I thought to myself, 'You know what, Pop, maybe we didn't do so bad, after all. God knows we could've been around more for our kids, and there's no excuse whatever for our self-absorption. But, I mean, there, at the end of the day, are those kids of mine—handsome and—and successful, and above all, good people. Maybe it's time I cut myself some slack here."

There were tears as he said this, and not only in Jack's eyes; with the standard exception of Rex, the others were moved by what they heard.

Lathon chimed in with his own kudos for Jack. "We should all get such praise from our children," he said. "And as for your epiphany about your wife, I'd say you *are* blessed to have her. Like the women in those old Westerns, she sure stood by her man—and I hate to think where you'd be if she hadn't.

"But having said that, and acknowledging how great she's been, I'm curious as to what brought this up," he said. "Did something happen recently—say, a fight, or a money problem—to inspire this guilty gratitude?"

Jack furrowed his brow, thinking it over a moment. "No, not really," he shrugged. "At least, nothing that comes to mind."

"Are you sure?" said Lathon. "Because it occurs to me that her name hasn't come up here very much. Which means you've either got one of the best marriages in town, or one of the dullest."

Jack let out a cheerless laugh, nodding to acknowledge the joke.

His absence over the summer hadn't made him much fonder of Lathon or eased the tension between them. If anything, the changes of the last couple of months had only increased his suspicions. Lathon's strange new outfits, the *"farkakte* art on the walls"—there was something kinky going on for sure. After session one night, he told me that he had a bad feeling about it, that his "AA radar" was tingling. Men of Lathon's age didn't do those sort of things—unless they were in some kind of trouble.

"Well," he said, "my marriage isn't dull, so I guess it'd have to be the other."

"Yeah, but now that you bring it up," said Rex, "I just realized how much I *don't* know about you. Like, how're you paying that million in back taxes when you're not really working that much? And how does your wife deal with being broke, after all those years of having money? You know, you make her sound like a saint or something, but I'm sure there's more to the story."

Jack stiffened in his seat, allowing a curt smile. "Boy, nothing like basking in the glow of a great moment."

Lathon shrugged. "Like you've said yourself, you're paying top dollar here. Be a shame not to get your money's worth."

Jack pumped his foot impatiently, as if preparing to make a dash for the door.

"Yeah, well, I guess there *is* something worrying me, in regard to finances. A check I've been waiting on since back in February, and it's not coming has caused me a cash-flow problem."

"What kind of problem?" asked Sara, brusquely. "Because, to be honest with you, I was wondering the same thing Rex was. How *have* you been supporting yourself these last six years, and what happens if they don't reinstate you?"

Jack's whole body winced, as though a current had passed through him. "I, ah—um, I don't . . ." He stopped to clear his throat, pounding angrily on his chest. The skin at his throat was scarlet. "I—

I really don't know how to answer that. In fact, I've had nightmares lately about losing my apartment, and people coming to take the rest of my furniture. . . ."

The others fell silent, stunned by the change in him.

"Is there any chance of that happening?" Lina asked. "In the immediate future, I mean?"

Jack stared at his hands, trying to make them stop shaking.

"While I was away on business last week, the landlord served us with papers: a—a, you know, notice to pay arrears, or be evicted," he whispered. "Marcia called me in Baltimore, frantic, in tears. She said, 'Please come back here now and do something.' Well, I—I couldn't just leave, y'know—it was a shoot for a BMW ad—but I did manage to get the guy's lawyer on the phone. I told him, 'Look, friend, please, there's a check due any day now; I'll be able to pay what I owe, plus six months' in advance.' And he was actually pretty nice about it, said, 'Well, you've been three months behind for a year, but if you square it by the end of the month, I'll stop the process.' So I tracked down my ex-partner, who's touring a show in San Diego, and said, 'Where the hell's that money, Fred? They're ready to toss me in the street here.' And he says, 'Relax, Jackie, I hear you, it'll go out by the close of business.' But meanwhile, *another* week's gone and still no check, and Marcia's so tense she can't keep solid food down. And so, yesterday, I—I finally did what I've been dreading for a long—"

He stopped and looked up at the high tin ceiling. His jaw trembled, until he clamped it shut.

"I . . . did something that I'd been putting off for a very long time—I hit up the one friend I hadn't borrowed money from. It killed me to do it—I mean, my oldest son's his godchild, and we've gone on vacations with our wives and families, and spent the Jewish holidays at each other's houses, and so on. . . .

"Well, anyway, he must've felt it coming, you know, because

every time I called him at work or at home, his line just rang and rang. I tried him first thing in the morning, and late at night and after dinner—I must've called him ten, twelve times. And each time I dialed, my hands would start shaking, and I'd curse myself viciously for doing this. Finally, I couldn't take it anymore, and went to Barry's office and waited for him—sat there from nine in the morning till three in the afternoon. And when he finally walked in, he—he was shocked to see me, and we just stood there, feeling rotten for each other. But, to make a long story short, he wrote me out a check, and today I went over and handed a money order to their attorney. And so now, thank God, I'm paid up in full, and when my check *does* come in, I'll give Barry back his dough, and hand the rest to the landlord and be done with him for six months."

Jack stopped for a breath, clamping his jaws shut tight. In the course of the last minutes, his face had puffed up, small pockets of swelling in a refractive scatter, the color and circumference of bruises. His head tottered on his shoulders and his foot tapped furiously, working off its ginned-up energy.

"Jack," said Lathon, "would you mind telling us again what you were arrested for?"

"Yeah, sure," Jack grunted, glad to be roused from his fugue. "Basically, in 1987 I started to run low on cash, what with my habit and some shows that had opened and closed. And so, to cover my expenses, I used money owed to investor A, and paid *him* with money owed to investor B, and so on. I did that a total of six times in twenty months, though eventually, I paid everyone back. But that's neither here nor there, of course, and doesn't excuse what I did. The bottom line is, I was charged with embezzlement, and pleaded no contest, and accepted my punishment."

"Yes, and that's my point," said Lathon. "You weren't taken down for drinking and drugging. You were suspended *because you couldn't stop hemorrhaging money*, and had to 'borrow' someone else's to stay afloat. You made two million a year—that's fifty thousand a week, folks—and yet you still couldn't pay your gas bill or the pool guy."

"Well, yeah, it's true I was careless—certifiably so. But what are you getting at?"

"What I'm getting at," said Lathon, "is that, beneath the addictions, there's an unresolved *money* problem. It's what killed you the first time and it's about to do so again, because you won't take a look at what it means. You started to last spring, talking about what being a high roller meant—buying dinner for all your buddies, essentially renting their attention. But then you went away to do that play all summer, and have avoided any mention of it since, telling us instead about your 'humdrum' life. Which makes me wonder what your peers are thinking, having listened to that humbug for two months."

Jack looked around from face to face, as if to gauge where the flak would come from.

"Well, I'll tell you how I feel," said Peter, glancing up. "I think it's really shitty that you didn't tell us the truth. I mean, how do you reconcile that you couldn't pay your rent, yet waltzed off to Williamstown for the summer? And how could you talk in generalities about your 'money problems,' when you had this *dire emergency* going on?"

Jack looked over at him, his blue eyes pooling. "Well, but I had to go where the work was, didn't I? I hadn't booked a *real* job since last November, so I went where the paycheck was."

"Yes, but that paycheck didn't even cover expenses," said Peter. "You actually lost money on the deal. And meanwhile, the fire's going from bad to worse here, and your wife is left alone to handle it. I mean, I can't understand what your thought process was. What did you *think* would happen?"

Jack sank back, seeming to shrink in his chair. "It wasn't what I was thinking, I was just trying to *survive*. To get through this one last, horrible year, and then hope I got reinstated. And if that check had come when it was supposed to, I would't've been in this spot. But it didn't and I fell behind, and I basically *carried* being behind till the check came in and I could—"

"But that's the same thing you did with your investors!" cried Peter. "You *still* have the idea that it's okay to do this, to pay off your debts with money expected tomorrow. Didn't you *learn* from that experience, didn't the embarrassment teach you *anything?* You can't keep kiting checks your whole life!"

There was another pause, this one ringing with Peter's censure. Jack looked back at him, trying to marshall an answer, but nothing seemed to come together.

"What *I'm* curious about," said Sara, "is how your wife felt about this. I mean, to work that hard and then be slapped with eviction papers—how could she not be furious at you?"

"Yes," said Lathon. "Get to the pain: what *consequences* has Jack's avoidance caused him?"

A third pause: Jack tugged angrily at his ear. "Well, with the same candor that I've answered all your other questions, I can honestly say that, as painful as this was for her, our relationship has still been loving. By which I mean that we've dealt with this together, instead of—"

"But you didn't *cause* it together," Peter railed. "You brought it on personally. You, Jack, second person singular."

"And believe me," said Sara, "if it were me you'd done it to, I'd've been out that door."

Jack seemed genuinely stunned by their rebuke. "I—I . . . I mean, I hear what you're saying, and I agree that I caused her pain. But—I, uh—I still just . . ."

He broke off there and stared ahead, his eyes dissolved in deep focus. His shoulders sank and the steam escaped him, as if he were a truck stalled out in the breakdown lane.

"Let me cut in here," said Lathon shortly, "because I think the point's been made now well enough: Jack's done a whole lot of suffering about money. We know that, for reasons tracing back to his father, Jack used money to prove his worth to people. Never mind that he was brilliant and had an eye for hit shows—that stuff's refutable, if you don't see the shows. What *couldn't* be refuted was the cash in his wallet; that you could quantify, and turn people's heads with. 'Oh, waiter: a bottle of Cristal for my friends here, and send another bottle over to table two.' Money was a validator, and it was also revenge: 'Here, Dad, have a new car on me; enjoy it and eat your heart out, you selfish prick.'

"But what happens when you throw around money is that, eventually, it runs out, and then the falseness of the story shows through. Without the fat wallet and the platinum cards, Jack felt inviable in the world. And so, for the last six years, he's gone into hiding, living like a ghost in the attic. And you know what the shame of that is? Nobody *cared* about his money. People liked Jack because he was fun to be with, and a loyal friend to his buddies. He could've shown up in a barrel and they wouldn't've said boo to him, other than, 'Hey, man, great barrel; where can I get one in *my* size?'

"No, if ever there was a case of 'optional suffering,' this would have to be it. Because it wasn't Jack's false story but his true one that people loved—his charm and his passion and his grade-A talent. If anything, all that spending did was keep people away, make it hard to get together with him and watch a ball game or have a meal. How badly his friends and wives must have craved that—and how much more so his four young boys! *They* didn't care how big a boat he owned, or which stars he had on his speed dial. All they ever cared about—all that anyone cared about—was the pleasure and privilege of his company."

Sometime in the last hour, a section of the overhead lighting had failed, blinking on and off per its own dictates. This cast the room in a kind of recurrent dusk, with a soft, gray glow and heroic shadows that flickered across the faces of the members. They sat there, stock-still, fixed in the gloaming, while Jack, beneath the window, wept silently.

"I let so many things go," he said. "All those people who cared about me . . . how could I have just turned my back on them?"

Lathon paused a moment before offering solace. "You didn't turn your back on them," he said softly. "What you did was hide out like a wounded animal, until the wound either cleared or killed you. So deep was the feeling of shame and loss that any contact with the world was unbearable. But it's six years later, Jack, and time has taken some of the pain down, and you're strong enough to come out of the cave you crawled into. And the way to bring about lasting closure is to make sense of how it happened. Yes, we know you spent all your money, but *when* and *how* did you spend it? What *feelings* triggered splurges, and what was happening at the time? Those are the kinds of questions that'll get to the truth, and we'd be glad to help address them in these last sessions. But maybe a better place to do so, slowly and methodically, is at a group like Debtors Anonymous. There, they delve into the mechanics of spending, and teach you to count your money like days of sobriety."

"Is that true?" asked Sara. "There's such a thing as Debtor's Anonymous?"

"Yeah, there is," Jack murmured, "and I'd been meaning to check it out. I've got friends at AA who say it's really helped them. Allowed 'em to get control of their spending."

"Well, not control," Lathon corrected him. "No one's ever in control. What they teach you, with practice, is to *manage* it. To keep a diary and jot down when and where you spend, which takes the compulsion out of it. I like to use the analogy of the cowboy and the bronco, where the cowboy is the cortex, or the rational mind, and the bronco is the body, with its primal impulses. What we're all trying to do is to stay on that bronco, to manage its kicks and thrusts with some grace, and hope it doesn't fling us on our head. But in order to do that, we've got to *pay attention*, to react to what the horse is doing. It's impossible for us to break him—and what fun would it be if we could? But if we're careful with him, and respect his will and energy, at some point, it stops being a constant battle, and we can ride, with a certain elegance, to where we're going."

nineteen
december

It had been a year, meteorologically, of such coups de théâtre—the blizzard in February that had stopped New York cold, and turned it into a prairie whistlestop for five days; and the run, six months later, of relentless heat, cooking up the streets in a stew of odors that singed the back of your nostrils—that it seemed a great letdown when, for the final session, the weather broke unseasonably mild. Instead of the sharp bite one expects of December air, it was a fiftyish evening with a tepid breeze and an insinuation of rain. There was nothing in it of sweep or resolution, no bracing shiver of the curtain coming down and a story racing on to its conclusion. It felt, rather, like a ruse; something meant to keep the year at bay, and life screwed down in its tracks.

In the group room, Lathon had the windows nudged open, and the trundling central heat turned off. The room was brighter than I had previously seen it, the light from the overhead spots up full, as if this were the penultimate scene of one of those drawing-room murder mysteries, wherein tonight all secrets would be revealed. There were fresh blue lilies in the Chinese urns, and a new rug beneath us from the Tibetan highlands, depicting, in recurrent triplets, a geisha, a dragon, and an emperor. It was a graceful addition, and not just because it covered the floor, whose pickled oak planks cast a glare. It also captured, in various tilts for primacy, the three characters in Lathon's cosmos—the victim, the victimizer, and the rescuer. In some scenes, the emperor had the dragon at sword's point. In others, the dragon overpowered the emperor, and was presumably set to roast and eat him. The only static figure was the frightened geisha, who stood apart from and seemed irrelevant to the action. In her stock passivity, she awaited the worst, as if the contest before her wasn't about love or death, but the right to become her captor.

Lathon greeted the group in what had become his new uniform: black work boots, black Levis, and a black leather vest over a dress shirt from Agnès B. It was a style shift that continued to puzzle the members, as they had told me in private meetings. Rex, ever one to think generously of people, surmised that Lathon had "crossed over to the dark side," and was now wielding a whip at the Mineshaft. Peter, whose loyalty to Lathon was total, worried that he was going through "some midlife thing," perhaps at the prodding of a young girlfriend. Lina also suspected a woman, and was troubled by a number of his recent "choices," the worst of which was displaying his art here. "If he wants to put it out there, that's fine," she said. "Just don't put it where *I* can see it. I'm his *patient*, for God's sake, not his friend. I don't want to see some statue about his mother."

Yet, despite their mystification, the members kept their eyes on the path. They were a self-contained unit, a ship under its own sail, and in some sense, Lathon had become extraneous. They didn't need him to figure out whose pain most needed tending, or how to get a stalled interview up and running. They were all well versed and invested in one another's stories, and what drove them now was seeing how they turned out. They wanted to find out if Sara would land a man, or hole up in her designer nunnery. They wanted to find out if Jack got his career back, or if, at sixty, he'd have to start over again. Whatever their feelings for one another—and these seemed to vary by the session—there was a larger narrative in which they all had stock: the group, and its winners and losers.

They were delighted to hear, then, when Lathon called them to order, that he was prepared to run overtime tonight. Three hours, four hours, whatever it took—he was willing to sit and listen until everyone had been heard from. Nor did it matter if some or most of them had to leave at nine. As long as even one person had unfinished business here, he'd be happy to keep the lights on and the coffee coming.

Dylan was particularly grateful for the offer. "As all of you know, I lost a lot of time here—basically, about half the sessions, thanks to my wipeout. But I have to say that even before that, I always felt somehow . . . rushed here. Like I had to talk, you know, really, really fast, so that the next guy could get in before the bell rang. Being as how we met only every two weeks, I felt like, 'Damn, I better get my story in, or it'll be *two more weeks* before I speak.'

"Yeah, I felt exactly the same way, you know, especially in the early going," said Lina. "Those first three months, when I was such an emotional wreck, I really needed to talk every session. I didn't want to hog things, but I had all this—*stuff* to spill, and when there was no time for me, I felt frustrated with this setup."

Lathon started, then put on a smile, as if it pleased him to be upbraided by his pet.

"Well, you're right," he said. "It *was* a design error. I should have made the sessions longer, or switched back to once a week. I mean, I did want you to think of this time as precious; to do the work at home and be ready to use every minute. But when you did that, I didn't give you enough minutes to use. And for that, I do apologize."

"Well, hey, good for you for saying that," Jack proclaimed. "That's the first time, in all my years of therapy, I ever heard one admit that he was wrong. Therapists do make mistakes and they should cop to it, instead of hiding behind that transference crap.

"Anyway, what threw *me* off," he continued, "was switching from the old office to this one. I've just never felt right here, it's like meeting in an airport—I keep waiting for them to call out my gate number. And I know it shouldn't bother me, but this place is just so—barren. Barren, and sterile-looking."

"Yeah, I agree," said Sara. "I was much more comfortable in the last place, and could never figure out why you left it."

"Ah . . . hah," said Lathon, still wearing a smile, but looking like he heard the thunder of hooves. "Anyone else with a bone to pick before we start?"

"Well, *actually*," said Rex, "as long as we're on the subject of your fuckups . . ."

This drew loud and sustained laughter from the others.

"Yes, Rex, by all means, let me have it." Lathon chuckled. "God knows, I've let *you* have it often enough."

"Ah, I never even felt it," said Rex. "I've been slugged by women twice your size."

"Yeah, and I'm sure you deserved it," said Lina.

"And *I'm* sure he paid for it," Jack called out. "In cash, with a fifty-dollar tip!"

This elicited much hooting and stomping of feet. Almost eleven months in and countless intimacies exchanged, and still nothing brought the group together like a laugh at Rex's expense.

"Are we done now?" Rex harrumphed, playing the picked-on innocent. "I'd like to get some *work* in, if you're all through clowning."

"Oh yeah, right," Jack bellowed, amid more laughter. "Far be it from *us* to waste your time!"

Presently, the kidding ran its course, and Rex got on with his point. He thought that the one-on-one interviews ran long, and that time could've been saved by opening the floor to the others, who usually had better questions to ask the subject. It was almost like Lathon was trying to *indoctrinate* them, to turn them into little clones of himself. Did they really need to learn, for instance, that whole diagnostic workup, or would they have been better off just cutting to the problem? Not that it wasn't interesting to know that stuff, but they got his point about listening long ago.

Lathon drew a breath and took this in, plying his patchy mustache. "Well, I'd argue that there *was* some value to that. I was trying to teach you not just how to listen to each other, but to make distinctions about what you heard. When you're out there living your life and a problem comes up, there's a way to pare it back and get to the nub of what hurts you. It's an essential skill, and not just for handling crises, but defusing them before they become critical."

This answer satisfied no one, including Lathon. Adopting a scowl, he composed himself for battle. That surprised but didn't rattle the members, several of whom seemed inclined to take him on. What had begun as harmless quibbling was about to boil into conflict when Peter stepped in to conciliate.

"You know, you're right, Dr. Lathon, that's a great skill to have, and I'd love to follow up on it sometime. Maybe do some sort of seminar or couples thing, where we bring in our spouses and learn it together. But I think what Rex is saying is there wasn't time for that here; not if we were going to keep to this schedule. You sort of had these two tracks going at once—the teaching part, which, as I say, was interesting, and the therapy part, which, of course, is why we came here. And it sometimes seemed like—without intending to—the one got in the way of the other."

Lathon sputtered, thrown back on himself. This last bit, coming from his other star pupil, stung him and put a shade on certain assumptions. Over coffee with me earlier, Lathon had been upbeat, almost celebratory. Despite some obvious bumps, he thought he'd brought this group a ways, he said. Lina and Peter had achieved brilliant liftoffs, and Jack was all but sitting on the launchpad. As for Dylan, the bottom line was that he was alive and breathing still, when all the early indicators had boded otherwise. Even Rex seemed to have benefited from this brush with reality, turning the page on some of his frat-boy buffoonery. Only Sara, in her recalcitrance, had

Lathon second-guessing himself. Perhaps he should have been tougher and turned the others against her, using their impatience as a cudgel. Or maybe he hadn't set enough tasks for her, allowing her to poke along at her own speed. You can't win 'em all, he shrugged, but Sara felt like a rout. "I'm kind of like a bug who went splat on her windshield," he concluded. "I'll bet there are a lot of us piled up under her wiper."

Whatever he had been expecting from the members, then, the last thing was to be fielding complaints. Nor could it have been of cheer to him that they had come far enough to rise in judgment. Their criticism was too broad to be read in context. They weren't just questioning his style or clock-management skills. What they were questioning was the very quality of his care.

"I guess what I hear you saying," he murmured, "is that I haven't been as good a listener as I can be. The truth is, it's rare to get a group this smart, and I see now that I probably got a little greedy. I treated you more like protégés than patients, teaching you what I've learned these last years. But, of course, you didn't come for that; you came to get your wounds treated, and I should've paid better attention."

A brief but complex silence set up, threading the air with strains of guilt. Looking around the circle at the faces of the group, I saw that they *had* meant to deliver a message to Lathon, though not, it seemed, by consensus or prior arrangement. Each, rather, had been nursing some private displeasure and was merely filing through the door that Lathon opened. But the doctor rightly sensed that their critique was more than the sum of its parts. It was a resounding thumbs-down to his new persona and its propensity for climbing onstage.

"Well, I'll admit there were some things that did worry me," said Peter. "The whole office thing, as Jack said, and then the goatee and the black outfits—I was starting to think you'd taken up

witchcraft like my ex, or had joined some weird sex cult, or something—"

"Yeah, the Psychiatrists for Satan," Rex cracked.

The others laughed at this, though with a certain discomfort. It
was perhaps a little too close to their own suppositions to be anything
as simple as funny.

"But then," Peter continued, "I remembered something you
once said that really hit home with me. You were talking about being
human, and you weren't trying to make any great point with it, but
you said that the first condition of being human is making mistakes.
And for some reason or other, that just really rang bells with me. I
thought, 'Of *course* everybody else here makes mistakes—why
shouldn't I be allowed to?' And I'm telling you now, that one little
thing right there took so much pressure off me. And so that was the
attitude I took with you. I thought, 'Yeah, Dr. Lathon's made some
mistakes, but so what, you know—he's human, too.' The bottom
line is, I got a lot of help here. Who cares if I don't like your
wardrobe?"

"I agree," said Lina, quick to chime in. "I, too, was more comfortable in the other office, and didn't know what to make of your
new . . . style, if you don't mind my saying so. I figured, hey, who
knows, maybe he's got a young girlfriend. I hear that's quite the
thing with men your age. . . ."

She paused for effect and gave a sly smile, letting the laughter
fill up around her. Even Lathon joined in, throwing his head straight
back, and clapping in slow percussion.

"Right, thanks for lumping me in with Anton," he said, cackling.

"Sorry," she laughed. "I guess that's the worst thing I can say to
someone: 'You remind me of my husband.' " There was more laughter here, and a decrease in tension, though the air still felt doughy
and trapped. "But anyway, when I look back on where I was ten

months ago, compared to how things are now—I mean, forget about it, you can't even compare the two. This group literally saved my life."

And with that, one could feel a break in the climate, and the canopy of tension draw apart. Dylan followed in, saying that he, too, felt grateful, and considered himself well ahead on balance. "I'm mostly just sorry I missed so many sessions," he said. "Because, for the time I put in here, I got a lot back out of it. Especially in these last three months."

"Yeah, I'll second that," said Jack, discharging a sigh. "As much fun as I had this summer, I also regret the sessions I missed. I was running from certain things and not taking responsibility, and this group really called me on that. I just wish it had happened sooner, which it might've if I'd been here, but that's hindsight, and we know what *that's* worth. The big picture is, I'm better for having done this, and I want all of you and *El Jefe* there to know that."

Lathon, who had been listening with a drawn face, roused himself to smile. "Well, thank you, Jack, that's very gratifying to hear. And I'm sure you mean *El Jefe*—'the dictator'—in the very best possible sense."

"Yes, I do," said Jack, holding his hand up in witness. "I'm just proud to be a peasant in your country."

As was so often the case with this group, its laughter now was sanitary, tidying up awkard moments. No matter their displeasure, the members hadn't meant to hurt Lathon, nor to have to spend good time now mending feelings. Prior to this evening, in fact, they'd seen no evidence that he *had* feelings, so exclusively did he seem to operate from the control tower of his mind. Yes, there had been flashes of temper and impatience, but nothing to suggest a softer side, a vulnerability beneath his bulk. Now, having glimpsed it, the group was backing up fast, trying to void the experience with their laughter.

"Well, anyway, thanks for the testimonials," said Lathon. "They mean a lot to me, though they feel a little unearned at the moment. And thanks just as much for your right-on criticisms; they're every bit as helpful as your compliments. If you'll remember, we started out by talking about 'grounded negative assessments'—how important it is to hear them, and not dismiss them or run away. We do all make mistakes, as Peter reminded us, and what distinguishes us is the courage to admit it. They may cause us shame, but the bigger shame is to deny them, to behave as though we were something other than human.

"And so, in the spirit of that truth, I acknowledge that I made mistakes here. There's no point in going over them again; let's just say that I acted out some unwise wishes, without thinking through their effect on you. As I've begun to see firsthand, there's a real pitfall in this wish-pursuit business. You can easily get caught up in your own solipsism, and trample on the wishes of people around you. We're bombarded on all sides now by the cult of self-actualization, by the idea that the self is the greatest possible good, and that it's our duty as Americans to be all that we can be. The problem with that is, it ignores the rights of others; to be governed, at least part of the time, by *their* needs and wishes. I hear it so often in couples therapy: 'If she would only agree to such-and-such, I could be happy, and then *she'd* be happy.' But that's just wrong, outside the context of partnership. It's happiness at the *expense* of someone else's.

"And so, what I've learned—or been reminded of—by my own mistakes is that happiness is usually negotiated. It grows, for the most part, out of a *conversation*, one in which both parties' wishes are respected. Unless you're a hermit, there's a balance to be struck, a rational weighing-out of the personal and the collective. I realize that that's probably un-American to say, but then again, as I've seen with my Wall Street clients, most capitalists make lousy spouses. They're much more interested in what the, ah, free market has to offer than with what they've got at home."

"Hey, now wait a minute," Rex growled in hurt half seriousness. "I happen to resent that remark."

"Well, if the shoe fits, wear it, I say!" cried Lina.

This time, the laughter was loud and unvarnished. Peter, sitting next to Lina, rocked in his chair, then laid a high five on her. Sara, two seats down, gave Rex a coy kick, cutting him a grin that said, Get over yourself. And Jack, across the circle, did a cowboy death scene, pulling an invisible arrow out of his chest. With this canny interval of laughter, and dumbshow, the group cleared the stage, finally, of the Lathon business, and got on with the evening's regularly scheduled program.

Lathon had designed the meeting as a series of reflections, asking each member to do three things: to calculate how far he or she had come in the last year; to say what remained to meet the goals that he or she had set; and to comment on the progress and prospects of the other members. The first two could be done in any order or style, but the third—the assessment of peers—was to be saved for last.

"You can use that time however you want," he said. "You can get something off your chest that you've been saving for months, knowing you probably won't see that person again. Or you could use it to make a final invitation to someone, help them see more clearly what kind of task they've got ahead of them. You now know these people next to you better than some members of their own families do. You could do them a favor by passing on what you've learned about them—or not. I'll leave that entirely up to you."

Lina raised her hand first, both because she had to leave at nine, and because she'd been ruminating about the end here for several weeks. Particularly in these last days, she said, she'd kept an eye on her feelings, in order to be able to put words to them before she left. In the years leading up to this group, she had grown fearful of her emotions. Her grief and rage were like a mass inside her, getting bigger and heavier each day. Even if there'd been someone to talk to, which there wasn't, how could she possibly squeeze that mass into something as small as words? It exhausted her just thinking about it, and so when she tried, in those early sessions, to tell her story, she would invariably break down after a couple of minutes. She wasn't just crying out of sadness and anger, but from choking frustration as well.

And so, with no way out, the pain had seeped into her body, hardening her joints and muscles. Her back was on fire, and her knees throbbed constantly, stabbing her when she jogged or climbed stairs. Walking to the office one day, she glimpsed a reflection in a storefront, and was horrified to see that it was her own. "I couldn't believe it," she said. "I looked like one of those old ladies on Broadway, trudging up the street with their bags of groceries."

But though scared to the point of panic in the early sessions, she continued to come in and tell her story. And as the weeks went by, something began to change, she said—a shift in her relation to her feelings. "What I found, as I learned to be able to tell them apart, was I could express them without falling to pieces. When something bad happened to me, I could say, okay, *this* is what scares me about it, or *that's* what hurts me, or *that's* what's making me furious. And as I got better at it, and started speaking my feelings to people— telling my son how angry I was at him for having drugs in his room, or telling my assistant she really hurt me when she forged a time card—gradually, I got the strength to stand up to Anton, and to fight for what I needed. At the time, he was like a giant to me, and I just stood there and took it from him. But when I finally spoke up to him and started to defend myself, I suddenly felt more like *me* again. Like the person I used to be before I lost my confidence.

"And you guys were so important there, not just for the advice and rah-rah stuff, but for helping me see that it was one small battle at a time with him. Before, I would lie awake and think, how am I going to do this? How do I beat a bully who's worth ten million dollars? Well, the answer is, you keep chopping at his ankles, until he finally keels over and starts bawling like a baby. And that's exactly what happened last week—he basically completely caved in, and signed over the apartment for five years. He said, 'You want it so bad? I'll even throw in the furniture, and the money that was in our joint account. Just please go away and leave me alone.'"

"Wha-at!" Jack grunted, after a moment of dead air. "He's giving up the apartment *and* the money?"

"That's right," said Lina, looking serene in triumph. "In fact, the money in that account is the least of what he gave me. After fighting me tooth and nail over idiocy like the dental bills, he suddenly called me at work—called *me*, you understand, not my lawyer—and said, 'What'll it take to be rid of you?' And I put down the phone and walked away for a minute, just so I could get my voice calm. I told him I was busy, and that I'd call him that evening, and then immediately got my lawyer on the phone. I was so excited, I was practically babbling with her, saying we had to come up with a figure right now so we could do this while he was still in the mood. And she said, 'Calm down, Lina, don't you get it? He's folded his tent up.' And so, we drew up a proposal with a lump-sum number, and language about keeping the apartment for five years. And as she was about to fax it to him, she called back and said, 'You know, as long as he feels like giving things, how about we ask for the joint-account money?' I said, ah, I don't know, what if he gets mad and walks away? She said, 'Number one, he's not walking anywhere, and two, it's poetic justice. Consider it his fine for being a thief and a liar, and an all-around, no-good shit.'"

"And he went for it?" asked Sara.

Lina pumped a fist like she'd won the French Open. "That night, when I came home, there was a message on my machine, basically declaring surrender. He said, 'Look, I know this has dragged on for years, but I just want peace again. It's been awful for the kids to see their parents like this, and I hope you and I can be friends.' Can you believe that crap—he wants to be *friends!* As if we were ever friends to begin with!"

"Or as if a friend would try to destroy you," fumed Peter. "Try to put you in the poorhouse."

"It's unbelievable," said Rex. "The guy's on another planet."

After a couple more gleeful shots at Anton, Lina finished the story. There had been a fax the next morning from his "imbecile lawyer," throwing in the towel. He had couched surrender, though, in distinctly martial terms, informing Lina's lawyer that the offer was only good until five o'clock sharp that day. Hearing this over the phone, Lina laughed so hard that she "almost fell and cracked [her] skull." "It was like that TV ad for those cheapo knives," she said. *"You can have this fabulous East Side co-op for just $19.95, but only if you act before midnight tonight!"*

The others broke out in applause and laughter. The news of Lina's victory was so deftly underplayed that it had taken them a moment to grasp it. Her long, corrosive struggle was over, and the defeat of her former tormenter was final. She had possession of his apartment and everything in it, as well as a cashier's check for the money he'd filched, a first-time-ever admission of culpability. Yet, out of concern for the feelings of the other members, she had tossed this off as merely another in a series of details. She understood, with the discernment that was her stock-in-trade, that nothing cloys faster than other people's good fortune. And, given her life with Jeffrey and its expansive joys, she must have sensed that she was verging on tilt.

"Now, I know it won't all be smooth sailing from here," she said. "The disease Jeffrey has is a serious one, though, for the moment, thank God, it's in a lull state. And I'm also sure that, knowing Anton, there'll be more crap to come from him—he isn't *near* done making my life hell. Last week, for instance, Jorie said she wanted to be a lawyer, and he told her—and I quote—'I don't think you've got the mind to be a lawyer. Why not think about being a therapist, instead?' "

"Hey, thanks a *lot!*" croaked Lathon, emerging from his funk. "Yeah, we all wanted to be plumbers, you know, but we couldn't figure out how to flush those toilets."

"Isn't he beautiful?" cried Lina, laughing along with the others. "It's hard to believe I lasted twenty years with him. My latest theory is he had me doped up on drugs. At night, when I was asleep, he would pour stupid-drops into my ear, and I would wake up the next day and go, 'Duh, but I *lovvve* him.' "

She made a goofy face, bugging her eyes and sticking her tongue out, and had a good laugh at her own expense. In that laughter, it suddenly occurred to me, there was no tincture of sadness, no trace of her former mournful trill. Free of old suffering, it said, The world is simple again. It can be counted on to mean what it says it means.

"But one thing I know," she said, when the group had settled in again. "And that is, never in my life will I keep quiet when something's bothering me. As much as I adore Jeffrey—and my love and respect for him grow daily—when something isn't right, I am completely up front about it. I mean, bang, that second, I come out with what I'm feeling, and we talk about it and make a decision as partners. Not that I'm turning everything into a federal case; far from it. But the one thing I've learned here and that I'll never forget is that silence equals suffering—always. And from this day forth, no matter what else happens to me, I am all done suffering."

Jack went next, after offering his compliments to Lina. "You know, as someone who grew up watching Broadway plays, I've always been a sucker for happy endings," he said. "I really do believe in the whole schmaltz of theater magic, in the idea that you can become whatever you want if you've got an honest heart. And that's what you've got, Lina: a really good and honest heart, and I can't tell you how your story has boosted my hopes. Not to mention my faith in our legal system."

"Well, thank you." She laughed, the color rushing to her forehead. "Although, with Jeffrey, I have to say, it was more about being lucky than good."

"Nah, see, there I disagree with you," he said. "What you did— and what Peter did, too, for that matter—was work the program here and make your own luck. You busted your butt in group, then went out and shook things up. Put yourself in a position where good things *could* happen. And not to fatten his head, but that's what the Big Cheese is always saying. You *didn't* just sit around, waiting for chance to provide. You put it out there, and made a new story."

"Well, thanks for the plug, Jack, if not the new nickname." Lathon chuckled. "I'm just wondering why I always feel ten pounds fatter after a compliment from you."

"Eh, you're paranoid," said Jack, laughing his booming laugh. "I would never stoop so low as to call you fat."

"Well, about Lina, at least, we're in full agreement; she has nothing to apologize for. Everything she has now, she got by showing up. By having the courage to go out and be herself, and say, 'I won't be defined by what scares me.' And what inspires me in that is, there *was* no magic. She did it the way anyone remakes their story: she rolled up her sleeves and *worked* it."

And with that, Lathon asked Jack to get on with the details of his own story. "You've got a funny way of doing that, you know—of avoiding the question, and putting it onto other people," he noted. "I know you've always thought you were the *real* therapist here, but just play along for one more night."

The others broke up, enjoying the joshing hostility. As far back as the first session, it had been clear these two disliked each other. Each resented the other's hubris, and his presumption of final authority. For months, they had skirmished in snubs and insults, each testing the other's patience. On two or three occasions, the conflict escalated, and they grappled across the circle like sumo wrestlers. But to the relief of one and all here, it had cooled in the late rounds, devolving into a kind of grudging truce.

"Well, unfortunately, I *don't* have that great an ending," said Jack. "The check I'd been waiting on finally came through, and I paid off all the bills that'd been piling up. Last week, in fact, I sent a check to my friend Barry, and it felt great to be able to pay him when I said I would. I've lost enough friends, you know, that I had to borrow from and couldn't repay, and I'm never going to do that again. That is *not* the kind of man my parents raised.

"On the other front, I still haven't heard from the D.A., and there's nothing I can do for that but wait. The suspension ends in April, but if they want, they could hang me past that, while they 're-view,' quote-unquote, my application. It's frustrating the hell out of me, but it won't help to lean on them, and it might just blow the whole deal out of the water. And so I sit and say nothing, not even to my attorney. He knows how bad I'm hurting here.

"Meanwhile, with the acting work, it's been, frankly, pretty disappointing. I signed with a big agent three months ago, and really got my hopes up that I'd start booking soon. But aside from a couple of commercials, it's been very, very quiet, and the truth is, my last guy served me better. I mean, it's nice to be able to say that my agent's the great so-and-so. But sooner or later, I'm gonna want to *eat* something, you know. I mean, just to keep my strength up while I'm looking. And while I've got enough dough to get me through the spring, if something doesn't break then, I'm gonna to have to pull up stakes. Let go of my apartment and find a place in Yonkers or somewhere, and go out and get a job doing . . . what? I've no idea."

The mood in the room came down very quickly from the high of Lina's valedictory. If there was any hope that the rest of the evening would be ceremonial, Jack put a stop to that. This was not to be a night of neat endings and best-foot-forward; not for him, at least.

What obtained on Broadway didn't obtain in *his* life, where loose ends and gaping plot holes prevailed. And in his voice now, you could hear that this baffled him. He had done the right things, performed the articles of his faith: not only made all his meetings but become an AA statesman, taking "newbies" under his wing and buying them coffee and hearing their stories, inducting them, with gruff kindness, into the fellowship of the sane. The rest of the time, he was out there scrambling for work, running around town like some gung-ho kid to the cattle calls and auditions. He had demonstrated, in these and other acts of rectitude, a good and decent heart, and yet where was the justice he thought was due him, the kind dealt out to Lina?

"For the record, though, I do feel good about my progress here, and the things we accomplished this past year," he said. "Now, maybe my gains weren't as dramatic as Lina's and Peter's—no, forget about maybe; they *weren't*—but that's sort of the way it goes with me. I'm the kind who goes by evolution, not revolution, because for me, at least, that seems to last longer. And that's what I care about, not where I am five weeks from now, but where I am in five years. You know, you hear people all the time say that life is short. Well, thank you very much, folks, but no, it's *long*—particularly if you've got work to do. My old man lived to be eighty-eight, and he was out chasing a story on the day of his stroke. And he also went out of his way, in those last twenty years, to try and make things right with me. Every chance he got, he'd say how proud he was, and that he loved me and was still kicking himself for not telling me that as a kid. You see, that, to me, is what a *man's* all about. To be a true-blue guy to the people you love, and to try to clean up some of the crap you left behind. And that's what I want to do with the time I got left. Be a mensch to my sons and let them know I love 'em, and that the dumbest goddamn thing I ever did in my life was not be there every night when they were growing up. And I also want to be a good husband to Marcia, who's been more than just a wife and friend to me. She's been my guardian angel, and literally kept me from harm, when harm was pretty much the only thing on my mind. And I love her for that, and feel blessed to have her, and if I ever, God willing, make some serious dough again, I'm gonna—"

Swept up in his feelings, Jack stopped in midair, and came back down to earth with a sheepish grin. "I'm gonna put it in the bank and take her out to dinner. Maybe splurge, and spring for a movie, too, with the large-size popcorn and soda."

Peter had brought something in a manila envelope that he wanted to show the group. Unfastening the metal nibs with nervous fingers, he pulled out what looked like a three-by-five negative and held it up for all to see. It was a photograph, hours old, of his child in utero, a souvenir sonogram.

"It's a boy," he said, laughing and twitching at the same time from the effort to contain his glee. "We were firmly decided that we weren't going to ask, that it would be better not to know in case. . . . But when we saw him on that screen, our big resolve went all to hell. Kara started crying and touching the screen, and even I, who usually only cry at my divorces, started tearing up pretty good myself.

"Anyway, the news is that he's totally healthy, and seems to like the cuisine in there a lot. And it's too blurry to really tell, but I think he's got more *hair* than me, which makes me feel *real* good about myself!"

Despite his attempts to stem it, Peter's joy was infectious. The group cooed over the sonogram, passing it around. Rex produced an expensive cigar, urging "Dad" to smoke it on the big night. Lina told Peter how thrilled she was for him, and that if anyone tried to tell her that therapy was bogus, she was going to grab them by the ear and drag them to Peter, because here was living proof that therapy *worked*.

306

"Hear, hear!" said Jack, breaking out in applause. One by one, the others did likewise, building to a warm ovation. From his seat by the window, Peter grinned and chafed, enduring it like a shower of iced Gatorade.

"Well, I feel a little ridiculous, being declared the big winner," he said. "I mean, if someone walked in now, I doubt they'd look at me and say, '*He's* the poster guy.' Unless it was, like, an ad for Rogaine, or a 'before' picture for the Hair Club for Men. . . ."

The others laughed, grateful for Peter's humility. If he was, in fact, the big winner here, it was hard to imagine a more modest one, or one less likely to inspire the envy of his peers.

"But at the same time, having said that, I can't tell you how excited I am to wake up every morning. There's this person lying next to me, and she's pretty and she smells great, and I don't even have to ask her and she scratches my scalp, which I could just lie there and have that done to me for *hours.* In fact, if I was any kind of businessman, I would invent a machine that rubs your head all day, and really gives the feeling of human fingers. It would make a fortune, and then I could retire and play golf, so that one day thirty years from now, I could crack the low eighties, and not three-putt the greens at my lousy course. . . ."

Peter laughed at his own joke, a wheezy pant that sounded like drowning. It was the closest he'd come to outright giddiness in the ten-month life of the group.

"And then, down the hall from us," he said, suddenly switching tracks, "is the room where the baby's going to go, which Kara's done all up in a wild-animal theme. And sometimes when I get home and I've got a splitting headache, I'll go into that room and just sit on the carpet, and soak in the feeling of him coming soon. You know, I always thought I'd be scared of being a father, of having this—creature next door that I had no control over, and that would just cry all the time and I'd never be able to escape it, and there would go the rest of my life. But instead, what I've been feeling is just this . . . calm and contentment, like he's lying there in his crib, looking up at me with these eyes. And as nervous as Kara's been, I feel totally relaxed; I just know that it's going to be okay. And I credit that to group, because I really learned something here—that most of my fears were groundless. When I get nervous now, I ask myself, what am I actually afraid of? And usually, it's something stupid, like, what if they stare at my bald spot during the presentation, or if they find out I fell asleep watching the Knicks last night, instead of working on those reports? And for whatever reason, that really calms me down, to the point where I'm completely off the Zoloft and Ambien, and can go to bed now at ten and be out by ten-fifteen, instead of lying there brooding for two hours. Even my *palms* have stopped sweating, which is a big development, because they've run like faucets my whole life. I know it sounds silly, but that caused me so much embarrassment, feeling like even my own *body* was against me. Now, I feel like I'm on my own side, like all the pieces are coming together. And I think, without making a big deal about it, that that reads to other people. At the office, some of the guys have been asking me to have lunch with them, and one of them even invited us to take a share at his ski house. In other words, there's *action* now, and I want to build on that. And above all, I want to remember what I've learned here and carry through with it. I like where I'm at now and never want to go back again. It was terrible living like that; it felt like being a ghost, where you're out there walking the streets and no one sees you."

By now, the group had gone almost an hour and a half and only made it partway around the circle. Sara was glancing at her watch every couple of minutes, and Lina had twice been beeped on her pager, ducking into the gallery to phone her daughter. Sensitive of the time, Rex and Dylan kept it short, each trying to get his piece said before others left. The text of Rex's remarks was that he had changed and earned no credit for it—had become the dutiful dad and husband, but was being dissed here as a skeezy player. His wife sure saw the difference in him, as did his family and friends; only in group, where he was most up-front about the changes, did he get no respect for having made them. And in a word, he thought that "sucked," and was part of the "p.c. drivel" here: no one believed you unless you got the waterworks going.

"I don't know why this was so hard to understand," he fumed, "but there *are* people who can change without crying about it. I am *not* one of those weepy, talk-show geese who go in for public displays of emotion; never have been, and never will be. But I do have a functioning head on my shoulders, and I used it to absorb what was being taught here. I listened to Dr. Lathon and learned what reasonable people do when they get themselves in trouble. And then I watched Dylan and saw what I *don't* want to do when the wheels come off the wagon. And I processed that data, and stopped drinking and hanging in strip joints, and the result is, I've never been happier in my whole life. My wife and I, we're like boyfriend and girlfriend again, except that we've got this fabulous daughter who's constantly cracking us up, and who runs around the house like a little white-girl Barry Sanders. And now that I'm not waking up with a scalding hangover every day—and by the way, it's been four months clean and sober, if you're counting—my performance at work has been off the charts; nearly twice the numbers I did, compared to last year. And to celebrate, we're going to Tuscany for two weeks, where I'll be taking a master cooking class. Now, I'm sure you don't believe me, and think I'll be up to my old tricks again. But that's okay, I understand. You just can't accept that there's other ways to do this—to reap the gain, without groveling in the pain."

For several shrill moments, no one spoke. So wide-ranging was Rex's insult that none of the others knew where to start. Could he really have been loutish enough to take a swipe at Lina, with his reference to "weepy geese"? Why the gratuitous shot at Dylan, who had redeemed himself with hard work down the stretch? Above all, why the sudden venom from someone who'd played it fast and loose here, and who'd clearly viewed these sessions as light comedy?

"You know, I've really gotta say, it makes me sick to hear that," Jack growled. "I mean, you waltz in here and crack jokes for twenty sessions, and hardly give up dick about your story, which, to *me*, at least, is like theft of services. And then, suddenly you've got the balls to say we stiffed you for credit? I mean, who the fuck are you to—"

"Uh-uh, not now," said Lathon, stepping in like a linesman. "Let's hold off on that till the final go-round. There are others who haven't talked yet and who we need to hear from before they start heading out. But don't worry, you *will* get your chance to respond, as will everyone who sticks around."

Jack cut a high-beam glare at Rex. "You planning on hanging around, or you going to leave at the stroke of nine?"

Rex shrugged, staring back at him. "Hey, I've got nowhere I got to be tonight."

"Good," said Jack. "Because I've got a *lot* I want to say to you."

Lathon called on Dylan, who was hurt and baffled, and needed a moment to get his bearings. "I, um . . . let's see," he said, shaking his head at Rex. "Well, I'd say that I've got a better grip on what knocked me down last summer. I've basically got a weakness for certain kinds of women: the birds-with-broken-wings type, as I call 'em. They had creeps for fathers, and got neglected or knocked around even, and grew up feeling lousy about themselves. And then I come along and try and fix them up, make 'em feel strong again, and happy. But what I've finally figured out is that some of these birds'll peck your eyes out. I mean, as much as I helped cause it with my drinking and feeling sorry for myself, this whole last year has been like a scene from that Hitchcock movie, where one minute, it's totally calm and peaceful, and the next, there's a million birds tearing you apart. And that's where we're at now, pecking away at each other with our lawyers, and wasting tens of thousands of dollars to do it. She wants some big, huge chunk of my retirement fund, and I want her to settle for something reasonable, like *a third—*"

He gritted his teeth and let out a hiss that seemed to issue directly from his gallbladder. But then, mindful of the time and the group's better opinion of him, he unclenched his jaw and went on.

"Anyway, the sale of the house went through, though I took a pretty bad beating on it. But still, you know, at least it's off my back, so that even with the loss, I save two grand a month. And hopefully, with the house thing out of the way, maybe I can strike a deal with Jeannie. Make her a cash offer, and cut the cord there for good. For *my* good, for the *kids'* good, let's just end it and be done. You go your way and marry some poor moron, and I'll go mine and find a woman that doesn't need fixing. There's plenty of them out there, I see dozens just in my neighborhood. Smart, pretty women walking to the subway each morning, and waiting in line where I get my bagel and coffee. You know, I'll stand there and look at 'em and think, *What was I doing?* Why was I stuck on this crazy woman, who was only happy when she was busting my shoes? Did I think, in some sick part of me, that she was the best I could do? That no other woman would want me? I can't figure it out, it's like some weird kind of addiction, where you know the stuff's killing you but you don't even care. All you care about is chasing that first high, where you spent the whole weekend in bed together, not bothering to get dressed or check for messages. . . ."

He paused for a breath, his eyes straying over the new rug. Admiring its icons, he lost himself briefly in the deadlock between master and slave.

"Dylan?" asked Lathon. "Were you done, or did you want to—"

"Oh, sorry," said Dylan, startling. "That's a pretty intense carpet. I was just trying to see which one wins."

"Neither of them does," said Lathon. "It's the suffering conversation—and, by the way, I got it on sale."

There was some scattered laughter, and the inevitable joke from

Rex, who said he'd seen a rug somewhere depicting the three kinds of pain. Glad for the pause, Dylan wrapped up his remarks. He had landed a job, he said, scoring the theme for a new kids' show. It was nothing to go nuts over, no network miniseries, but it was great to be back in the studio again, after ten or eleven months out. It did feel strange at first, picking out some basic chord structures without Greg sitting across from him, riffing back. For twenty-odd years, they had done this together, and there were echoes and flutters in every inch of that booth. But bit by bit, some of the weirdness was starting to fade, and in any case, the big thing was being back there. Because, within the confines of those walls, he wasn't a recovering drunk or a single dad. What he was was a guy with a singular talent, an ear for the infectious tune. And after a year in the sewer, it felt great to be a guy with talent again. In fact, he said, it felt like a privilege.

At long last, it was Sara's turn, to her great relief. As usual, she was beautifully and severely turned out, in a man-tailored suit of tight, black melton, and Manolo Blahnik shoes with spike heels. Her hair, piled high on top of her head, gleamed like something lacquered and spring-loaded. Even her makeup was ominous, with magenta crescents and shadows, and lips drawn darkly in deep bronze. She could have been on her way to a Bryant Park fashion show or a vampire rave at one of the Goth clubs. Instead, she had a date with a guy she'd met on a ski lift, and was already in danger of running late.

"First off, I want to say—and I don't know whether to attribute this to the group—but I have met more men in the last four weeks than I did in, like, the four years before it. Last week, it was this great-looking guy at a fund-raiser. The week before, I had a whirl-wind with a complete stranger at a dinner party. A half hour after meeting him, we were holding hands and making eyes, which might've had *something* to do with my accidentally taking a hit of Ecstasy—"

"Wha-at!" cried Rex, forgetting the no-cut-in rule. "How do you 'accidentally' do *that*?"

Dylan laughed, happy to hear someone else's drug story. "Do you think you could 'accidentally' get some more of it?"

"Hey, that's not funny," Jack chided. "You shouldn't even be joking about crap like that. When you've got a couple of years' sobriety, *then* make jokes."

But Sara was a good sport about her indiscretion. "Well, I vaguely remember that someone gave it to me over the summer, and I forgot about it and left it in my pill case. And then, the night of the party, I was feeling jumpy and reached for a Xanax, and the next thing I knew, I wanted to *marry* this man. I thought, My *God*, he's so beautiful, and everything he's saying is such brilliance—and then I saw him ten days later, and he's like a *food stylist* from Long Island. I mean, for a week, I was thinking is this it, is he the *one*, finally? Have I lucked out and beaten the clock? Because the day after we met, he'd left town on business, and I was mooning over a guy whose face I couldn't even remember, and thinking, now what did he say that was so riveting? And then he came back and I saw him for dinner, and he looked like Fred McMurray on *My Three Sons*. It was all I could do not to shoot myself."

Jack, like the others, was amused by the story, but somewhat perplexed as well. Two sessions earlier, Sara had announced to the group that she'd ended her affair with Christian. In breaking it off, she'd come to the decision that self-respect mattered more to her than anything—even, yes, having a baby. No longer would she tolerate insults from men just because her clock was ticking. Nor would she settle for half a loaf for the sake of not sleeping alone. She wanted the whole deal, and nothing less.

"That's a funny story, Sara, and you'll tell it brilliantly at parties," Jack was saying. "But I sort of had the idea that you were gonna get serious now. Buckle down and find something long-term."

Sara blinked, her good cheer flagging a bit. "Well, but I *am* looking," she said. "I've put the word out to friends, and I'm not sitting home on weekends, like I was."

"Yeah, but I mean, a guy on a ski lift? And this other one, a food stylist?" Jack shrugged. "It doesn't sound like you're looking in such great places."

"Well, but where should I look, then? Should I stake out museums, or—or hang around in yacht clubs, looking available? I mean, where do you go if you're not twenty-one, and you want someone your own general . . . caliber?"

The others traded glances, surprised to be back here, at the place they'd begun with Sara. "You know, not for nothing," said Jack, "but Peter didn't do so bad answering a personal a—"

"Aiiee, *again* with the personal ad?" Sara groaned. "What's the deal, are you all on commission, or something? I *don't* want to run an ad in *New York* magazine."

A testy silence settled over the group. Jack gave a shrug, as if washing his hands of the matter, and stared out the window at the rain. Rex, with a snarky, disengaged smile, picked at the liner of his bottle cap.

"Look, I *know* that there's more I could be doing," Sara conceded. "I could go to one of those dating services, the high-end kind, and put my picture in their video files. Or I could get involved with some organization and do fund-raising stuff, which is supposedly another way to meet men. But, I—I don't know, it just feels so—*desperate* to me, like something my mother would do. Even with what I am doing, I feel totally transparent, like people can see right through me. And normally, I'd just stop and say, the hell with this; if it's meant for me to meet someone, then I will. But I've done that, too, and it didn't get me anywhere—and besides which, that would be going backwards. And so I guess what I'm trying to say is, I'm doing what I can. Maybe other people would do more, and maybe I should, too, but . . . but I'm doing what's within me to do."

Peter put his hand up tentatively. "I don't know if it's okay to make a comment now . . ."

"Sara, was there anything else you wanted to add, or should we turn it back over to the group?" asked Lathon.

"No, I was more or less through," she said. "Except, I—I did want to say I've taken hope from some of you guys. Obviously, people *can* change—at least other people can—and I'm trying to implement that in my own life. I'm making an honest effort to be nicer to people I deal with, be it the photographer at a shoot or the guy at my dry cleaners. Which is another way of saying, I'm more aware of how I sound, and I'm trying to soften my edges. And if that's all I actually get from this, and a small improvement in my love life, I guess, you know, I would call that progress."

Lathon was about to comment when a hand went up again. "Yes, Peter, I'm sorry. You had a question for Sara."

"Yeah, I did," said Peter, swinging around to face her. "You know, when you were talking before about the thing with the food stylist, I was remembering my first impression of you. And that was, I never had the *slightest* idea what you were feeling, especially when you talked about your childhood. I mean, whether you were describing your doll collection, or—or when your father threw a knife at your mother, it was all in this jazzy, upbeat voice, as if you were talking about some movie you'd seen. And at the time, I was thinking, what is *wrong* with this person, that she could be so disengaged from that?

"Anyway, back to tonight, when you were talking about your love life, and it was like I was listening to another person. Your frustration and anxiety, it was right out in front of us; I could tell exactly what you were feeling as you said it. I mean, that sense of wanting something so bad you can taste it, but not knowing where to look for it—boy, can I relate to that. I was flashing back to the year of my divorce, when I was eating Popeye's chicken in my little shoebox apartment, and the only phone calls I got were from my mother and sister. I mean, basically what I'm saying is, I find you so much more . . . *real* now. Someone I can root for and—and connect to, and care about what happens. And I do care what happens to you, Sara, I find myself thinking about it between sessions. And I just wish you could see yourself as you really are, instead of fixing on those ten extra pounds you think you're carrying. I mean, this may not mean much to you, coming from a bald man in glasses, but on the scale of looks and brains, you're in the top two percentile, and—"

"My God, *stop* already," cried Sara, in horror. "I'm having a sugar panic!"

The others laughed at her arch discomfort, perhaps mistaking it for false humility. "Hey, the truth hurts," said Rex.

"But it's *not* true, I've never felt so fat in all my life," she protested. "I'm barely at the gym now, I have wild cravings for sweets, and—" She stopped and looked at Peter searchingly. "Do you really think I've changed that much?"

Peter tilted his head back and studied the moldings, picking his words with care. "Yes, I do," he said softly, "and I wish there was more time here—in fact, I almost kind of wish we were starting over. If we could just attack this head-on, this idea that you're unattractive, and—and a ditz who takes after her mother. I mean, it's just so *wrong*, Sara, and such a waste of your life, and we never really pursued it in depth. Because if we had, you'd've seen that it's just lies from your father. Just a bunch of crap from a guy who hates women, and who couldn't stand to see them happy. And I'm convinced that if we'd done that and hammered away at it, you'd've come to the realization that he's a first-class jerk, and that you're someone who's worthy of being loved. In fact, you're more than just worthy; you're at the head of the line, and—and I really hope you manage to see that."

It was by now after nine, and for some, the hour was closing in. Lina kept glancing at Lathon's desk clock, having promised to help her daughter with an essay. Dylan, who had his two girls down for the week and had dropped them at their cousin's for dinner, needed to get them home and packed off to bed before it got much later. But Sara, who'd had an eye on her watch since the group got started at seven, suddenly seemed becalmed and nailed to the spot, all her attention on Peter.

"First of all, I want to say—well, thank you," she said. "You're really sweet to say that, though, as you know, I'm not good with compliments. I always just assume that it's some kind of ploy, or that the person who's saying it is . . . um, ah—"

"An idiot?" Peter laughed.

"Well, no, not an idiot." Sara blushed. "More like someone who's never met me before."

Everyone laughed at this, including Sara, who seldom found her own jokes funny.

"But I did want to tell you that you're right about one thing— I'm much more close to my feelings now. And I'm not so sure that that's such a great thing, because I'm really open to *bad* feelings, like hopelessness. And when I get those feelings, I don't know what to do with them; I almost think I was better off being numb. At least then I was too spaced to know I was miserable—although, actually, that's not true, either."

"No, it's not," said Lathon. "You were numb *and* miserable, which is just about as bad as it gets. Now, at least, you know where it hurts, which is a big step for someone in ether. And we applaud you for that, because it took guts to turn the gas off; the fact is, you were almost comfy in that life. You had the great job and the fabulous apartment, and the close circle of friends in the same predicament—as compromises go, that isn't so bad, and a lot of people would've taken it in a minute.

"But now, having weaned you off the anesthesia, we urge you to take the next step—or actually, two steps. One, take a good, hard look at the false story, and see how dated it is. The fact is, you're not the helpless girl under your father's thumb. You're a bright, beautiful woman with your own real power, and you don't have to live in fear now. Which brings me to step two, which is to challenge the false story in the way you live your life. You walk, I think you'd agree, a pretty narrow line, wearing the same basic colors each day, and going to the same dull dinner parties, where you have the same conversations you had years ago. Well, you told us once about a wish you had—you wanted to wear a beautiful red dress. For one special night, you wanted to shed the black clothes and be the belle of the ball in red. But no, you said, you could never pull it off; you'd have a heart attack before you left the house. Well, *we* disagree; we think you'd be stunning in that dress, and we urge you to put your wish into action. *Buy* the red dress, wear it to a fancy party—take some *chances;* be *available;* put the *sword* down. The moral of this group is to make your own story; to become who you are by practicing it. You've had lots of practice being who you don't want to be. Now, we urge you to go out with charm and energy, and practice being the true Sara, for once."

Sara sat still, saying nothing for several moments, her eyes boring in on him. For the length of that pause, all systems seemed to halt—every neuron, phagocyte, and car horn. It was as if Sara, at full intensity, had the power to stop time, in order to review the film of her life.

"You're right," she said flatly. "I've got to get out of this bind. For the last—whatever, I've been in a constant state of fear, always terrified of one thing and another. Whether it was losing my assistant to another magazine, or—or growing old and dying alone, I've always got some nightmare scenario going. And what I need to be doing—what I *will* start doing—is to challenge those fears head-on. I don't know what it'll be yet, but I know it'll be something; you give me my marching orders, and I *move*. That's what I've been needing

318

here, some explicit instruction, and now I've finally got it—*take risks."*

And with that, she and Lina got up almost at once and began to gather their things. Both women were sorry and truly wanted to stay longer, but time and prior commitments, et cetera. Suddenly, the others, just a second ago in stop-time, were all up on their feet and talking at once. After counting down the ten-plus months together, working toward this moment with purpose and fixity, they had somehow arrived at it in rank confusion, and were uttering good-byes in a dazed, slapdash way. There was a lot of milling around in the center of the room, the men leaning in to shake hands with the women and extend best wishes and pleasantries. The women received these in their way—Lina reaching across to hug Jack and Peter, and Sara twisting away to avoid all contact, extricating herself untouched. There was a moment when she and Rex came face to face with each other. They smiled, he in his seductive way; she, for an instant, considering it. Then she slid by him, murmuring something inaudible, and was on her way out the door.

For a moment after they left, no one spoke. The men stood in place, staring in the direction of the door, or glancing at one another's feet. It was as though the women, in parting, had taken something with them—the collective affect, or the power of speech.

"Wonder what they're saying on the way down," said Rex.

"Probably how much they both hate you," said Dylan, laughing.

"Yeah, well, they weren't so crazy about *you*, either," said Rex. "Besides, Sara is secretly in love with me."

The others guffawed at this, including Lathon, who said it was such a secret that even Sara didn't know. Glancing at his watch, he suggested they spend a few minutes finishing up. The men stretched and yawned, wearily taking their seats again.

"Well," said Lathon, "the reason I kept you after class is . . ."

The four of them let off a sluggish laugh. Clearly, they were running on fumes now.

"Actually, what I thought we'd do is give a couple of minutes to Rex. It seemed like he had something to say to you all, and you had something to say back."

The hostilities of half an hour ago had cooled considerably, and, with the departure of the women, seemed irrelevant. Far from lying in wait for each other, Rex and Jack were eyeing the exit, uneager to resume a fight that would settle nothing. But Lathon had called them out and there was no simple way to back down, and so they checked each other dimly across the circle.

"Well, what I was trying to get across," said Rex, "was that I've got my own way of handling things. I usually don't share my feelings with strangers, or with people I see twice a month. If I share them with anyone, I do it with my family—people I really care about, and trust. But that doesn't make those feelings any less valid, or the changes I made less credible. If anything, I'm like the kid who says nothing in class, but studies hard and gets an A on the final. And I'm sorry if that's not the *approved* way of doing it, but—"

"That wasn't the point, and you know it," said Jack. "The point was, what did you contribute? You took from me and from Dylan and everyone else in the group, but what did you give back? I mean, aside from your sarcasm, what'd you actually *bring* to the party?"

Rex's jaw set. "What did I bring?" He squinted. "Well, a hell of a lot more than you did; at least I *made it in here* half the summer. And I don't know how you define *contribute*, but I think I did my share here. Does it mean taking part in an effective dialogue about other people's grief and problems? I *did* that. Does it mean making intelligent and on-time assessments, and getting praise off the hook from Lathon? I *did* that. But if it means going down on both knees and crying 'Mammy,' not only did I not do it, I *can't* do it. That isn't the way I'm built, or the way anyone in my tribe is. Yeah, I know we came over from Genoa, but we're more like WASPs than wops, and tears just ain't our bag."

"Or so you keep telling us," Jack retorted. "But you've got tears in you, believe me; you just haven't cried 'em yet. And when they do come, watch out; you won't even know what hit you. They'll have to hose you up with a Shop-Vac."

"Yeah, well, you know what? I'm not too worried; I've got my ducks in a row. You see, I, unlike you, am good at counting my money. So, even if something *does* happen, I'll cry all the way to the bank. But thanks for watching my back."

And with a shuck of his head, Rex gathered his things, pulling on a leather jacket. Before he could get it buttoned, though, Lathon coaxed him back, saying they'd all be sorry if he left now. The reason he had brought this up again was he sensed hurt feelings that had gone unspoken. Yes, Rex was angry about not getting strokes from the group, but something else was eating him, as well. And whatever his grievance, it needed to be aired before he left here, because not airing it would taint the work done.

Rex sat down again on the edge of his chair. With his hands in his coat pockets, and his cheeks flooding with color, he looked, as he sometimes did at odd moments, like a boy sitting alone on a porch step.

"Man, it was, like, so long ago, it seems *ass* to even bring it up now," he muttered.

"Well, try us," said Lathon. "I'm sure it's still timely—or whatever the opposite word of *ass* is."

Rex sunk further inside his jacket. "It's just that there're certain crimes that're acceptable in this group, and certain crimes that're not. Like when I came up out of my beer coma and realized I was a drunk, that was all well and good here. Everybody was real positive about it, and clapped me on the back; it was almost like welcome to the club. But when I tried talking about my sex stuff—man, I was like a warm shit sandwich. That night I was telling about my girlfriend Erika, and how I was with her while my wife was pregnant— boy, you could just *smell* the hatred. Sara was saying how they ought to lynch me, as an example to the other ones like me. And Lina says something like, 'Well, why didn't she just *shoot* you,' meaning, I would suppose, my wife. And I'm like, *wait* a fucking minute, where am I, in Texas, where they lethally inject you, then ask questions later? And how come my crime is worse than Jack's, who, after all, walked out on four wives—"

"Actually, three," Jack corrected him. "I'm still married to number four. And number two walked out on me."

"Yeah, well, whatever," said Rex. "I'm not trying to be snide; I'm just saying that it blew my mind. And from that point on, I thought, the hell with it, why bother; they don't want to hear my problems. Obviously, there's a code of what's acceptable here, and apparently I fall outside it."

This last came out with a whoosh of feeling, a cadenza of hurt and sourness. It seemed to stun the others, who stared off and said nothing. For several moments, the only sound came from elsewhere: the *whoomp* of car tires threading a pothole.

"Jeez, I don't know what to say," groaned Peter. "I feel awful that we shot you down like that. I mean, the last thing you want is for someone to feel he can't talk here. I just wish you'd said something then, instead of waiting all this—"

"Yeah, me too," said Dylan. "It blew right over my head; I wonder if I was even here then."

"Actually," said Rex, "you were worse than the others. I tried to talk to you another time about how they scam you at strip clubs, and your response, basically, was to go fuck myself. I was saying, 'Look, I've got some experience in that area, having been ripped off for thousands myself.' And you were all, 'Aah, what do you know? You have no *idea* what suffering is.' So, I said, fine, whatever, if that's your attitude. I'll just sit and re-swab my Q-Tips while you drown."

Now it was Dylan's turn to look hurt and puzzled. "Wait a minute, are you sure you're talking about me? I have zero memory of this conversation—I mean, I would've been *thrilled* to get your input. God knows, I was out of hand there, dropping thousands I didn't have. When did you think I was—"

"No, you said it," Peter affirmed. "I remember it word for word. It was one of those times when you showed up drunk, telling us about your 'adventures.' And I remember thinking it was brave of Rex to talk to you about that, considering how we'd attacked him about his stripper girlfriend."

"And I remember the Lina thing, where she said you should be shot," said Jack. "I thought she was kidding, because she said it with that weird laugh of hers. But then I saw she was serious; she really wanted to watch you *bleed.*"

"And I'll take some of the blame for that," said Lathon. "I heard it, too, and chose not to pick up on it, for reasons that now escape me. Then, later that night, Lina beeped me at home, and was very upset about it. She asked for your number and wanted to call and apologize; she said she was thinking of her husband when she said it. And I said no, I'd prefer it if she held off till the next session, when we could deal with it as a group matter, which it was. But the two weeks went by and I guess she forgot about it, as did I. And I'm sorry about that now, and about the stink bombs we sent you. It was *my* job to see your feelings were taken seriously."

A last, long silence descended now, brewing with strains of the unsaid. Hanging above us was the nebula of the year together, the vapor of experience reshaping itself. Events were being reviewed and animosities revised in light of these developments. Peter, ever solicitous, was gaping at Rex, as if drafting a formal apology. And Jack, sapped of anger, had lost his focus, and was frowning in self-reproach.

"Well, I have to admit, it was ass of me not to say something," said Rex. "And also, I did have an attitude coming in, which is maybe why you frosted me out. As you could probably tell, it wasn't *my* choice to come here; it was basically an ultimatum from my wife.

And I guess I was pissed off and saw this as jail time, and said, 'Hell, I could do it standing on my head.' Which was possibly not *the* most mature thing to do, so I guess I'd have to take some of the blame."

"That's right," said Lathon, "although I'd delete the word *blame;* better to say that suffering is a two-way street. We, for our part, bought your bad-boy act, and thought you were trifling with us, while you bought into our irritation, and thought we were freezing you out. And as we've seen so many times here, that's how suffering operates—it's trains going round the tracks of an old story. I suspect, for instance, that as a kid in that 'model' family of yours, if you ever had negative feelings, no one listened to them. In a house where they were going from 'wops' to WASPs in a little under sixty seconds, nobody wanted to hear from the family drinking problem, or from a kid under pressure to be perfect. And I further suspect that's why that 'perfect' kid went berserk when he got to college— selling coke by the carload, and shoving it up the ass of his family. Because I'm a strong believer that if you close your ears to your kids, they'll reach you through some other orifice. And by then, it won't be words but a pipe bomb they're using, and *boy,* will you be sorry you didn't listen sooner."

For the span of several seconds, there was stifling silence, the kind encountered in the noonday desert. Then, from somewhere in the circle came a low, dull groan, which built and redounded on all sides. Another moment passed before I could tell it was laughter, and that it came from the four men before me. Thick and unaspirated, it seemed to issue from some deep place in them, and then to rise into the air above us. There it curled, perhaps a foot below the ceiling, where all things, resolved and otherwise, took up residence.

epilogue

One sweltering evening, some two and a half years later, I found myself sitting in an uncooled basement with fifty other shirt-soaked souls. The building was an ancient row house on Pearl Street, and the amenities in the room were provisional. There were yellow utility lights swagged the length of the low ceiling, a cracked casement window housing a Fedders low on freon, and a john whose spring door had warped in the heat, rendering it impossible to shut.

But for all its retro-shtetl charm, the room drew a flossy crowd. Slumped in the gray metal folding chairs were men wearing Paul Stuart banker's suits and hand-stitched British wing tips. Sipping iced lattes, they scanned the folds of their *Crains Daily*s, or scribbled on palm-sized digital assistants, issuing the world orders via fiber optics. Most of the women present were similarly engaged, jotting down memos in Filofaxes or making calls on slender Nokias. Here and there were others less prosperously groomed—a man in an old Mets hat, the brim bar-graphed with salt stains, and a group of young women seated together, tucking bra straps under their tank tops. But at this six-thirty meeting of Alcoholics Anonymous, most of the attendees were Wall Street professionals, including Rex, who was sitting on my left.

Owing, no doubt, to the oppressive weather (and the futility of the old air conditioner) the meeting was not very rousing. There was a blustery speech from one of the Wall Street chaps, complaining that he hadn't gotten his "sobriety dividend." Though clean for ten months now, he felt bored and rootless, and unable to relate to his grown children. Nor could he seem to get rid of his beer gut, despite hours of due diligence in the gym. Next up was a prolix pastry chef, who was having trouble deciding if she was gay. On the one hand, sex with women "only went up to three on a scale of five"; on the other, no woman had ever beaten her bloody. That was important, because being battered was one of her "triggers," a thing that sent her "running, not walking," to the nearest bar. And so, she sighed, if sleeping with women was the price of sobriety, then it was a price she was willing to pay.

Thus it went for much of the next hour: a series of mostly sad and maladroit stories, interspersed with reports of small progress. Through it all, Rex sat mum but irritable, crossing and uncrossing his legs. He'd put on a few pounds in the last couple of years and was plumply uncomfortable in his ice-blue dress shirt. The heat, however, was not the source of his pique, as he made plain in a speech before the break.

"I know that it's hot in here, and I talked to the repair guy again, and he swore he'd have the AC fixed soon. But still, you know, this has been a real piss-ass meeting, with everyone bitching about how hard their lives are, and how no one ever cuts 'em any slack. And I'm like, look around the room, people—there must be forty million in cash here, not to mention all the boats and summer houses. And I'm thinking, whatever happened to the joy of being *sober*, of getting up in the morning without being sick to your stomach, and putting on nice, clean clothes after your shower, instead of the shit you slept in yesterday. And whatever happened to *gratitude*, of thanking God or whoever you pray to that you're alive and breathing, instead of mauled in some three-car pileup you caused. Because, believe me, *I'm* grateful; I'm grateful every single day, and let me tell you what I'm grateful for. I'm grateful that I have eyes, so that I can see my beautiful kid, and read *Curious George* to her, and *Good Dog, Carl.*

And I'm grateful that I have ears to hear her talk, and tell me that when she's older, she wants to be a doctor, so that she can give her Mr. Potato Head a nose that stays on. And I'm grateful for other things—to my wife for not divorcing me, and to my parents for not booting me out of the family. But above all, I'm grateful that I've made three years sober, and that there's a place like this that helped me do it."

Outside, during the break, a number of people came over to Rex to thank him for his comments. Several were young women, and he flicked on the charm, kidding them about being "thirteen-steppers." The term refers to a species of pickup artists—AA veterans who cruise the newcomers, preying on their fragility. The joke, of course, was that this was the wolf accusing the sheep, but the women didn't seem very insulted. A couple even murmured that they'd call him at home, a thing I brought up to him later on.

"No, I am not having sex with them," he said with a laugh, in the chauffeur-driven Town Car crossing Chambers. "That'd be like child abuse, taking candy from a baby. Besides which, I am the very *picture* of a faithful spouse."

"Then what's with all the flirting, and the phone calls at home?"

"Oh, well, you gotta keep in practice, in case of an emergency. But you are *so* not right about me, I am such the loyal dog now. An hour with me, and you'll throw up from boredom."

Several hours later, after fine duck salad, and a naked *pas de seul* by his daughter, Marisa, I sat drinking coffee with Rex and his wife, Claudia in the larger of their two living rooms. Drained from a ten-day stint at The Hague, where she'd coproduced a story about the Balkans rape trials, Claudia was sprawled across the width of their lavender sofa with her feet propped up in Rex's lap. He had removed her shoes and was kneading the soles of her feet, knuckling his way up the arch.

"Would you look at this *service:* first dinner, then a foot rub," she cooed. "Do you believe this is the same Rex Dimauro?"

I laughed, casting a look her way. "The question is, do you?"

"Well . . . ?" she teased him, taking her time thinking it over. "Actually, I do think he's turned a new leaf. I mean, if this is just an act, he's kept it up for a long time, and got everyone fooled, including his folks."

"It's not an act," he said. "I am such the real deal. I could teach the *Marines* about 'ever faithful.' "

Claudia laughed and stuck a foot in his ribs, jiggling the sides of his paunch. "Forget the Marines, you need to go to the *gym*," she said. "That, or run laps on the golf course."

Rex heaved a sigh, affecting patient dignity. "She's just chafed 'cause I'm down to a seven handicap, while she's still struggling to break ninety."

I sat back and laughed, enjoying the chummy ease between them. I'd seen none of it on a visit here three years earlier, when they'd occupied opposite ends of the room, like warlords dragged to a parley. Rex had been holding forth about the prospects of his new company, bragging that he and his partners would be "titans" in five years. Claudia, meanwhile, had quietly tended the baby, cutting looks laced with sarcasm at Rex. I'd been unable to gain a sense of her beyond a woman marking time, weighing out her options by the hour. Now, she and Rex seemed undetachable, like two genes on the same DNA strand. I asked her what had made the difference.

She looked him over with an appraising smile. "Well, I hate to say this, because he completely denies it, but it had to be that group. I mean, for years, he'd promised me that he would stop drinking, and be more responsible around the house, but it never happened. And finally, I was just *over* it and told him, 'Fix this or leave; I can't have this craziness around my child.' And maybe it was partly that, but something got his attention, and I think it was the group."

"But of course it was *not*," said Rex, feigning insult. "That clown Lathon had nothing to do with it. It was all about me, and my will of iron. When I come to a decision, it's lights-out."

Claudia smiled and sent me a wink. "Then how come you didn't make it until you joined the group?"

"Pure coincidence," he said. "Totally unrelated. The amount I learned from *them*, you could fit in an eyedropper."

Claudia cackled and kicked him again, driving her heel into his thigh. "Welcome to my world, and meet my husband, Rex," she said. "He's not *really* a bad guy, or an insensitive jerk; he just plays one on TV."

Not surprisingly, the other members were more charitable about the group. Peter, whom I met for lunch one Friday, had nothing but praise for the experience. Passing across pictures of his toddler son, he marveled at the changes in his life. He had twice been promoted at his large accounting firm, and was now heading a department of twenty people. In keeping with his new power, he had turned over his wardrobe, and sat before me clad in a three-button suit, with tone-on-tone tie and dress shirt. And, throwing caution to the wind, he and Kara had overpaid for a "classic six" apartment on the West Side. It needed a lot of work and the maintenance alone was boggling, to say nothing of the mortgage they'd assumed. But there was a thirty-foot balcony and a view of the whole park, and three doors down from them was the Beresford, where Peter's hero, Jerry Seinfeld, had just bought.

"It's a little hard to separate it all out right now: how much I owe to Lathon personally, and how much was the group," he said. "I mean, I *met* Kara as a result of the one-on-one stuff, but it was group that gave me the tools to see it through. And they also gave me the confidence to promote myself; to go out and shop my skills to other firms. You know, when I look back on where I was then, I almost get the chills; I was so lost, I didn't even know to ask for directions. I could easily have wound up as one of those people who flails around, and after a while, just gives up and stops fighting. I mean, it wasn't to that point yet, but I was pretty depressed, and felt like I had no—ally; no connection."

"So group was sort of like a compass then? A place to get your bearings?"

"Well, yeah, but it was more than that; it's where I found my strength. I mean, for most of my life, I was sort of used to getting less. Getting less than my sister, getting less than my friends—I mean, it sucked and made me furious, but there I was. And then I joined the group and saw that all that was crap, that I was as good as anyone else and deserved respect. I mean, I'm still feeling my way, and have to remind myself sometimes that now *I'm* the boss and they answer to *me.* But the thing I always go back to is what Lathon told me: if you have self-respecting wishes and put them in action, the world can't help but take you seriously."

Lina was another member with high marks for Lathon. At a trattoria on Third Avenue, she squeezed her husband's hand and said she thanked God for the group. She and Jeffrey were so happy that it had become a joke around the house. Every time her daughter caught them hugging or smooching, she marched over and separated them, saying she wasn't running a bordello here. Laughing, Jeffrey reminded Lina of the gift her son had given them. Wrapped in pricey paper and a Bergdorf box was a five-dollar rubber bucket. The card read: *In the event of heavy petting: 1. Fill with cold water. 2. Pour over heads. 3. Go and get a room!*

"Seriously, though, this is even better than I expected," she said. "My kids love being around Jeff, and go to ball games with him, and Jorie even dragged him to a concert, didn't she? To see that one with the sad voice and the exposed navel."

"Jewel," he said, helpfully.

"Right. Jewel." She shook her head waggishly. "Eight jillion records, and she can't afford a last name. Or a shirt that tucks into her pants."

Picking up again, she extolled the virtues of her new marriage, the most surprising of which was its effect on her ex-husband. He had been a much better dad of late, especially with Jorie, whom he'd gone out of his way to spend time with. "It's like he suddenly realizes he's got competition, and that if he wants his kids to like him, he'd better shape up."

"Well now, I can't take credit for that," said Jeffrey. He was a tall, rangy man with a broad nose and a slight stoop, and a seemingly permanent smile. "Don't forget that he's gotten remarried, too, and he and Caroline seem very happy. But otherwise, yes, I accept all praise. It's hard, being this wonderful all the time."

Lina laughed, slipping an arm around him. "Good; I'll buy you a cookie on the way home."

Now, *he* laughed, and leaned in close for a kiss. I felt as superfluous as a bellhop at a hot-sheet motel.

"Well, not to short-change the group," I said, "but it sounds like the best medicine was meeting Jeffrey."

"Yes, that's true," she said, "but I doubt I'd have *met* him without group. I mean, I was so beat down then, both physically and emotionally, I could barely get out of bed in the morning. The *last* thing I'd have done is join some tennis club, and if I hadn't . . ." She paused, looking up at him.

He smiled, squeezing her hand for reassurance. "Eh, don't worry, I'd've tracked you down." Turning to me, he said, "You know, as terrific as she is, and as smart and together, it's hard for me to believe that she was in such bad shape. . . ."

"Well, but it's true," she said. "This man was a witness. Tell him what I looked like when you met me."

I nodded, recounting my first impression of Lina. "Looking back now," I asked her, "what do you think turned the tide, and allowed you to see yourself differently?"

She sat back and pushed away her plate of pasta. Looking over my shoulder, she surveyed the bustle in the room, the tables full of canoodlers and self-proclaimers.

"I can't say when it happened, but it finally got through to me: most suffering really *is* optional. I mean, if it's end-stage Alzheimer's or you're crippled from the neck down, that you can't do much about. But if your health is okay, and you're not saddled with nine kids, then suffering comes down to a choice. You can sit and do nothing about it, or you can get up and help yourself. But either way you go, it's your decision—and I decided to stop sitting there."

I had no substantive contact with Sara, per her own request. She'd wanted little to do with me during the course of group, and still less following its breakup. Now, as before, she assured me it wasn't personal, nor had anything to do with Lathon. Rather, she was simply "maniacally busy," and hadn't time now for even her friends. In the course of our ten minutes on the phone, however, I was able to glean some things. One, she was glad she had done the group, and had learned "some useful facts about [her]self." (Asked, though, to list them, she laughed and curtly declined.) Two, she had not yet reconciled with her father, to whom she mainly spoke about investments. Three, there was still no man on the scene, nor any compelling prospects. And given the demands of her workload, one would "have to literally fall from the sky" for that to change, she said.

Before hustling me off the phone, she asked about the others, none of whom she remembered by name. She was encouraged to hear about Lina and Peter, and surprised by Rex's stability. "I would've given his marriage another year, tops," she said. "But then again, no one ever called me a relationship expert."

It took me months of trying, sadly, to turn up Dylan. He was deep in one of his "blue periods," he said, which meant—he needn't have added—that he was drinking. The voice on the line sounded lost and distant, though he was calling from a bar on Forty-third Street. He wouldn't say why he had picked up again—indeed, wouldn't answer *any* of my questions straight, responding with a species of tetchy sarcasm that ran the conversation in circles. But through all the wisecracks and circumlocutions, an answer began to emerge. He still drew an income from his work in reruns, which, while modest, was enough to support him. More, his ex-wife had recently remarried, saving him the cost of alimony. She even allowed him to see his kids now and then, provided that he taper off beforehand. This meant, practically speaking, that he drank because he could; had set up a bleak but sustainable lifestyle around it. No one hassled him for the rent money or child support, because he had an accountant who handled all that. And no one groused that he wasn't working, because the world of work had lost tabs on him. It is easy to disappear if you really want to, and for Dylan, getting lost had become an art.

Obviously, there was no point in asking about the group, or about any lessons he might have learned. Rather, the lesson went the other way. He was teaching me about the vanity of trying to help someone who has all the escape routes mapped out. When it got dull drinking beer at nine in the morning, and hanging out in bars with retired cops and widowers, he'd find something else to do. But for now, he was seemingly in his element, in the company of friends and peers.

"Yo, do me a favor," he said, before hanging up. "If you talk to Lathon, would you tell him . . . I'm all right. I know that he worries about me, and feels like he let me down. So tell him I'm good, and that everything worked out. Tell him it's all under control."

"Hey, you know what I say?" said Jack, when I told him about Dylan. "I say four out of six ain't bad."

We were sitting in the back of Chez Josephine, where he liked to grab a precurtain dinner. With one play in previews and another in development, he was grateful for a good meal fast. He ate with quick bites, laughed in short bursts, and kept glancing at his plastic Swatch. Despite earning a solid living, he still wore the cheap watch, as a reminder of where he'd been and what it had cost him.

"I mean it," he said. "I'm no fan of Lathon's, but give the guy credit where it's due. To get four success stories out of that bunch— you gotta tip your hat to him."

He crunched the last of his *pommes frites* and sat back, exuding adrenaline. Two-and-a-half years ago, within a week of his reinstatement, he had been hired by a team of veteran producers to develop Off-Broadway shows. The first, a British import, went up for an Obie; a second had been held over for a month. Clearly, he still had the golden touch, and something else to go with it—the hunger of a twenty-year-old. He lived and breathed now to put on shows, to find the next big voice out there. No longer for him the *"farkakte* musical," the flash-and-trash greasepaint pageant. What he was on the hunt for was something dangerous, a play that "knocked you out of your seat into the aisle."

"Well, obviously, you're one of the four success stories," I said. "Although I'm not sure what group had to do with it."

He grunted ruminatively in the way I remembered, a plosive syllable from the gut. It was a complex utterance with a list of ingredients, and laughter was chief among them these days. "Me, either." He laughed. "Why give *that* prick the credit? It's enough that he's got my dough."

"But on the other hand, you're not demanding a refund," I noted.

"No, that's true," he allowed. "Group did do me good. It clarified my craziness about money."

"In what way?"

He grunted again, more from exhaustion than laughter, implying that it was hard work to unpack these things. "Well, after group ended, you know, I finally took Lathon's advice and checked out Debtor's Anonymous. I only lasted four months there—I couldn't do

that *and* AA, not when I went back to work—but I did go long
enough to see his point. What I saw was I spent money when I felt
bad about myself; it was my last line of defense against feeling shitty.
I mean, it's no accident I joined group only *after* I went broke. As
long as I still had dough to burn, why submit to that? But when that
tank hit empty, it scared me shitless, and I swallowed my pride and
came in."

I was about to reply that he hadn't swallowed all of it, that there
had been plenty of his pride in evidence in those sessions. But as I
was opening my mouth, our waiter appeared, and slipped the check
between us. Both of us glanced at it, and then at each other. I don't
know which of us laughed first.

"Hey, you're damn right you're paying half!" he cackled, going
for his wallet. "There's no free lunch with Jack Perlman anymore."

In his peremptory way, Jack was right, of course: four out of six
wasn't bad. In fact, by any measure, it was a solid triumph, even
with a group this advantaged. Granted, its members were hand-
picked professionals who were, by and large, prosperous and well ed-
ucated. None, moreover, with the possible exception of Dylan, had
problems that could be called life-threatening. None were in flight
from a violent spouse, or on the cusp of suicide or homelessness.
And none had brought in pain so acute that it required hospitaliza-
tion. What they presented, instead, were the quotidian concerns of
affluent, midlife adulthood: Who am I? How am I valued in the
world? What am I meant to accomplish?

But within its own terms, the group had done a great deal. In the
span of ten months, its members had peeled back the husk to arrive
at the germ of their suffering. And by a two-thirds majority, they had
done something useful to resolve or reduce its grip. Rex confronted
his drinking problem, and salvaged a tenuous marriage. Lina out-
lasted her boorish first husband, and found the courage to meet a

true partner. Peter made repairs to his self-respect, and gained a wife and an enhanced career. Jack came to terms with an old compulsion, and resumed his place in the world.

If that were the sum of it, then, I could close the book on a fanfare of happy ending. But I am grieved to report that there is more to tell, and that what follows still pains and confounds me.

About a year and a half after group broke up, I completed a draft of this book. To mark the occasion, I stopped by Lathon's office, intending to buy him a drink. Actually, I had two motives, the other being to check up on him; he hadn't returned my calls in over a week. I got no response when I knocked on his door, and was surprised to find it unlocked. Inside, the gallery was gray and unswept—the blinds pulled down against the midday sun, and a haze of dust in the air. Alarmed, I poked my head into the studio, where I saw Lathon slumped on a couch. He started awake at the sound of my voice, but fell over trying to get to his feet. At eleven o'clock on a splendid June morning, he was profoundly—morbidly—drunk.

On the phone in the gallery, I dialed a friend of his whom I'd met on several occasions in the previous office. The man, a colleague and former partner of Lathon's, was saddened but unsurprised by the call. He informed me that Lathon was an alcoholic whose drinking had spiraled in the last year. Where once he'd been continent, if not abstinent, during the week, of late he would go missing for days at a stretch, stranding his patients without notice. Their calls went unreturned, their prescriptions unfilled; groups sat, stunned, in the lobby. As a result, he'd lost most of his clientele and faced eviction for unpaid rent.

It would strongly understate matters to say I was stunned. For days, I walked about in a kind of somnolent fog, unable to process the news. How, I wondered, could I not have seen what was a year or more in the making? It is true that I'd had less to do with Lathon after group broke up, and that such contact as I did have was con-

ducted mainly over the phone. It is also true that at our handful of
meetings he'd been on his best behavior. Kempt and clear-headed,
he talked about his work and about plans for a book about child-
rearing. He ate with avidity, had a glass of wine with dinner, and
gave no blinking sign of a man in free fall. Yes, there were calls that
he took days to return, and the odd meeting canceled at the last
minute. But Lathon's excuses were never less than plausible, having
to do with his breakneck schedule. Even at the end, when he
dropped appearances with his neighbors, he took pains to hide his
plight from me, nursing the hope that this book would somehow
"save" him.

But it is also true that I wasn't looking very closely, and saw no
advantage in viewing him closely. The facts of Lathon's life were in-
convenient and clashed with the "truth" of his authority. How, after
all, to square his clinical effectiveness with his behavior in the last
months of group? The grandiloquent new office, the bizarre change
of costume—clearly, his actions were at variance with his counsel,
and the two were not easily reconciled. Moreover, there was a preening hyperbole I hadn't heard as his patient. This was his *best group
ever*, the *smartest*, the *most eloquent*—he was as much its impresario
as its priest.

Later that month, less at the beseechment of friends than at the
pending seizure of his license by the authorities, Lathon checked
into a rehab facility. It was an in-patient unit in another state, with
a separate and distinct protocol for doctors. As I learned in a visit to
its rolling campus, dozens of addicted physicians were in residence,
and their treatment was lengthy and arduous. The customary stay
for other residents was four weeks. For doctors, it was a minimum
of three months. At the end of ninety days, many were transferred
out for a year or more of long-term care. The reasons for this were
several, said Lathon's therapist. First, she explained, doctors made
difficult patients, presenting strata of denial and grandiosity. There
was a mantra you heard from them—*I'm too smart to be a junkie*—

as if addiction were a correlative of intelligence. Second, they were in positions of public trust, and many had betrayed that trust. They had performed surgery while high or rendered treatment decisions drunk, and posed an ongoing risk to patients. Third, they had access to pharmaceuticals, and the potential for abuse was great.

Lathon spent three months at the out-of-state clinic, then returned to New York in the fall. He enrolled in an after-care program in the city and began going to twelve-step meetings. As I write this, he has been sober for twenty months and abiding by the terms for reinstatement. He sees an addictions counselor weekly, attends a group for recovering doctors, and submits to regular urinalysis. His psychiatric license has been provisionally restored, allowing him to see up to ten patients a week under rigid supervision. He has been told that if he continues to meet these conditions, he will soon be cleared for a full return.

As for me, I've been occupied by painful questions, and the one that keeps nagging is the most obvious. How could a man as troubled as Lathon be as lucid and useful in group? That he was sober during session I have no doubt, but it does not speak to the question. Nor does his assurance, solemnly offered, that his addiction didn't snowball till group ended. The fact remains that he was steeped in suffering and incapable of thinking his way out of it. Had he raised it in group—or anywhere else, for that matter—the answer would have been blunt and forthcoming: *seek treatment.* After all, the keystone of his practice was the banality of addiction—the flight from pain and complication into the refuge of indulgence. He was equally skilled at gauging the suffering it masked and depicting it in language that got through. How he could be acute with others and blind to himself is a matter I can't work out.

In the end, though, I will take instruction from Lathon's triumph, not his failure. These are tenuous times for the "talking cure," and its detractors range on all sides. The managed-care companies have all but disallowed it, making it a luxury for many who most need it. The temple of Freud is in steep decline, assailed by radicals and the rear guard alike. Drug companies press the market solution, positioning Prozac like psychic Bufferin. I do not begrudge them their products or profits; far from it, I am in their debt.

But what I saw in the course of events described here confirmed my own experience: that in the hands of a skilled and sentient practitioner, there is nothing like the power of talk therapy. It deepens and ramifies, is generous and generative, and confers the power of moral gravity. For me, its chief value, in an age of puerile narcissism, is the lessons it teaches about adulthood. Probity, judgment, respect for others: these are the kinds of qualities a good therapist imparts— even in that unhappy instance when he does not fully embody them.

about the author

Paul Solotaroff's first book was *The House of Purple Hearts*. His work has appeared in numerous magazines, including *GQ*, *Esquire*, *Rolling Stone*, and *Vogue*, and has been collected in *The Best Sports Stories of the Century*. He lives in Brooklyn with his wife and child.